NEWT
THE CO...
THE CON...
THE POLITICIAN,
THE MAN

He has become one of the most extraordinary and compelling politicians of our day. Yet Speaker of the House Newt Gingrich remains a mystery. He is a champion of "family values," but was born of a teenage, single mother, and raised by a remote stepfather, and has a checkered marital record. He's railed against congressional privileges, but climbed the political ladder with the aid of the most effective money-raising machine in American politics. He has infuriated many with his statements on the state of society and government but has inspired millions to join him in his fury for change. Now his plans to revolutionize government may change the face of modern America, and most Americans don't even know who he is or what he has in store for them.

That is why this book was written. That is why it must be read.

NEWT GINGRICH

SPEAKER TO AMERICA

Judith Warner

AND

Max Berley

A SIGNET BOOK

SIGNET
Published by the Penguin Group
Penguin Books USA Inc., 375 Hudson Street,
New York, New York 10014, U.S.A.
Penguin Books Ltd, 27 Wrights Lane,
London W8 5TZ, England
Penguin Books Australia Ltd, Ringwood,
Victoria, Australia
Penguin Books Canada Ltd, 10 Alcorn Avenue,
Toronto, Ontario, Canada M4V 3B2
Penguin Books (N.Z.) Ltd, 182–190 Wairau Road,
Auckland 10, New Zealand

Penguin Books Ltd, Registered Offices:
Harmondsworth, Middlesex, England

First published by Signet, an imprint of Dutton Signet,
a division of Penguin Books USA Inc.

First Printing, April, 1995

10 9 8 7 6 5 4 3 2 1

 REGISTERED TRADEMARK—MARCA REGISTRADA

Printed in the United States of America

Contents

INTRODUCTION
Warming Up the House

"Hey, Newt!"

The shouts of greeting were everywhere he turned on that Friday, his first day back in Washington after his 1994 congressional victory in Georgia.

Washington had never before so truly been his city, his spiritual home, as on that day, as he cruised around town in his black Cadillac Fleetwood Brougham (soon to be replaced by a bullet-proof van).

Red, white, and blue flowers filled his office. Supporters clung to him. Smiles were thrown in his direction: *that* was an unaccustomed sight.

"Hey, Newt!"

A doorman at the Willard Hotel stopped him for an autograph. Cameras appeared everywhere.

He was talking to a room full of businesspeople from the Washington Research Group. It was a typical speech: "We simply need to erase the slate and start over.

". . . What is ultimately at stake in our current environment is literally the future of American civilization. It is impossible to maintain civilization with twelve-year-olds having babies, fifteen-year-olds killing each other, seventeen-year-olds dying of AIDS, and with eighteen-year-olds ending up with diplomas they can barely read."

It was the kind of statement that everyone agrees with. And if anyone had raised a dissenting voice with the implications, if not the exact words, of Gingrich's oft-repeated doomsday saying, this wasn't the group to do so. This wasn't the time. This wasn't even the city. Not anymore.

The liberals were out to pasture, licking their wounds from the trouncing they'd just received at the polls. "Speaker Gingrich. Deal With It" T-shirts were sprouting up around the Capitol. And for a brief time, a moment really, there were no dissenting voices.

"Hey Newt!" The calls started up again as soon as he stepped outside.

Two months later, the friendly cries had turned to shouts.

January 4 was a notably loud and raucous day in the House. The press gallery was full to overflowing. Children played in the aisles of the House chamber, staring up curiously into the eyes of the depressed-looking Democrats.

Democratic and Republican congressmen, called in name order alphabetically, shouted out their choices for House speaker. "Gephardt!" the first voice rang out.

"Close the vote!" Representative Gary Ackerman of New York, a Democrat, then shouted, in a game attempt at graveyard humor.

Richard A. Gephardt, the Democratic congressman chosen to hand the gavel over to the new Republican victor, sat, gaunt and drawn from recent surgery.

By the time of Gingrich's swearing-in, the shouts had reached a roar. One minute after the newly sworn-in members of the 104th Congress had cast their votes for the new speaker, the Republican freshmen had started shouting: *"Newt! Newt! Newt!* It's a whole Newt world!"

He received three standing ovations. One Democrat, Maxine Waters of California, walked out. And one Republican, Senate Majority Leader Bob Dole of Kansas, remained nonplussed.

Dole watched the vote quietly, and exited quickly as soon as the swearing-in was over. Asked for a comment by *Time,* he merely said, "I'd better get back to work."

Another Republican appeared less than jubilant, too. Robert Gingrich, a lieutenant colonel in the United States Army and the new speaker's stepfather, had remained seated throughout all his son's standing ovations.

"It was a forgone conclusion," he growled at *Time*.

"I just didn't feel like standing up. After the third standing ovation, it gets a little old."

A few weeks before the swearing-in, Newt had called Bob Gingrich to extend a personal invitation to the event.

"I want to thank you for being an influence in my life," Gingrich had said as Bob listened silently. "You had a great deal to do with me being where I am today."

It had been a grand act of diplomacy. His swearing-in speech was one, too. Speaker Gingrich credited the Democrats for doing the great work in the civil rights movement. He hailed their great president Franklin Delano Roosevelt. He said: "Here we are as commoners together, to some extent Democrats and Republicans, to some extent liberals and conservatives—but Americans all." He was the statesman that supporters always said that he could be. He was the "kinder, gentler Newt" the pundits thought they saw coming ten years ago—and who never arrived. He wasn't *manic,* not vindictive, wasn't smirking like a nasty boy in the back of the class—as he would do during President Clinton's State of the Union speech a month later. He just, for once in his life, looked happy. Things might have been perfect. If only his stepfather could have lifted himself up out of that chair.

His mother sat, too, not daring to defy her husband. Such was the lot of a military wife. Gingrich could accept that. He could accept it when his stepfather made the kind of statements that fueled the fires of his opponents' gossip mills: "*He doesn't even like his son!*" He could accept that the observing world wouldn't understand Bob Gingrich's logic: "A standing ovation from your peers is worth something. A standing ovation from your father and mother is worth nothing. And that's the reason I did not stand."

He could accept it. Just like he'd accepted it, thirty-three years earlier, when his parents hadn't come to his wedding. He'd been too young. Bob had thought, only nineteen. "I never held it against her; I never held it against him," Gingrich has said.

He never *saw* all that much of them again, either. Friends he made after his first wedding all thought that he was like a man without a past, without any permanent sense of home. He was a man obsessed with the future, and with only one goal: becoming speaker of the House. He was set on remaking the world—remaking his world—all for the Good of America.

"He has a thoroughly American attitude toward things," says Gordon Wood, author of *The Radicalism of the American Revolution* and a professor of history at Brown University. "He's a thoroughly Emersonian character, in the sense of believing that you can re-invent yourself, you can re-invent the culture, you can make over yourself, you can make over people."

It was good for Newt Gingrich to make history. "Renewing American Civilization," as he would call it, had given him a place in the world.

In the House now he *is* at home.

"How'd you like the speech?" he asked his parents amicably in passing, like a host at his own House-warming party. And whisked off to go throw some bombs.

Newt Gingrich has made his life out of a quest to make history. Now he's hellbent on "revolution."

"It is our goal to replace the welfare state," he says.

"Not to reform it, not to improve it, not to modify it, to replace it. To go straight at the core structure."

On January 4, 1995, he swung into action in a fury. In fourteen hours, he led fifteen roll call votes, without a single Republican defection. He drove his troops to work until 2:23 A.M. And, as the first day passed into the second and he'd been written into the history books as having made his start as a statesman, he denounced the Democrats as "narrow and foolish."

A former congressman, surveying the scene, called it "in-your-face" politics.

"This ain't business as usual," Gingrich's longtime close friend and ally Congressman Vin Weber cheered.

One Democratic congressman, remembering the speaker's promises of work schedules scaled back for "family time," grumbled about *Addams Family* hours. But he was a liberal anachronism; all the clocks had been reset, and were running on revolutionary time.

Gingrich is an odd type of revolutionary. He topples hierarchies only to climb up to the top. He fights elitism only to become part of the nation's ultimate elite. He calls himself a "conservative futurist," which basically means that he's for anything but the status quo.

He's a man full of contradictions.

He's a man who rails against big government, who claims that welfare, as an entitlement, is dehumanizing, and yet has lived his entire life subsidized by the state and federal government: as an army brat, as a student on a Georgia State scholarship and a National Defense Education Act fellowship, as a professor at a state college, as a member of the United States House of Representatives.

He's a man who once railed against President Gerald Ford for playing partisan politics—and then became the most divisive pit bull fighter on the House floor.

He is a man whose first campaign promise was to keep all his fund-raising activities out in the open, and who has assembled one of the most complex and secretive money-raising machines the country has ever seen.

He's a man who has assailed the patriotism of Democrats ranging from Ted Kennedy to Tip O'Neill, has called for quadrupling the size of our military, has said he believes in "universal military training," and has belittled President Clinton's ability to serve and lead the armed forces—yet sat out the Vietnam War with student and family deferments.

He's a man who tells the House of Representatives that "ideas matter" and then tries to dismantle the Corporation for Public Broadcasting, the most democratic disseminator of ideas in America.

He is the most successful congressman in the House—and has authored no significant legislation.

He's been called a "cherub with a chip on his shoulder," a "case study in careerism." He protests: "I'm not interested in preserving the status quo; I want to overthrow it," he said in 1991.

What makes Newt Gingrich run?

Some people say it's sheer bile. Some say it's a pure power lust.

Gingrich himself admits to monumental ambition: "I have an enormous personal ambition," he once said. "I want to shift the entire planet."

Mary Edwards Wertsch, author of *Military Brats,* a study of adults who, like Gingrich, were brought up as army brats during the Cold War, suggests that anger is a prime mover in many men like the speaker. "Anger is the core of every military son whose father was abusive or distant," she writes. "And what spills over into the world is likely to be fiery as well: a quick temper, pugnacity and choice of career that channels aggression and allows for plenty of confrontation."

Newt Gingrich has ridden an angry crest of history to victory. The "Contract with America," is a statement of faith for those who feel priced out, pushed out, squeezed out of the easy American dream life they'd thought was their birthright. Gingrich speaks for people who miss a time when you didn't need an

Ivy League education to get a good job, when you didn't need the best job at the best firm with the best salary to be a respectable person. He shows people, "just folks," that you don't have to always worry about beating the elites—intellectuals, authorities of any stripe, politicians, presidents—at their own game. You can *change the rules of the game*.

He has. Newt Gingrich, who bills himself as the ultimate anti-elitist, anti-establishmentarian, has *become* the Establishment, and is appointing his own elite. He changed Congress from a genteel gentleman's club into a gladiators' ring. When he didn't like the way the networks covered the Republicans, he took his message straight to the public through C-SPAN. When he didn't like the way the Republican Establishment dealt with the Democrats, he formed his own counter-group, the Conservative Opportunity Society. He threw bombs and started firefights and held prayer vigils and staged walkouts and took no prisoners, forcing out former House Speaker Jim Wright, outlasting the gentlemanly party stalwart Bob Michel and consigning old-time leader Bob Dole to the dustbin of history as a "tax collector for the welfare state"— until, finally, his outrageous outbursts became the order of the day, and he woke up one day to find himself speaker of the House.

His detractors call it "skinhead politics." And worse.

"At heart, Gingrich is a nihilist," Jim Wright wrote about him in November 1994. "Throughout his career he has been intent on destroying and demoralizing the existing order. He proudly calls himself a 'systematic revolutionary.' He has nothing in common with Karl Marx but much in common with Guy Fawkes, who tried to blow up the British Parliament. He is a bit like those who burned the Reichstag in Germany so they could blame it on the 'Communists.' "

Is Newt Gingrich a rebel without a cause? Or is there really something behind him, something beyond his internal demons, his backbiting tactics, his sometimes megalomaniacal, sometimes touching attempts to be a larger-than-life figure in history? *Whom* is he really speaking for? And what is he *really* saying?

"As a historian I understand how histories are written," he told the *Atlanta Constitution* in 1985. "My enemies will write histories that dismiss me and prove I was unimportant. My friends will write histories that glorify me and prove I was more important than I was. And two generations or three from now, some serious, sober historian will write a history that sort of implies I was whoever I was."

Who Newt Gingrich is matters right now. Because his personal politics—of anger, of resentment, of revolution, call them what you will—are now our nation's politics. In Newt Gingrich's Congress, ideas that until recently were unthinkable to many mainstream Americans—doing away with the progressive income tax, doing away with welfare, doing away with public television, putting children in orphanages—circulate with approval. These ideas have the potential to completely change American life as we know it.

Who Newt Gingrich is, what he believes in, who is the company he keeps, matter a great deal right now. For Newt Gingrich doesn't just speak to America; as the highest-ranking member of the people's House, he ostensibly speaks *for* America. And so it vitally matters if his mother says he calls Hillary Rodham Clinton a "bitch." And it vitally matters if his lieutenant, Dick Armey of Texas, calls his openly gay fellow Representative Barney Frank "Barney Fag." Were these just "innocent" slips of the tongue, or were they unconscious renderings of what Gingrich's vision of "renewing American civilization" is all about? The answer is vitally important. For as long as Newt Gingrich continues to speak for us all, we need to know what lies behind his words.

NEWT GINGRICH

SPEAKER TO AMERICA

1

A Cold War Childhood

When Kathleen Daugherty McPherson Gingrich, mother of the Speaker of the United States House of Representatives and burgeoning media star, was just plain Kit Daugherty, the sixteen-year-old daughter of a freight conductor from Royalton, Pennsylvania, the best thing going in town on a Saturday night was the local skating rink. That was where her friends went, where the boys were, where she found company after her father died in a car accident, and her mother started dating again.

At the skating rink, she met a boy named Newton C. McPherson, Jr. Newt was nineteen, attractive and attentive. He was a mechanic, originally from a farming family from a rural area near Lewistown, Pennsylvania. And when he asked Kit to marry him, she said yes right away. Why not? she thought. It *was* what was supposed to happen, after all—and she held her breath and thought: we'll just be engaged. I'll always have time to change my mind.

Time ran out faster than she anticipated. Kathleen's mother sent an announcement of the engagement to the local newspaper. Kit felt the clock was ticking; her future was taking form. And it wasn't shaping up to be all she'd ever dreamed. Newt had a dark side. He had a quick fuse, a cruel streak. He drank too much. He'd broken his nose running into a bakery truck playing football in the street, but everyone assumed he'd had it broken for him in a fight—he was that type of a guy. He had a tendency to fly off the handle.

"I was afraid of him," she says. "I was standing in front of the soda fountain one night talking to a young man who lived in town. Big Newt was not supposed to come in for maybe an hour. So I felt safe. Well, he got off. And he came in from work, and he grabbed a pipe out of this guy's hand and he said, 'I don't ever want to see you close to her again.' The guy took off."

Kathleen got cold feet.

She went home and told her mother she wanted the wedding called off. Impossible, her mother said. "It's being announced in the paper tomorrow."

"But I don't want to marry him. I want to break it off," Kit insisted.

"You can't," her mother said.

With her mother pushing her out, and Big Newt drawing her in, Kit went with the flow. She didn't really know what else to do.

"My father had died, and I didn't have anyone to go to," she says. "My mother was young, she was dating, having a good time. And wanted, I guess, to put me out on my own."

The Daugherty-McPherson wedding took place early one chilly morning in Middletown, Pennsylvania.

"I had it at seven or eight in the morning," Kit recalls. "I didn't want anyone to come."

The bride wore a velvet dress, gray velvet—"Marry in gray and you'll live faraway," she mused—and after the wedding the couple moved in with Newt's parents. The first few months passed smoothly enough. But in the third month there was a rude awakening.

Newt had spent the night out drinking at the pool hall with friends, and did not want to wake up when Kit tried to rouse him for work at the Hershey chocolate factory. She insisted. He hit her. Luckily for Kit, her father-in-law intervened.

"His father came in and said, 'If you ever put your

hands on her again, you'll never come back into this house,' " Kit recalls. The ultimatum sat badly with Newt. Three days later, he left for the navy.

Married, pregnant, but more or less homeless, Kit stayed with her in-laws until her son, Newton McPherson, was born on June 17, 1943. Then, after a series of hospital mixups in which wrong babies were taken out of wrong bassinets—errors which, if uncorrected, could perhaps have saved the Clinton presidency—she went home to her mother's, filed legal papers, and waited.

When Big Newt came home on leave, she told him she'd filed for a divorce.

"He laughed," she says. "And he said, 'Thanks for all the letters. There were too many to read, so I threw them overboard.' "

"How I got together with Big Newt, I don't know," she reflects today. "The only good thing was I had Newtie."

The country went to war. The local men went away to the army. Kit wanted to go too. She tried to join up as a WAC. But the recruiting office told her that to do that, she'd have to give her baby up for adoption.

She refused. "Newtie was all that I had," she says.

She took a job working as a junior mechanic in a war factory. The Rosie-the-Riveter lifestyle suited her well. She was proud to be part of the war effort. Her life wasn't unpleasant at all. With her mother working as a schoolteacher, her own salary, and Big Newt's navy allotment, she could afford a baby-sitter for little Newtie, who was spending a very happy toddlerhood dividing his time between his grandmother's house and the home of his Aunt Loma and Uncle Cal, his father's sister and brother-in-law, who were childless and lived nearby.

Newt's grandmother, he has always said, taught him to read; his Aunt Loma and Uncle Cal would teach him to vote Republican. But despite the importance of these early influences on his two grand passions—reading and politics—his mother still made the deepest mark on Newt in those early years. They were intensely close. Which may be why, when Kit, now a strikingly pretty and stylish nineteen-year-old, took to skating once again and met up with Robert Gingrich, a tall and handsome army artillery officer, and eventually brought him home as her husband, Newt was less than overjoyed. His reaction to the new man in the house was to give his mother a well-aimed kick in the shins.

"He got his tail whopped," Kit recalls. "And he should have."

True, Newtie hadn't been consulted on the marriage. But then, he was only three. And no one, after all, had really done all that much talking about it anyway.

"We just danced," Kit says of her six-month courtship with Robert. "We danced the whole time. We didn't really talk."

Lieutenant Colonel Robert Gingrich, a career military officer at the height of the Cold War, was a man of few words. He is still the same today.

"Talk is just that—talk," he says. "Unless I'm talking about something I'm interested in, I'd rather not talk about it at all. But when I say something, you know I've said it."

Straight away, Robert said that he wanted to adopt Newt. He himself had been born to an unwed teenage mother, and was "taken to raise," as the local expression has it, by a Pennsylvania-Dutch family in Hummelstown who gave him their name and accepted him as one of their own—but didn't legally adopt him until he was seventeen years old.

"I wanted to give him a sense of belonging," Robert says. "It was especially important to me once our girls came along."

Newt's father took some convincing, but when Kathleen and Robert argued that all their children ought to be able to start school with the same last name, he agreed. The adoption came through when Newt was three years old.

Marcella McPherson, Newton McPherson's second wife, says that in later years her husband came to regret having allowed his son to be adopted by Gingrich.

"Newtie was so small when Bob Gingrich adopted him that he didn't really realize that Newt was his real father and Bob was his stepfather," she says. "When he was little and he used to come and visit with us, my mother-in-law and sister-in-law used to point to Newt and say, '*This* is your father,' and he'd say, 'No, no, it isn't.' His father regretted it very much then that Newt had been adopted."

When asked once by the *Washington Post* about his childhood, Gingrich said, "You could write a soap opera." He elaborated: "I spent probably into my forties coping with the whole process of being adopted and having to sort it out. Marianne [his second wife] helped me come to grips with being human at that level, because I had literally dealt with all sorts of issues by making them mechanical and outside myself."

Newt Gingrich has described his relationship with his stepfather as a "classic psychodrama."

Exactly what he means by this has never been clear. He has offered more by way of hints than actual explanations. For instance, he's said that he could never finish reading Pat Conroy's classic novel *The Great Santini,* about a teenage boy's frustrated efforts to win the admiration of his emotionally cold, even abusive, military father, because it was just too painful. Kit Gingrich has told reporters that Newt went out of his way to try to win his stepfather's favor, over and over again. Filling in details, she tells of how, when thirteen-year-old Newt was given money to spend on himself in a gift shop in Shannon, Ireland, he used it to buy a bottle of whiskey for Bob. She also remembers how the two would go out back together and toss balls, Bob yelling and berating Newt because he couldn't catch them. "We didn't know that he couldn't see," she says.

"He was domineering," Kit says, then amends herself. "He was *different*. He had a *different* way of showing appreciation."

Roberta Gingrich Brown, Newt's forty-four-year-old sister, now the home economics program specialist for the Pennsylvania State Department of Education, tells the story of how Newt and Bob went away together once on a Cub Scout camping weekend: Bob pitched a perfect tent, Newt tripped over a cord and brought it crashing down, and Bob let out a string of "some things the Cub master asked him not to repeat," she says.

Bob Gingrich, too, has stories. He told the *Washington Post* of how, when he was stationed in France, Newt once went into town after he'd been told not to. When he came home, Bob picked him up, held him off the ground against a wall by his shoulders, and asked him what he had to say. "It's pretty hard to be aggressive with your feet a few inches off the floor," was Newt's response.

The stories are funny today, ancient history now that "Newtie" is Speaker of the House and Bob Gingrich is an older, greatly softened, almost wistful-sounding retiree who looks back on his life with some disappointment and speaks of Newt with some admiration. But they probably weren't very amusing when they happened, not to a teenager or a little boy whose father towered above him in his uniform, communicated in orders, and dominated the mother he'd once claimed all for his own. And it wasn't funny when the derision and humiliation continued after Newt was a young man.

Lee Howell, a Griffin, Georgia, journalist who met Gingrich when he was the editor of the West Georgia College student newspaper and worked with him throughout his early campaigns, chiefly as a speechwriter, remembers conversations with Newt from the early 1970s, when the two men shared stories about growing up with career military fathers.

"I was saying something about being opposed to the

war, and saying my father didn't approve because I didn't join the army and volunteer,'' Howell recalls. ''And Newt said, 'Yeah, I had that problem, too.' Our fathers had a tendency to think of us as wimps.''

''He looked at Newt as not being manly,'' another friend from the period agrees. ''Newt represented everything that his stepfather found objectionable. He wore glasses, he *talked*. I think he considered him a sissy.''

Bob Gingrich was a military man: an austere, no-nonsense officer who saw the world in black and white, right and wrong, with very little room for the gray area of childish behavior.

''Military life is pragmatic,'' he says. ''You do what you have to do when you have to do it, and you do it as well as you can.''

But the military austerity that clings to him didn't just start with the army. His life was always a bit rough around the edges, unindulgent. Bob's adoptive father, Morris Pitt Gingrich, was a railroad brakeman. His family lived in a house without central heating and with a privy in the backyard. Bob began adulthood working on the railroad, and might very well have spent his entire life doing so had it not been for World War II (a war he almost missed, thanks to a hernia that branded him 4-F until near the very end of the fighting), and the GI Bill, which offered a path into a middle-class life for so many men of his generation.

Shortly after marrying Kit, Bob enrolled in Gettysburg College. The family moved into a split-level apartment over a gas station on the main street of Hummelstown. Kit's mother moved in to help take care of the children, now Newt, Susan, and Roberta, later, Candace—staying on until 1970. Kit went to work in a men's clothing store, and at age twenty-six Bob became a freshman. He studied biology and chemistry by day, tended bar at night, and drove fifty miles back and forth from home to school and work, all the while maintaining a B average. He declared a premed major, and dreamed of becoming a doctor, until a school admissions officer looked over his finances, his three children and his expiring government scholarship, and told him to forget it.

"I busted my butt to get my education," Bob Gingrich says. "Then I got smart enough to find out that I didn't have the money and there was no way I could swing it."

It was the first, perhaps seminal disappointment in a life that would brighten but never, as Robert Gingrich saw it at least, really shine. In the early 1950s, with medical school out, he rejoined the army. Because of his college degree he was told he could expect a bright future as an officer. But bureaucratic snafus got in his way—and though he did at the end of his career become an infantry instructor and a colonel, he never made general—a failure, Kit says, that fuels his self-criticism to this day. Just forty-nine years old when he retired from the army, he brought Kit and Candace back to Pennsylvania and went through a series of unsatisfying jobs. He collected tolls at the Gettysburg interchange of the Pennsylvania Turnpike, and worked as a security guard briefly, until he complained that he just couldn't stand it anymore. Now he's retired.

"In the past I had no time for hobbies," he muses. "Now I've got nothing but hobbies."

To a certain extent, Bob Gingrich's black-and-white world has faded to gray; the son he once disdained for his lack of physical strength is now third in line to the Presidency, his youngest daughter is gay (and a Democrat), and he stays at home now, sometimes, tending to young granddaughters quite happily—and he seems at peace with the world.

Kit, a staunch conservative Republican, describes the moment when she discovered that her youngest daughter was a lesbian: "I found a flier in her bedroom. And I read it and thought, 'It can't be Candace. It must be one of her friends.' When she came home from college, we stopped to have a bite to eat. I said, 'Candy, are you trying to tell me something?' She said, 'What do you mean, Mother?' I said, 'The book in your bedroom.' And she said, 'Well, you may as well know. But think of it this way: you don't have to spend the money for a big wedding.'

"I don't think Bob even talks about it," Kit says now. "Just accepts it."

It wasn't always this way.

"We were terrified of Dad when we were growing up," says Newt's sister Susan, who works in the Medical Assistance Program in the Pennsylvania Department of Public Welfare. "He was your typical military, in-command type of person—really the boss of the family. He's a lot more mellow now than he used to be. He's a lot easier to communicate with, a lot more human now than he was then."

"I could be pretty imposing in a uniform," Bob Gingrich himself admits. "But I don't know why anyone would have been scared of me."

He *was* different. He showed his concern for his teenage daughters by refusing to teach them to drive. (Kit and the neighbors taught them, on the sly.) He showed his playful side by encouraging one of his girls to join him in a swim in a freezing mountain pool. He bought Kit a house without asking her where she wanted to live (she dreams, to this day, of homes in the subdivision one over, with their red brick and white-trimmed exteriors and cozy fireplaces). He preferred, Kit has said, doing crossword puzzles to talking.

Roberta strongly disagrees with the portrayal of her father as a cold and crusty authoritarian. "It's a misnomer," she says. "The things that I remember are snowball fights in the house. I remember a tease, a devil. I remember being tickled. I remember many times just sitting down and telling him what was going on in my life." All the same, she does agree on one thing: to hold your own in Bob Gingrich's family you needed to have an agile tongue and a quick mind.

She recalls how the family used to sit around the dinner table for hours, avoiding the dishes, talking and debating, and getting out the encyclopedia to challenge their father on points of fact—always to lose the point in the end.

"Thanks to Dad, all of us are outspoken," Roberta says. "None of us are yes-people. The intellect, the thinking things through, the planning, the belief in responsibility—we all got it from him."

Many observers who have observed Newt Gingrich over the decades also think that his stepfather is to thank for his single-minded determination to become a powerful politician.

"It's all about his psyche," one longtime Gingrich watcher says. "It's all about never earning the love of this stepfather. It's this need to be able to say, 'I am somebody. I am worth something.' What triggered him to channel it all into politics? I'll tell you why: because the military always has to respond to civilian authorities."

It's true that however much artillery officer Bob Gingrich controlled his family and his troops, his own life and the fate of his family were largely out of his control. He didn't see much of the family during Newt's early years, when he was stationed at Fort Monroe, Virginia, and in Korea. He kept up with the boy's advancement through Kit's faithful letters. In elementary school, Newt developed his first two passions: reading and animals. Bob bought him an *Encyclopedia Americana,* and he devoured it night after night. His grandmother gave him a leather jacket, and he painted it with white stripes to look like a zebra. He read the works of the German animal specialist Carl Hagenpeck, originator of the "bar-less zoo" theory, and became obsessed with the idea that Wildwood Park in nearby Harrisburg would be the perfect site for a public zoo.

When he was ten, he told his mother one afternoon that he was going to the library and instead went to the mayor's office to make a plea for the zoo. After his first visit the mayor sent him home in a state car. Newt came back almost every day, better and better read in his subject and more insistent, until the mayor finally came up with a solution. He sent Newt over to the nearby Telegraph Building, where the *Home Star,* a local paper, was headquartered.

"Tell it to that fellow over at the *Home Star,*" he told Newt. "He has a little newspaper and will listen to your ideas. He has the time, which I don't."

Newt showed up at the newspaper on deadline day and introduced himself straightaway to "that fellow," Robert Walker, a longtime newspaper man. Walker listened, his eye on the clock, then decided to save time by asking Newt to sit down and write up his ideas as a piece for the paper.

"But I've never used a typewriter," Newt said.

"All the better," Walker thought.

He didn't yet know Newt Gingrich. Newt wrote the piece and the paper ran it. Walker made him an honorary staff writer.

"He was good for a new idea every day," he later recalled. The newspaper eventually recommended him to the state museum, where he worked as a volunteer. When a local reporter caught up with him a few years later, he'd become a kind of local celebrity:

"Newton Gingrich, an earnest young man of twelve, has filed another appeal for public-spirited Harrisburgers to support his movement for a zoo," the story ran.

Newt showed a mastery of facts and figures: "There is no reason why every town of 100,000 inhabitants should not have its zoological garden," he said. "That just fits Harrisburg."

He estimated that the initial cost of a zoo would be $15,000, and annual operating costs would be $150.

"We could start out with the smaller animals," he said. "Don't you know an African lion costs only $250. And it's easily gotten." A kinkajou, he said, cost only $75, and monkeys went for about $50, "except for the chimpanzees, of course."

In a move he'd undoubtedly revile today, he suggested that the city pick up most of the tab, and that zoo admission be free. But, with the seeds of parliamentarianism budding within him, he added, "Everything would be easy if we had a committee."

The newspaper man concluded: "A few minutes' conversation with Newton leaves an awed adult with a flying start toward an inferiority complex."

Bob Gingrich, receiving the clipping out in Korea, was less impressed. "Keep that boy out of the papers!" he wrote Kit.

When Newt's plans for public funding didn't take, he began canvassing neighbors for private funds. He tried to talk a local funeral director, Harry Trefz, into lending him seed money. When that didn't fly, either, he found other ways to bring his love of animals to the public. He talked a local pet store owner into advertising by displaying his animals on TV. He then talked a local television station into letting him get on the air, and, unbeknownst to his family, started doing his own five-minute, weekly TV spot, giving lectures on zoology to the local viewing public. Once, just before the family was to leave Pennsylvania for Kansas, Kit was called to the TV by an excited neighbor. Newt was on the air, talking about their new home state.

She was shocked.

"Will you just keep him home?" Bob growled.

By 1953, Bob Gingrich was back from Korea. The family was sent on its first military posting, to Fort Riley, Kansas. The three children, parents, grandmother, and dog—Kathleen's Pride of Riley, which Newt saved from drowning in a frozen lake by diving under the ice to catch it—moved into a two-bedroom row house, and settled into the unsettled, peripatetic existence of military families. While Bob didn't much relish giving up his and Kit's bedroom to his mother-in-law, Newt and the girls enjoyed the life of the army base. Life was secure and neighborly; there were children everywhere, sleeping over and eating at one another's houses and even sleeping out on the front lawns in the summers. Newt began organizing fossil-hunting excursions, and would lead his sisters up onto the Rim Rock formation, where they'd rock hunt and build "igloos" and dams.

"It was easy to make friends, but you didn't keep them," Susan Gingrich Shurskis says. "Once you left a place, you really didn't keep in touch with anybody. It made us very close as a family, very dependent on each other. We were like the three musketeers."

In a 1990 interview with an *Atlanta* magazine reporter, Newt Gingrich stated that his family's constant moves left him lacking a feeling of long-term attachment to people. "It actually led to an exaggerated sense of being without friends," he said. "It took me years to get over it."

The children's world was insular yet multinational. It was secure yet bordered by extreme danger. An army father could be called off to war at any moment—and might not come back. And, once the family moved to Europe in 1956, setting up base in Orleans, France, and Stuttgart, Germany, they also had to contend with the ever present danger of living in ground zero in the case of nuclear war.

"The soldiers of [Robert Gingrich's] generation were prepared at all times to deal with any contingencies that might come up in the Cold War," says Steve Hanser, a West Georgia College military historian and close friend and adviser of Newt's. "If you're in the military, you're on twenty-four hours a day. And the contract, the implicit contract, is your willingness to be shot, bombed, mutilated, blinded, or killed in the performance of your duty. It lends a certain piquancy to the situation."

In Europe, the Gingrich family was issued a set of evacuation plans. They had to keep a box packed with the basic necessities: blankets, towels, soap. There were routes laid out for dependents to follow if they had to evacuate their homes. They knew that if bad news came, they would have to leave their Doberman behind.

"Newt was in high school, maybe eighteen miles

away. And all I could think of was 'How would we get to Newtie?' " Kit says.

Ultimately, in order to survive in the pervasive climate of insecurity, they simply blocked out the fear.

"It was always there in the back of your mind," Bob Gingrich says. "But all in all, you got on with your daily life, and if it happened, it happened."

"We just took it for granted that everything was going to work out," Kit says. "And it did."

The army was a nation unto itself, and its culture set the children's horizons, permeated their imaginations, flavored their games. While other kids played Capture the Flag and Post Office and House, these kids played Army and Passport Check and PX. "We'd sit in the car for a couple of hours playing Going on Trips," Susan says. "We would play Commissary."

"We were cliqueish. We all stuck together," says Roberta. "We couldn't believe it when we lived with civilians and they didn't know the difference between a corporal and a captain. We didn't believe they could be so stupid. We were precocious. We thought we knew everything. We'd have teachers trying to teach geography to people who had lived in the places they were talking about. I remember once at Fort Leavenworth having a French teacher to whom we kept trying to explain that he was not teaching French."

The Gingrich children's acculturation was specific and strange, unusual and wholly typical of the experience of military kids in the Cold War years that Mary Edwards Wertsch documented encyclopedically in *Military Brats*. Wertsch describes military brats as nomadic, resilient, forcedly extroverted people who quickly learn to "travel light" both physically and emotionally through their rootless lives. They are people who often seem to have both missed a few steps in their socialization and are precocious at the same time.

Military brats, and particularly the boys, who were drawn into the deepest drama of identification and conflict with their fathers, Wertsch says, tend to develop a rather unique set of personality traits: a great awareness of class differences and hostility about them, an "outsider syndrome," accompanied by a great tendency to divide the world between us and them. Military brats, she writes, "don't invest heavily in relationships," and often seem to have an "undeveloped interior life." She elaborates: "We children of the Fortress frequently arrive in adulthood bearing some similarity to the spacious old homes one finds on many a military base: impressive, sturdy, well tended, and with a certain air of déjà vu—but without much in the way of interior furnishings."

It's easy to read into that description a kind of laundry list of traits that Newt Gingrich has shown, both on a personal level in his many broken friendships and as a larger-than-life character on the political stage. How much of that, though, is really due to his military upbringing, and how much is a synergy of army brattiness with professional deformation is hard to say.

In Newt's own personal lore, his life as a teenager in Europe can be summed up in a single, terrible word: Verdun. On Easter weekend 1957, the Gingrich family paid a visit to a childhood friend of Bob's from Pennsylvania who was stationed with the army in France near the World War I battle site. Bob Gingrich's friend had been drafted into the army in 1941, had been part of the Bataan death march, and had served three years in a Japanese prisoner-of-war camp. The horror of the friend's recent war stories was still reeling in Newt's imagination when, one morning that weekend, he stepped onto the hills and furrows of the now desertlike former battlefield, which had seen one of the worst slaughters of the twentieth century. In the battle of Verdun, the Germans assumed the French would defend their stronghold to the death rather than admit weakness, and the French took the bait. The battle raged for ten months, at least seven hundred thousand men were killed, and neither side at the end could claim victory. "It was an indecisive battle in an indecisive war; the unnecessary battle in an unnecessary war; the battle that had no victors in a war that had no victors," the historian Alistair Horne has put it.

When the Gingrichs visited Verdun, many buildings in the surrounding town still bore the scars and pockmarks of war. Walking along the road leading to the battle site, Newt found the rusted helmets of French and German soldiers. But nothing chilled him more than the ossuary—a stone monument overlooking the battlefields in which the bones of the unclaimed war dead lay in a mass basement grave. They lay behind windows that had once been painted black but had been chipped away enough to provide a view of rib cages and skulls, thousands and thousands of bones, thrown together in a heap.

Newt left Verdun amazed at the awesome power of politicians to cause such destruction. In his 1984 book, *Window of Opportunity,* he would write that the "sense of horror and reality" that overcame him looking into the ossuary became "the driving force which pushed me into history and politics and molded my life. . . . I left that battlefield convinced that men do horrible things to each other, that great nations can spend their lifeblood and their treasure on efforts to coerce and subjugate their fellow man. I was absolutely certain that what had happened before could happen again."

If Verdun struck Newt quite as strongly at the time, he did not say so. His mother doesn't remember Verdun as the defining memory of their years in France. Nor do his sisters recall Newt spending much brooding over the decay of the West. Their memories of France are of a much brighter nature: for one thing, after years of drab army base housing, they rented a charming country villa in Beaugency, near Orleans.

"A chateau," Susan remembers.

"It wasn't a chateau," Robert insists.

The house—"Belle fleur du desert," Susan says; "Belle *vue* du desert," Robert snaps—was set behind a great wrought iron gate. It was approached by a circular gravel drive. In the back, French doors and a set of steps led past urns of bright flowers to an apple orchard and, a bit farther on, to the river.

There was a gardener and a maid ("No maid," Robert says), and a woman who ironed, and the children were given a playroom with a gilded ceiling painted with angels.

"I had dreams about that house years after we lived there," Susan says.

It was a great time to be an American in France. If you had dollars, you were rich, you were "liberators," and, if you spoke French, it was easy to make friends. And even if you didn't, and insisted, like an Ugly American upon calling the statue of a horsebacked Joan of Arc in the center of Orleans "Joanie on a pony" and another statue of a seated nude "Dotty on the potty," as many Americans did, the French were tolerant. Bob learned to speak French well enough that he made friends with townspeople, particularly a couple who ran a nearby bar and restaurant. He was so popular in town that when the family was delayed once in returning from a camping trip in Spain because he had badly sunburned his foot, the local firemen held off on holding their July 14 parade until he could join them in marching. He, in return, fed them hot chocolate, corn, and toast, and even bought an American toaster at the PX one Christmas for his close French friends.

By that time Newt had discovered girls. In Spain there was a girl who ran a concession stand ("He drank a lot of Coke," says Susan), and in Beaugency he fell in love with a girl named Jeannette. She gave Newt a pink chiffon scarf that he proudly showed off to his young sisters, forbidding them ever to touch it. They wore it every time he had his back turned.

Newt was a boy who could watch *The Sands of Iwo Jima* three times in an afternoon. When he got a new bike, he immediately took it apart to see how it worked, then spent days trying to pick all the misplaced pieces up out of the gravel driveway. He loved

Red Skelton and Jerry Lewis. Despite the fact that the family hated living in Germany (there were games of Army in the Black Forest, lots of castles and museums, but still, as Gingrich says in his Renewing American Civilization lecture series, "The number one fact about Germany is, there are a lot of Germans"), he learned the language well enough to be able to read German medical texts in the original.

There is no doubt that he was passionate and single-minded. But did he really spend the ride on the military transport ship that brought the family home to the United States nursing his psychic wounds from Verdun and planning his political future? Roberta's memory of the crossing is of ten days of seasickness and an endless craving for peanut butter sandwiches. Newt remembers a soul-sickness and the start of a calling. "I saw this would consume me; it would destroy me. It was an epiphany, he told the *Los Angeles Times* more than thirty years later. "It was the most amazing decision of my life," he told another reporter. "And it gives me certain inner strengths that other politicians don't have, because I see this as a calling, as something that someone has to do if America is to keep the freedoms we believe in."

Did he truly, the following fall, hand in a 180-page paper on the balance of world power to his English teacher and announce his intention to go to Georgia and form a Republican party and become a congressman?

He says he did. And according to Nando Amabile, who taught English at the American School in Stuttgart, Germany, when Newt was there, "he was precocious. He was a man-child."

Newt came back from Europe intellectually precocious but socially awkward. He was finally wearing glasses—big, thick, horn-rimmed ones. He was more comfortable with adults than with other teenagers. He wasn't entirely happy.

"When Newtie came home from Germany, he was like an altogether different boy," Marcella McPherson says. "He was more like an adult, and he and his daddy used to talk for hours and hours and hours. They'd sit up at night and talk politics and sports. He wanted to be with my husband constantly."

Newt had always spent a good deal of time visiting the McPhersons before his family had moved to Europe, Marcella says. But now the quality of that time grew different.

"He and his father got to be very, very close," she recalls. "He wanted to come and live with us. But [his mother] had had him from the time he was real small. . . . It wouldn't have been right for me to say yes."

Newt's relationship with his stepfather was clearly less than golden. But was it so bad that he wanted to leave home? Or was it just that he wanted, after the rootless years on army bases, to have a sense of place? Or was he looking for another, non-military, role model?

No one is saying. But the McPherson family—"Big" Newt's son, Randy, his daughter, Kathy Evans, and Marcella, all of whom have remained close to Newt—strongly refute the notion that Newt McPherson was in any way the violent man that Kit depicts. He was tough, they say, and big, but never abusive or cruel.

"He demanded respect. He would yell. You knew he meant business when he yelled. He could be a physically intimidating person to some people," says Randy, twelve years Newt's junior. "But he never was abusive."

"Newtie was very close to his father," says Marcella. "I don't think his mother kind of wanted to acknowledge it. . . . They were both so young when they got married."

Newt Gingrich, however, has made the presence of a tough, hard-fighting natural father part of his personal mythology. "Newt described him to me as a large, brawling man who would go into bars and get into fights," former representative Vin Weber of Minnesota told the *Washington Post* last year. "Newt was proud that that was his background. He liked knowing that he's combative and confrontational by birth."

The McPhersons' memories suggest that some re-writing may have gone into Newt Gingrich's life story.

"My father was very, very well read," Kathy says. "And Newt always had a book in his hand. Their favorite thing to do was sit around the kitchen table or out on the front porch and talk about world affairs, share points of view. They used to have big discussions."

Maybe Newt was in search of his roots—he's always liked to wear a McPherson tartan tie and speaks reverently of Robert the Bruce, unifier of the McPherson ancestral home of Scotland—or maybe he was just indulging in the eternal teenage dream of running away from home. In any case, in 1960 he moved with his family to Fort Benning, in Columbus, Georgia, then the largest American military base in the world.

Columbus, Georgia, was the first permanent-seeming home the Gingrich family had ever known, and they settled into it gladly. Life on the military base was secure and neighborly. The girls took dance classes and became active in the Junior Army Daughters. Newt quickly established himself as a star at Baker High School, a highly reputed school with many international students, about ninety percent military brats, and no blacks. With his heavy glasses, short-cut hair, white and plaid shirts buttoned up to the top and worn with pens sticking out of their pockets and a slide rule, Newt Gingrich didn't have the look of the popular crowd. He had a funny way about him, too, a kind of professional self-absorption. He would exclaim, "Question here!" when he raised his hand in class. He'd read while he walked on his way home from the library, and if a family friend stopped to give him a ride on the way home, he wouldn't put his book down until he was dropped off.

"He was the epitome of a nerd," says Mike Kocian, a former classmate who is now an elementary school teacher in Georgia. "But it was when being a nerd was respectable. We looked up to him."

He was a "thespian" and a debater. He tutored a school beauty queen. He wrote and directed the senior class show. He was excused from classes his senior year, provided he kept up his grades on his own. He was called to the school principal's office sometimes four or five times a day to give advice on academic issues. He was a National Merit Scholarship semifinalist. An essay he wrote won the *Time* magazine current-events award.

"He's probably the most intelligent human being I've ever met up with," says Kocian.

"He wasn't an A student," Robert Gingrich attests. "He was test-smart. I am, too. And if it was a test on something he was interested in, he scored well. If it was something he didn't care about, he scored low. He wasn't the class pride."

Baker High School was a bomb-proof school built like a fortress just two miles away from the Fort Benning reservation. It was the kind of school at the time when boys wore their hair slicked back into a d.a., wore Ban-Lon shirts and pegged pants, and girls wore bobby socks and won awards for their sewing. It was the kind of place that had clubs like Beta Tri-Hi-Y—"a group of outstanding Christian girls banded together to create, maintain, and extend high standard of character"—and Newt's own Beta Kappa Hi-Y—"outstanding members in their classes as well as in their church and community." It was the kind of place that made "Beauties" a section of the yearbook, featuring pages of blushing girls in strapless taffeta ballgowns, like "Miss Arrowhead of 1961," who "reflects a beauty symbolic of the freshness of youth, representative of the young people of our school, our nation, and, indeed, of our world."

Columbus was the kind of town where the students from the three white high schools spent their weekends going to sock hops and "cruising" the strip between their respective drive-in hangouts. The boys would take offense when soldiers came off base and tried to pick up local girls, and what few non-military sons there were hated the army for that.

Newt didn't cruise; he couldn't dance. He tried to go out for football, but he debated with the coach on the validity of every play, then developed chronic headaches, and then was told by a base doctor that he could go blind if he continued to play. He cried, then quit the team.

"He was a terrible football player," Kocian says. "The coach would say, 'I want you to go down fifteen yards and turn to the right.' And he'd say, 'Why?' No matter what you told him, he'd say, 'Why?' Everything had to have a purpose. It had to benefit somebody, or he wouldn't consider it. But he tried."

Physical activity wasn't really his thing. He swallowed a mouthful of Clorox once when he tripped while carrying an open bottle down the stairs, eager to take a stain out of a rug. If his father kept him close to home for discipline's sake, it was probably for the best. At home, he cooked popovers and made marshmallow and peanut butter and banana and mayonnaise sandwiches ("We used to call him the human garbage disposal," Susan says. "And he wasn't heavy then!"), teased his sisters, and amused himself with his wood-burning set. And he read.

He also met his first soul mate. Jim Tilton was one of the only students around who could match Newt in intelligence and academic achievement. (Newt and Jimmy tied for highest scores in Muscogee County on the National Merit Scholarship Test.) Jimmy, like Newt, was an army brat. Newt told of his fear of Bob Gingrich—and Jimmy, understandingly, agreed.

"From the first time they met, they were sympatico," Roberta says. "They could say things that had a meaning to them that they didn't have to the other people around them. They could say anything to each other. They had complete trust."

Newt and Jimmy spent afternoons walking for miles

together to Republican Party meetings. Both campaigned hard for Richard Nixon.

Media-savvy on the cusp of the TV campaign age, Newt befriended the local TV station owner in Columbus, winning him over with his moxie and smarts and Jimmy Tilton's not inconsiderable charm.

"Newt walked into my campaign headquarters one day and told me that he was going to be a politician and that he would do anything I wanted him to do," Marilu Blaney, then president of the Republican Women's Club in Columbus and a Republican National Committee worker, recalls. "He had a lot of confidence. And he sure wasn't shy."

Perhaps the apogee of Newt Gingrich's high school career was Jimmy Tilton's 1961 campaign for student president. Jim Tilton wasn't a long shot to start off; by the end of the year he was elected "Best All-Around," "Boy of the Year," "Most Representative," and "Most Likely to Succeed" in his class (his campaign manager was elected "Most Intellectual"), but Newt took no chances.

"Newt printed bumper stickers, he printed handout sheets. He had pencils made with Jim Tilton's name on them," Kocian says. "He took the job of Tilton's campaign manager as seriously as if he were Bush's campaign manager. Put the name in front of everybody. Over and over and over again!"

Not surprisingly, Jim Tilton won. And Newt had his first taste of politics. Friends from high school say that it was then that he started talking about his dream of being Speaker of the House.

The Gingrichs stayed in Columbus for six years—longer than they had lived anywhere else. "Georgia was home. We never wanted to leave," Susan says. But eventually the family did leave, everyone but Newt. The Gingrich family went on to Baltimore, back to the Harrisburg area, to Fort Leavenworth for a year, then to Indiana, Pennsylvania, and Panama. But Newt stayed in Georgia, though it could be argued that he did continue to "travel light": keeping emotional entanglements low-key, making friendships that were easily sloughed off when the time came.

He kept most of them light, anyway.

In the mid-1970s, one of Newt's closest high school friends, Calvin Rousch, died in an auto accident. He was thirty-three. In 1993, Jimmy Tilton, then a lawyer in Washington, died of pancreatic cancer. A few months before Tilton's death, Gingrich spoke at a Salute to Newt rally in a Holiday Inn in his district. He talked about high school, recalled playing football, and spoke about his two closest friends, Calvin and Jimmy. He mentioned that Jimmy Tilton was then lying in Georgetown Hospital with cancer. He didn't say that he was dying. But he turned his head away from the microphone, and he sobbed for twenty or thirty seconds. As he composed himself, the room was silent. No one had ever seen this Newt Gingrich before.

"In the length of time that we lost three Americans in Somalia, we lost forty-eight in Washington, D.C.," he began again, abruptly, haltingly.

He held firm for a moment, then veered again into the personal. Bob Gingrich, he said, "helped teach me that life is vital and real . . ." He trailed off again. And resumed: "What we are about is having our children and grandchildren pursue what they want in a society where the rules are followed by everyone."

His voice rose. He was back.

2

Education of a
Political Animal:
Rebel Without a Cause

Newt Gingrich hadn't been totally asocial in high school.

In fact, as girlfriends went, he scored about as high as any boy in his class possibly could. Other guys, like "best all-around" Jimmy Tilton, might date beauty queens. Newt went out with his geometry teacher.

Her name was Jackie Battley, and she was twenty-four years old. She was born and raised in Georgia, a devout Southern Baptist, a traditionalist in everything except, it would seem, her taste in younger men. She was pretty, slightly chubby—"five-four, five-five, either way you measured her," Mike Kocian laughs. She was the subject of untold numbers of military brat crushes.

Newt Gingrich wasn't one to sit back passively and fantasize.

On his first day in Miss Battley's math class, he turned around and told Jimmy Tilton, "I'm going to marry her." Soon he was taking time out from tutoring a class beauty queen to make "top-secret" phone calls to Jackie. They began dating secretly during his senior year. And when Jackie took a new teaching job in Atlanta, Newt soon followed, enrolling as a freshman at Emory University.

Newt didn't go to Emory to be near Jackie; the

university, often called "the Harvard of the South," has a highly reputed history department. It had resources far more tempting than those at Columbus College, where Newt had taken some courses. Emory offered Newt a partial scholarship. It also offered him an entry point into the world of the intellectual elite.

A letter he wrote to his Aunt Bea soon after arriving at Emory clearly suggests that thoughts of Jackie were not foremost in his mind: "I manage to go on dates several times a week, run around with the boys whenever I want to, watch TV down in the lounge two or three nights a week, and in other ways lead a rough life," he wrote, noting that, in addition to conducting his social life, he was attending class fifteen hours a week, spending three hours in physical education, two hours at ROTC, and spending seven hours a day studying and reading. He was somewhat miffed about the fact that the coaches at Emory had put him into an archery class filled with girls. Then, his tone softened: "I try to keep my ideals high," he wrote. "When most kids go to college they learn a great deal about life that reveals its more complicated and, sometimes, darker side and their idealism and romantic ideals of life are destroyed. I do not think I will be bothered by this because my romantic notions and dreams of the 'simple life' were destroyed a long time ago . . ." And he ended on an unabashedly happy note: "College life is wonderful . . . I am enjoying it more than anything I have ever done. I would venture to say this is the happiest time of my life. . . ."

The letter is genuine and touching—and sad. Perhaps what makes it sad is the clear memory of youthful disillusionment that lingers around its edges. Or perhaps, with hindsight, it's the happiness.

For happy was not a word that anyone would soon attach often to Newt Gingrich—and is not a word that leaps to the lips of anyone who describes him today.

"Newt's life was never much fun," says David Kramer, professor of social policy and vice rector of the School of Social Work in Berlin, who would become Newt's best friend at Tulane a few years later and is one of the few friends to have remained close to him since. "I don't even think he expects a lot of fun in life."

Living in Atlanta took Newt away from his family. It liberated him both from his stepfather's criticism and from the bond that tied him to his mother, whose marriage to a distant, overbearing, often absent man made Newt almost unbearably precious to her. "He was a joy to have around. We would do the dishes; I would wash and he would dry, and we would talk about everything under the sun," she recalls. "I cried when he left to go to Atlanta."

Newt didn't cherish his freedom for long. Maybe he didn't end up liking it so much on his own ("He was always very scared of traveling alone," his mother says). He might just have fallen madly head over heels in love. Or maybe he wanted at last to throw off his stepfather's iron rule and express himself, establish himself, play the rebel—by doing the one thing that everyone in his family had told him was wrong ever since the day he was born.

He would be just like his father. He would get married at nineteen.

Jackie Gingrich remembers things a bit more romantically. As she told David Osborne of *Mother Jones* in 1984, in an interview that would be the start and finish of her talking to the press, Newt showed up at her door one day not long after he'd arrived in Atlanta.

"I'm here," he announced.

"Yeah?" she said.

"Yeah, I came. I'm here."

"He had made up his mind," she told the reporter. "We dated and went together for that year, his freshman year in school, and we got married the next June."

He was very "persistent, and persuasive," she said.

"He put a major rush job on her," a friend elaborates. "It was kind of a touchy operation."

Newt Gingrich has since called his first marriage "a

random accident." It was anything but that. With trademark single-mindedness, Newt set his mind upon the wedding.

"If you live your life as a hostage to everybody else's decision, you either have to live a very narrow life or you have to spend a lot of time in pain," Gingrich told the *Washington Post* last December. "I hoped my mother would come, but I also understood that she . . . had to live with my stepfather. She only had to love me."

He got his stepfather's goat. There was nothing that the colonel could say or do to stop Newt.

"He did not discuss it. He just told us that it was going to happen," Bob Gingrich recalls. Typically, he said virtually nothing about it at the time. But he decided that he would not attend the wedding. The wedding day came, Jimmy Tilton dropped by with an unused corsage for Kit, and the girls, playing softball outside the house, watched him come and go in his tuxedo and wondered what was going on.

"I don't know if I was even that aware that it was taking place," Roberta recalls.

"I was upset that we didn't go," Susan says. "We had met Jackie and we liked her, and we just didn't understand. I understand now that Dad wanted to be a doctor but ended up with three kids and needed a job and was not able to fulfill his ambition," she adds. "He wanted something different for Newt."

"I *was* disappointed," Bob Gingrich now says, with control. "I was not understanding. But I was not angry. And once the first grandchild came along, that was the end of the fighting."

Kit was heartbroken. Faced with a battle of loyalty between her husband and her son, she was paralyzed. "I was in the middle," she says simply.

Jackie and Newt were married on June 19, 1962. Their first daughter, Linda Kathleen, was born nine months later. As a college student Newt staid true to his high school ways: he studied, he politicked, he went home. He cut out hijinks. He did his course work and was quiet in class. His center now was Jackie. His life was history and politics. He was looking forward. He didn't have to look back. It was as though he'd decided there wasn't anything to look back to.

Ben Branch, a professor of finance at the University of Massachusetts at Amherst, who founded the Emory Young Republican Club with Newt during their freshman year, remembers him as someone who seemed to have no past and was almost exclusively focused on his future life in politics.

"Newt had a lot of ideas. He was very articulate, he said a lot of thought-provoking things, but he didn't talk a lot about his past personal life," he says. "He was an intellectual sort of guy who wasn't really focused on the social scene. It was my sense that his wife was his best friend."

Though it would be a lonely sort of life for most nineteen-year-olds, Newt Gingrich didn't seem to mind. He was too busy. He and Branch worked hard to bring the Emory club statewide Republican recognition. Once established, they threw themselves into a petition drive to get Edward Smith, a Republican, on the ballot as a candidate for governor of Georgia. This was no small feat. Georgia had not elected a Republican governor since Reconstruction. It was a Democratic state, run by a well-oiled and fiery Democratic political machine, and when Gingrich and Branch got involved, the Republicans didn't even field candidates at the state and local level.

Smith was the first Republican to have even run for the governorship since Reconstruction. Newt hailed him as a candidate for change, and denounced his two Democratic opponents, Marvin Griffin and Garland Byrd, as guardians of an antiquated order.

"Neither of the Democratic candidates offer the voter a chance to turn to the future, to a highly industrialized, wealthy and heavily urban Georgia," he told the Emory *Wheel*. "We [the Republicans] are against the corruption fostered by the smug one-party atmosphere presently extant in this state, and we are against the reactionary attitude displayed by many of the state's Democratic politicians. . . . The Republican Party is essentially a conservatively oriented party, but we have plenty of room for all who wish to join regardless of their position on the spectrum.''

Unsaid, but understood, in that speech was Gingrich's message that the Republican party would welcome anyone, regardless of race. There was no better way to strike at the Democratic establishment than that.

''The Republican party at that time was much more in favor of civil rights than was the vast majority of the Democratic party in Georgia,'' Branch says. ''The governors at that time all ran on segregationist planks and were all trying in one way or another to slow down or stop the efforts to integrate the schools. The Republicans were trying to reach out to the black community and bring them in.''

Smith would die in a car accident before the election. But Gingrich's star would rise nonetheless. He made himself a fixture on the local political scene. He loved to organize and was good at it.

''Newt was the only person I knew who had multiple phone lines coming into his apartment [in college] when he was essentially just a kid,'' Linda Tilton, Jimmy Tilton's wife, told a reporter last year. ''He'd frequently be talking politics with [two] people at once, running from one phone to the other to tell each person what the other one was saying.''

In choosing to align himself with the Republicans in such a solidly Democratic state as Georgia, Gingrich all but insured himself rapid recognition and instant exposure.

''Most places where he might have tried to establish himself would have had a lot of people who were further along in getting to the point of where he wanted to be,'' Branch explains. Newt's choice to be a Republican, he says, was only ''partly ideological. He saw a chance to help develop a party and get in on the ground floor.''

Newt Gingrich was a natural-born Republican. The Harrisburg area where he'd been raised, now as then, is as hard-core conservative GOP as a region can get ("Democrats seated in the rear," reads a sign in a restaurant close to the Gingrich parents' home in Dauphin; billboards on the local roads advertise the PTL club, and a town banner in their tiny town proclaims "Christ Is Our Savior.") Newt's mother's family where old-line G.O.P. loyalists dating back to the time of Newt's great-great grandfather, who fought in the Civil War. On his father's side, his Uncle Cal and Aunt Loma, with whom he lived in the summer during the Fort Riley years, were vocal Republican supporters. His grandmother, too, was an outspoken Republican and, as Newt looked on, cried with his sister Susan when Kennedy was elected president. Only Bob Gingrich was a registered Democrat—a great admirer of Franklin Roosevelt and Harry Truman, though he changed his registration to Republican around the time Reagan was elected.

"I could see the handwriting on the wall," Bob says.

Newt lived and breathed Republicanism. It flowed in his veins. By his sophomore year at Emory, he was giving campus speeches on misappropriation and waste of taxpayer money. There were five imperative beliefs of the Republican party, he told his Young Republican faithful. They were: "belief in personal freedom, limited government, the federal system, the law, and capitalism." He blamed a negative image for the reason that the G.O.P. did so poorly in Georgia.

He made it his mission to try to rectify that image. He befriended Reg Murphy, then political editor of the *Atlanta Constitution,* and kept him tuned in to Young Republican activities at Emory. He tried to have himself made state chairman of the Georgia Young Republicans.

"It was a very unusual thing for someone still in college to do," Branch recalls. "The position normally went to someone in their twenties or thirties."

Gingrich and Branch arrived at the state convention all prepared to propose his candidacy, but let it drop at the last moment when it became clear to them that it was a lost cause.

In 1964, he had a chance to strike again at the Democrats when he and Jimmy Tilton managed the Ninth District congressional campaign of Jack Prince, a wealthy chicken processor from Gainesville. Prince was challenging Democratic congressman Phil Landrum, a powerful member of the House Ways and Means Committee, and a strong ally of Lyndon Johnson's in the War on Poverty. Prince ran considerably to the right of Landrum—as had Zel Miller, the current governor of Georgia, in the Democratic primary. In the end, though, Gingrich's campaign for Prince was less about ideology than a changing of the guard. Landrum was establishment—Gingrich wasn't.

Gingrich graduated from Emory in December 1965 with a degree in history, applied to Princeton, was rejected ("Princeton sent me a rejection letter so elegantly worded that I still think of myself as an alumnus," he once said) and, after spending a semester at Georgia State University, transferred into the Ph.D. program at Tulane, in New Orleans.

Tulane, in the late 1960s, was a far cry from Columbus, Georgia, or even Atlanta. The college had been integrated. New Orleans was multi-ethnic and cosmopolitan. There were foreign-sounding names, foreign-seeming foods, foreign-looking people. There was some campus activism—nothing like the paroxysms that shook Berkeley and Columbia and Madison—but there were protests against the war and ROTC.

Gingrich ate it up. It was a cultural awakening. In some ways, although he was married with two children, he hadn't changed all that much from his Baker High School days. He was still crossing streets with his nose in a book and sticking six pens in his shirt pocket. He'd taken a course on speed reading, which meant that even his favorite activity made him look bizarre. He was odd-looking, stocky, with a thick shock of black hair, a round face and thick horn-rimmed glasses.

"He looked," one friend recalls, "like a malicious teddy bear."

"Newt was the anti-hipster," Tulane friend David Kramer recalls. "Polyester pants, maybe a turtleneck, maybe a white shirt. Some kind of stupid socks that didn't match. He had these huge glasses and would push them around on his nose, talking a mile a minute, which was a comic spectacle. When I first met him, I thought, 'This guy is the most outrageous nerd that I've ever met!' He didn't care back in those days. It took me awhile to realize that I was very interested in what he had to say and that I liked him a lot."

There was something oddly unsocialized about Newt Gingrich. He seemed never to have done any social mixing before. He was the type of person who went to a dinner party and made rude comments to the hostess without realizing that he'd done so.

"The graduate students would get together before a football game or for hamburgers or for beer in the basement of the University Center, and I had the impression that these were kind of new experiences for Newt, and that he was watching to see how people handled social experiences like that, and behaved and related in that kind of environment," says Blake Touchstone, a fellow graduate student of Gingrich's in American history at Tulane. "Newt, though extremely bright, had not been exposed to as much of the wider world as one might think somebody of his age might have been."

"He was inept," Kramer says.

He was different. And he was changing. What Newt Gingrich was soon getting out of graduate school was only in part an education in history. It was also an education in being young in the latter half of the 1960s, and Newt inserted himself in it—whether through socializing or social protest—with the kind of hunger he normally reserved for reading.

"It was a period of enormous change, and Newt

was sucking it all up," Kramer says. "He was very interested in it. He was sorting it out. I think that he was open to the idea that American politics might change in a new direction."

Kramer was perhaps the single most influential person in broadening Gingrich's horizons at Tulane. He was a moderate Republican from California. His wife had been a graduate student at Stanford. Kramer told Gingrich stories about wild California ways, and he watched his eyes pop out. He told Newt about a band he'd heard play at Stanford called the Jefferson Airplane. Then he took Newt to one of their concerts. He also, one afternoon, gave him detailed instructions on the Beatles' *White Album*.

"I don't think it did any good," he says.

Newt even smoked pot.

There were some things that he wasn't open to. He got very upset when a woman graduate student joined one of his seminars. He had no time for feminism, and snarled at Jackie, a heartfelt homemaker, when she said anything that sounded vaguely women's liberationist. Jackie was generally having a harder time relating to the student culture than was Newt. Her age made her a stranger, as did the preoccupations of raising children. She organized the family's social life, as much as possible, around their Southern Baptist church. (Newt, baptized a Lutheran, had converted.) She spent a great deal of time with the Fosbergs, an older couple who lived next door.

"Jackie was, in her whole manner of acting, a good deal older than Newt," Kramer says. "She had a hard time relating to the student culture." Newt was very close to the Fosbergs, too, and referred to them as "my other mom and dad."

Gingrich was in his element in graduate school. Lots of other people were "nerds." He didn't mind the relative poverty; it was a privilege, after all, to be poor while studying on a National Defense Education Act fellowship, and his daughter, Kathy, attended nursery school for free thanks to Head Start. He loved the intellectual debates, the verbal one-upmanship, the push to excel at arguments.

"He'd inject himself, he'd go out of his way to enter into a debate," recalls Pierre-Henri Laurent, Gingrich's thesis adviser and now a professor of history at Tufts University. "He loved that. That was his milieu. In the university you can take on your professor, and he did, but always in the right way. And you could see the difference in how he took on his fellow graduate students."

When the Tulane administration blocked the campus newspaper, the *Hullabaloo,* from printing two "obscene" photographs, Kramer and Gingrich helped organize a massive week-long student demonstration. As part of a group called MORTS (Mobilization of Responsible Tulane Students), they led students in a series of marches, sit-ins, and boycotts. Groups of students picketed businesses like Merrill Lynch, the Pierce Fenner and Smith brokerage firm, WDSU-TV, the National Bank of Commerce, and Maison Blanche, all of which had executives who sat on the Tulane board. Gingrich threatened that MORTS and its backers would stop classes for weeks if the university did not give in on printing the pictures.

"It is now a question of power," he told university president Herbert Longenecker, according to minutes of a meeting that *Newsweek* discovered in the Tulane archives. "We are down to a clash of wills."

The nude pictures in question were to have been printed in a weekly arts supplement to the *Hullabaloo*. One showed an art instructor, Gabor Gergo, seated nude before a giant ceramic sculpture of a nude male and female with enlarged sexual organs. It was to have been captioned: "Making an ironical statement on the fad for nudism." The other picture was by the Baton Rouge artist Shirley Reznikoff, and was part of an exhibition that had been raided by Baton Rouge police on obscenity charges. It showed a sort of machine surrounded by symbolic representations of various human body parts including sexual organs. There were some mathematical sums in the picture, with the words "Total 69" at the bottom. The caption on the Reznikoff picture said: "The quantification of sex along with the quantification of everything else in our industrialized society."

When Longenecker and other university officials charged that the protests were the work of "outside agitators," MORTS refuted it. When the director of the Office of University Relations suggested to reporters from UPI that the two statuary figures in one of the photographs were "engaged in sexual intercourse," MORTS denied it and threatened a libel suit. They presented a list of student grievances and threatened weeks of disruption. The administration eventually promised to allow greater student participation in university policy. The pictures didn't run.

Such was the career of Newt Gingrich the student radical. As generational warfare went, it was a limited engagement.

"I never even saw the pictures; it would surprise me if Newt did," Kramer says. "We were not very interested in the pictures; it was the principle. We thought that New Orleans—although a lovely city— was being run by a bunch of incompetent dopes. And that included Tulane University. And we thought it was a good idea to take on incompetent dopes wherever you encountered them."

In 1968, Kramer suggested to Gingrich that they take a job helping to coordinate Nelson Rockefeller's 1968 presidential campaign in Louisiana. Rockefeller was a liberal Republican, with a strong commitment to enforcing the new civil rights laws. He was more than a long shot in the South. Much has been made of this flirtation with liberalism on Gingrich's part. To hear Kramer tell it, the affair wasn't that serious.

"Newt was not highly motivated pro-Rockefeller even then," he says. "He was really down on Nixon. It was basically a kind of rabble-rousing operation, basically an effort to unseat Nixon, or to stop Nixon, and we actually came very far with it."

Gingrich did, however, feel strongly about increasing the role of blacks in the election process. In fact, he was a staunch supporter of civil rights. He even sent his daughter to a mostly black Head Start program, invited Ernest "Dutch" Morial, who later became the first black mayor of New Orleans, to speak at the discussion group he ran with history department friends, and worked with Kramer to enlist large numbers of blacks for Rockefeller.

Gingrich and Kramer enlisted black voters to their cause by arguing that Democrats were the pillars of the racist Old South.

"What we did was, we discovered that there were still a lot of blacks in New Orleans who were registered Republican but didn't participate, and we simply made an all-out effort to get them to the caucuses," Kramer says. "We made quite a stir. The Nixon people got very worried about what we were doing, which was a very anti-elitist thing in those days. Everybody thought we were nuts. After all, there was nobody who was likely to have any less impact whatsoever in southern politics than Nelson Rockefeller."

Gingrich went to the Republican National Convention in Miami that year. He had no chance of swaying the Louisiana delegation to Rockefeller—Nixon supporters controlled the entire Republican Party in that state—though he certainly tried hard enough. And in the end he got what he wanted: he raised the hackles of the establishment. He ruffled feathers in the Nixon camp and got himself noticed. One observer, U.S. District Court Judge Martin L. C. Feldman, would take away from the convention an image of Gingrich as "a bantam rooster."

Four years later, he would be named the Georgia state head of the Committee to Reelect the President. (McGovern, he would say, was "too frightening for most solid citizens to even think about.")

Friends from that time suggest that Gingrich approached his political activities at Tulane much as he

approached his social life: more through observation
than engagement. His political participation, people
who knew him then argue, had less to do with belief
than with a desire for experience. Some found this offensive.

"I felt he had no moral or political principles," Kit
Wisdom, Newt's co-chair of the Louisiana Rockefeller
campaign and the daughter of John Minor Wisdom, a
Republican Court of Appeals judge known for his
historic civil rights rulings, told the *Washington Post*
last year. "Newt liked Rockefeller because he so
disliked Nixon," she said. "And also he wanted to
advance his own political career."

The patterns that would characterize Gingrich's political and historical thinking in his later life emerged
very clearly at Tulane. He assessed issues like racism
and Vietnam less in terms of their overarching moral
worth than in terms of their *efficacy* as political strategy. Racism to him was "simply not viable in the
South," Kramer explains. "It *was* possible to believe
in those days that racism was a viable strategy for
conservative politicians. Newt thought exactly the op-
posite, and thought that racism was deadly and acted
on it. It's not like it was like a moral crusade, although
I'm sure he felt morally about it," Kramer said. "One
of the first things about Gingrich is you've got to take
him the way he is, and there's always a political
calculation in it."

Similarly, Kramer says, the Vietnam War was to
Gingrich "a mistake."

"Neither of us were against the war in the sense
that it was a terrible colonial war," he says. "I think
both of us felt that it was muddled. It was not clear
what we were doing; we were eventually not going to
accomplish much of anything."

Gingrich's take on the war, which sidestepped moral
issues entirely, would, with the passage of time, grow
increasingly self-serving (in his 1984 book, *Window of
Opportunity,* he would write: "The greatest failure in
Vietnam was our own government's underestimation

of the speed with which the American people would tire of conflict'').

Gingrich sat out the war at Emory and Tulane, first on a student deferment and then, after 1966, thanks to his wife and two daughters. When later asked about why he did not serve in Vietnam, he said it would have been "irrational" with two young children. He also said, to Jane Mayer of the *Wall Street Journal*, "Part of the question I had to ask myself was what difference I would have made. No one felt that this was the battleline on which freedom would live or die. Tragically, it was the kind of war fought in the U.S. Congress, not the battlefield." Explaining his choice to enter politics instead of the army, he told Mayer, "There was a bigger battle in Congress than in Vietnam"—a statement that would make more sense had four years not elapsed between the end of the war and Gingrich's ascension to Congress. Taken at face value, his answer seems to suggest that his decision not to go to war was aimed at keeping himself alive so that he would be *able* to go to Congress. At which point one wonders how highly the 55,000 young men who *died* valued their futures.

Gingrich's doctoral dissertation, on Belgian education policy in the Congo, showed the same signs of this kind of indifference to moral issues. Unlike most graduate students, who agonize over their thesis topics and choose themes that obsess them, Gingrich was steered to his dissertation field by his history professor Pierre-Henri Laurent. Gingrich wrote about the final years of a colony that, under King Leopold II, had seen some of the most vile atrocities committed in Africa by the European powers, but practically without any overarching critique of imperialism.

"To have developed a semi-modernized, semi-educated but politically innocent colony was one of the twentieth century's lesser sins," he wrote. He criticized the European rulers not for having seized the land and resources of Africans in the first place, but for having done so poorly. "Belgian colonialism left the Congo with a solid infrastructure, an encouraging basic welfare and education system, but a pathetically inadequate leadership cadre," he wrote. The thesis even contained a glimpse of the anti-government talk that would dominate his politics a decade later: "It is now clear that the dream of technocratic planning had all too many hidden limitations and so became a nightmare."

Laurent has called Gingrich's thesis "nothing earth-shattering." He suggested that Gingrich rewrite and expand upon it in the hope of getting it published. Gingrich declined.

"Involved as he was with it, he thought of it just as an interesting exercise," Laurent says. "He was not going to take it further than that. And once he got to Carrollton and was teaching, and was interested in futurism, the interest in taking it further, or even of following up with more historical studies, just faded."

Laurent says he never expected Gingrich to make a life as an academic. "He was a deviant from the model graduate students I knew at the time," he says. "They all wanted to teach, to get tenure. He was another breed."

His teaching at Tulane certainly deviated from the norm. As a teaching assistant, strapped for time, he found a way to get away with not having to lecture or even to bring notes to his classes. He called his method "total feedback." It was structured around team presentations that were entirely student-led and evaluated. Arguing that "there is no penalty great enough to compel people to learn," he told the *Hulla-baloo*, "the lecture is medieval. . . . I expect the students to rely on the text and outside reading for factual material. . . . I am a guide, not a god." Some might just have called him lazy.

As a student of history, it sometimes seemed that he was more interested in the present and future than in the past. At Tulane, Gingrich developed a fervent interest in science fiction, discovered Alvin Toffler's *Future Shock,* and became an ardent devotee. He was fascinated by Toffler's depictions of the far-ranging physical, psychological, and political effects of the rapid technological changes in late twentieth-century society. He was drawn to his populist visions of "social futurism." "Political democracy, by incorporating larger and larger numbers in social decision-making, facilitates feedback. And it is precisely this feedback that is essential to control. To assume control over accelerated change, we shall need still more advanced—and more democratic—feedback mechanisms." This would spark Gingrich's imagination and resurface later in his constant use of C-SPAN and call-in television. He was passionate, too, about the burgeoning communications revolution, avid about its potential to de-hierarchize society. When students took over the university center, and "liberated" it from the administration, setting up a "free university" of non-tuition, non-credit courses, he taught a class on the Year 2000. The course featured required reading from some of his current favorites, including management guru Peter Drucker's *The Age of Discontinuity: Guidelines to Our Changing Society* and the futurist Herman Kahn.

It was clear to everyone who knew him at Tulane that Gingrich's interest in history was far from purely academic. He needed to master history—to understand it, personalize it, and find a way to insert himself into it.

"Newt's idea of history is you kind of put yourself in it, and you kind of walk through it," Kramer says. "We used to spend a lot of time talking history, and Newt's approach was always, 'I *am* Abraham Lincoln. So what do I do?' or 'I *am* Benjamin Disraeli. So what do I do?' "

Gingrich was drawn to historical figures who had taken unpopular positions and been proven to be right. He was also drawn to outsiders.

"Disraeli was a guy who was a completely unlikely candidate as a leader in the British establishment, and yet was one of its more important leaders," Kramer says. "That is the kind of figure that Newt has always identified with. He always thought that his road to influence in America was not to keep his mouth shut and follow around important men. His role was more of an unorthodox one."

The Ph.D. degree was like training wheels for the life Newt Gingrich planned to live in history's eye. He wanted to learn history in order to know how to *use* it.

"Debating ideas in class is part of the game of graduate school," Laurent says. "It was not simply a game with Newt, however."

Some acquaintances soon started to say that Newt Gingrich didn't just use causes for his own personal education and enhancement, but that he used people, too. He was starting to grate. Some people found him empty, thought that his single-minded preoccupation with politics had drained him of personality. Others found him calculating and loud-mouthed.

"He would pick people's brains a lot while he was here," the wife of one of Gingrich's former fellow graduate students says. "And if he found someone who knew something that he didn't know, then he'd cultivate him until he learned about it. He really was not interested in being that person's friend. He didn't want to not know about something that someone else knew."

Blake Touchstone recalls one evening when he, Newt, and a few other history graduate students took a break from studying and grading papers. They sat around a friend's kitchen table, making idle conversation over beer.

"What do you plan to be doing fifteen years from now?" the friend asked.

"Teaching history," a unanimous chorus of voices replied. All but one.

"I'm gonna be the U.S. Senator from Georgia," Newt Gingrich said. No one disbelieved him.

And by the time he was Speaker of the House, only one would still call him his friend.

Gingrich's odyssey through late 1960s student culture seems, in the end, to have done less for opening his mind than for increasing his social currency. He learned to relate. He learned the vocabulary of youthful revolt. He learned how "to make himself more presentable," Kramer says. He gained polish, gained sophistication. By the time he reported to work at his first job, teaching history at West Georgia College in Carrollton, Georgia, he passed perfectly as a progressive, sympathetic, "with-it" young professor.

Something, however, was missing.

Something having to do with human connection.

According to *Newsweek*'s Howard Fineman, in 1972, when his father would lie dying of lung cancer, Gingrich would visit and lecture him so devoutly on the evils of self-pity that his own mother would "cringe" in embarrassment. In 1982, when his "other dad," Irving Fosberg, would die, he would fail to send his condolences, Fineman reported.

Some kind of human connectedness failed to develop in Gingrich as he poised himself for his launch into politics. He'd lose touch with his mother and stepfather for years. He would glorify the image of himself as a man struggling alone, facing world-shaking issues unencumbered.

"We would talk for hours about what being a leader was all about, what leadership meant, what politics were all about," Chip Kahn, who met Gingrich during a touch football game at Tulane, told *Mother Jones* in 1984. "He would tell me about talking with Jackie about what would happen if she or the kids were kidnapped. He thought he would be in a position of power someday, and might have to make decisions about things like that. He knew he would have to be tough. He and Jackie agreed that if it came down to that, he would have to make decisions for the society, not for his family."

Patriotism aside, Gingrich's concerns were megalomaniacal. There was something very empty about his ambition.

There was something very empty about him. Something chameleonlike.

"He reveals what he wants to different people," Gingrich's former speechwriter Lee Howell says. "When he needed me, he wanted to reveal his idealism, his moderate-progressive streak, and he'd want to appeal to me in language I could interpret. Once, on election day, he invited me to come to his house and 'toss a football around the yard.' I knew he was joking. But he knew that would appeal to me because I was very fond of the Kennedys. He would use images that he knew would strike chords with me."

A childhood of rootlessness had created a very mutable adult personality. There was a bizarre lack of interiority to Newt Gingrich. A political consultant who advised Jackie Gingrich on how to deal with the media recalls an interesting conversation: "I asked Jackie; I looked at her, I said, 'When he was dating you, a little 17, 18-year-old kid, did he ever show weakness or softness or, you know, express a fear or confess a need?' And she just smiled, shook her head 'no,' and said, 'He's just always been driven and always been focused on one thing.' "

An interview Gingrich gave to *Atlanta* magazine in 1990 put the peculiarity in his own words: "If you said to me, 'What are your hobbies?' they would be reading, going to the movies, going for long walks, animals and the outdoors. But the truth is when I read, I am reading about something that relates. When I go to the movies—I saw *Parenthood* the other day—I think, 'What does that tell me about America?' In a sense, I am almost always engaged. And that has a disadvantage to really break out of that and stop to think, All right, how do you have a private life?"

He's still looking for the answer.

3

From Carrollton to Congress: An Agent for Change

Newt Gingrich didn't end up at West Georgia College by accident. He knew that Democratic Georgia, with its weak Republican party, offered great opportunities for him to rise up through the ranks quickly. And he knew that with the changing times the election of Republican statewide officials wasn't that far away. Bo Callaway, after all, had won election to Congress as a Republican in 1965.

On the one hand, 1974 was just about the worst time possible to launch a career as a Republican. The party had been demoralized by Watergate, and the electorate was disgusted with its leadership. Voters were apathetic and cynical. Any Republican who would try to galvanize them behind new, optimistic platforms was sure to run into great skepticism. On the other hand, though, there was a good deal of anger in the air.

There was anger at inflation, frustration with Congress, disillusionment with a government that had lost a foreign war and had seen a president forced to resign. It really was a time of "malaise"—the word that Americans would revile a few years later—and malaise was good for Newt Gingrich. He understood it. He could use it. He knew where it came from, what it felt like, and how it could be galvanized as a force for change. The Republican Party needed people like him.

In 1972, two short years after returning to Georgia, and four long years since his work for Nelson Rockefeller, Gingrich was asked to be state chairman for the Committee to Re-Elect the President. He said he didn't want to be state chairman; he wanted to be chairman for his congressional district, the Sixth. He was told that there weren't going to be congressional district chairmen.

"There will be if you want me," he said. The party wanted him.

In canvassing for Nixon, Gingrich got his own name out. He made his face known, and his views—if often in somewhat unconventional ways. He'd have a liberal, hippy-ish West Georgia College friend drive him to Nixon campaign events, then would seat him at the back of the room. About two-thirds of the way through his speech, he'd point and say, "You want to know what a McGovernite looks like? See that bearded fella in the back of the room? *That's* what a McGovernite looks like!" Two years later, he'd have quite a time explaining to those same crowds why he had the McGovernite working for him.

At the time Gingrich's Sixth District stretched out to rural areas near the Alabama border, down to working-class southern suburbs of Atlanta near Hartsfield International Airport, and through the rapidly growing boom areas in Fayette County. The South Fulton area was heavily black, Peachtree City was full of retirees, and the suburbs were rapidly filling up with yuppies, fleeing Atlanta in the first wave of white flight. The district included a large number (for Georgia) of Republicans, especially Goldwater Republicans, and Democrats who were so conservative that they differed from Republicans only in name.

In the 1970s, it was a changing, expanding district. And it had had the same Democratic congressman for two decades: John J. Flynt, Jr. Flynt was the ultimate insider, a lifelong public official, self-serving and laughably corrupt, a segregationist—a true pillar of the Old South. He'd gone to Washington in 1954 and had stayed there longer than any other member of the Georgia delegation. He had reportedly stopped holding regular delegation meetings in 1972, when Andrew Young was elected to Congress from Atlanta, because he didn't want the meetings to be integrated. He had a terrible record on environmental issues. And his ethics were considered a joke. Longtime residents of Griffin, Jack Flynt's hometown, laugh at the mention of him even today. Their favorite story is of the time when he sold a five-and-a-half by twelve-hundred foot strip of land rather than have his road paved.

Flynt also was involved in some funny business with the Ford Motor Company. In 1972, he leased one hundred acres of his farm to Ford, which needed land to store three thousand new cars whose engines did not meet federal environmental standards. Flynt collected $12,500 from Ford for two months' rent on the land. Although Ford officials said they had come upon Flynt's land by accident, and Flynt said he had asked for a mere dollar in rent but that the company had insisted on paying the "going rate" of $6,250 per month (Gingrich claimed that local farmers said they would have charged only $1,000), the story raised eyebrows, particularly when Flynt collected $200 each from two members of the Ford family, and afterward made one of his rare House floor speeches in support of easing up on tough auto-emissions standards.

Flynt also allegedly spent many weekends hunting in Maryland as the guest of Rockwell International Corporation, makers of the B-1 bomber, which he had strongly advocated in Congress. Flynt had put his farm manager on the congressional payroll as a part-time employee in his Griffin office. And he routinely took all-expense-paid flying junkets on corporate airplanes, including one vacation trip on a plane provided by the Beech Aircraft Company, which bid on millions of dollars of defense contracts every year that were funded by Flynt's Military Appropriations Subcommittee.

When faced with these charges, Flynt was adamant in his defense. "I couldn't be bought with a whole airplane, much less a few rides in one," he told the *Miami Herald*.

Jack Flynt was a perfect foil for Newt Gingrich. He was an icon of the Democratic establishment. He was ripe for overthrow. Who better to set things right in the changing, modernizing, diversifying Sixth District than a young, future-oriented, *Republican* anti-establishmentarian?

"Jack Flynt is not a man of our time," Gingrich would say on the campaign trail. "He's just the classic example of everything wrong with the politicians of his generation."

At West Georgia College, a little-known state school in Carrollton about forty miles west of Atlanta, Gingrich had already established himself as an agent for change. He co-founded an environmental studies program which featured courses like "Alternative Lifestyles" (people living in teepees, vans, shacks), introduced future studies, taught science fiction and Marshall McLuhan, and brought Alvin Toffler as a visiting lecturer to the campus. He supported the psychology department's embrace of the new and controversial "humanistic psychology," and taught his classes in a circle on the grass.

He was overwhelmingly popular with his students. He was considered laid-back, even cool. His hair was now on the long side of short, his clothing no worse than anything anyone else wore in the early 1970s. He would invite students to his home for philosophical rap sessions and spent time hanging out with them at the student center. He was known as an easy grader.

"He had more counterculture students than anybody else," recalls Glyn Thomas, who taught in the environmental studies program with Gingrich. "They all had long hair and beards and sandals and granny glasses, the whole thing. And they all loved him."

Thomas thought highly of him too: "I always found him a really good conversationalist," he says. "He was interesting. And always wanted to do something new and different. And I always found him to be very tolerant in those days. I didn't realize the mean streak until after he got into Congress. I'd never seen Newt mean. He was combative, but I don't remember seeing him ever be just mean."

During registration time, students would lie, cheat, and steal their way into Gingrich's classes. To limit enrollment he held one class, called "The Future," in the cafeteria at seven o'clock in the morning spring semester. The students came anyway.

"Mr. Gingrich would make you think things you never would think about. He stretched you in every possible way. He'd completely overwhelm you with his mastery of communication," says Joseph Cerniglia, a former student. "The bell would ring, and if we weren't finished we'd just keep going and people would be late to their next class."

Some of his colleagues gave him more mixed reviews. Don Wagner, for one, a professor of political science at the college who used to participate in faculty meetings with Gingrich, found his ideas more than slightly erratic.

"He was right on the edge," Wagner says. "You could feel the energy, the intensity. Sometimes he'd generate ideas the way a volcano spews out lava. A lot of that stuff was nonsense, but every once in a while there was something extraordinarily insightful and really bright, really brilliant."

Benjamin Kennedy, chairman of the history department when Gingrich arrived at the college, found him downright megalomaniacal. Kennedy resigned his chairmanship after a year in which Gingrich attacked him publicly in open meetings and went behind his back and over his head to the college administration over a disagreement in hiring policy.

"He was then what he is now: extremely ambitious and conspiratorial," Kennedy says. "His way of get-

ting to the top is by destroying other people, building
alliances behind the scenes, fighting just to advance
himself, to make himself look good. He didn't do the
sort of things that academics do. He didn't publish, he
didn't do research, he wasn't collegial. He advanced
his own cause."

One year after Kennedy resigned as department
chair, Gingrich applied for the position. He was
twenty-nine years old, had done no scholarly publishing, and was soundly defeated.

"That wasn't ambition, that was presumption. It
wasn't the appropriate thing for a young assistant
professor to do," says Richard Dangle, retired dean
of the arts and sciences. The new department chair
would be Steve Hanser, the University of Chicago-
trained military historian who specializes in nineteenth-century Germany and has since become
Gingrich's intellectual mentor.

Writers like Toffler and futurism as a sub-field of
history impressed academics much less than they did
undergraduates. Some found the idea of the "history
of the future" somewhat contradictory. Gingrich circulated a proposal for a master's program in "Futures
Studies," noting, in his outline: "The program might
well fail but it would be a truly experimental and new
type of failure." One colleague, unimpressed by the
pitch, bemusedly scribbled at the top of his copy,
"How much do we know the present?"

"It certainly wasn't appreciated particularly well by
the traditional history professors in his department,"
says Dangle. After several years in history, Gingrich
asked to be transferred to the more friendly geography
department, and the historians happily complied.

Geography was a five-professor department. History was the campus's second-largest. Gingrich's ambitions, however, did not downsize with the move.
Without a single book or scholarly article of note to
his name, Gingrich applied to be president of the
college. His application was laughed off the campus.

"There are no limits to his ambition," Kennedy says.

No one protested too loudly when Gingrich began spending more and more time away from the college and devoting himself to bringing his agenda of change to the people of the state. His obvious teaching talents aside, he was making no effort to prove himself as a serious academic.

"His prospects for tenure weren't very good. He never evidenced any of the kind of interest in doing scholarly research and writing that he would have needed to be tenured," Dangle says. In 1978, when Gingrich's seven-year probationary period as an assistant professor would be up, Dangle would encourage him to resign. "He chose not to do that, and he was terminated. He never applied for tenure," Dangle says.

His thoughts were elsewhere. Canvassing the district for Nixon had given him a sense of what voters wanted and how he could sell it to them. One morning in 1973, he showed up at the home of his fellow history professor Mel Steely with piles and piles of polling research, and over blueberry pancakes he mapped out a campaign strategy to defeat Jack Flynt. He wasn't the only one interested in running. Tracy Stallings, dean of men at West Georgia College and a future state representative, was thinking about it, too. But he had a wife and small children, and he didn't want to give up life with his family for politics. Gingrich was a family man, too, but he didn't see a problem. The presence of a family would never cause a politician grief in conservative Georgia, he knew—provided you had the right sort of family, and used it well. And Gingrich did.

He had diluted his northern blood by marrying a Georgia girl. He had converted from the Lutheran church to her Southern Baptist. He would end up being ordained as a deacon of Carrollton's First Baptist Church just one month before the 1974 election. The church's pastor, Reverend Brantley Harwell, would soon bring his whole family out to campaign for him, writing to all the ministers in the district and telling them what a "good churchman" he was.

Gingrich spent the winter of 1973 canvassing the district, talking to small groups of powerful Republicans in the hopes that he might win the party's nomination for Congress without a primary challenge. He did. He then took a leave of absence from West Georgia College and declared his candidacy.

In Watergate's wake, and in a Democratic district, relying too hard upon party allegiances was problematic. Rather than play Republicans off Democrats, Gingrich focused on an enemy he knew was shared by all disgruntled voters: Congress. He announced his candidacy for the Sixth District seat by lashing out at the "incompetency and indifference" of a Congress that was "more interested in party squabbling than in problem solving." He rallied voters behind his attacks on "a Congress that will not act on impeachment or anything else."

"There are two games in this country," he said. "One is played by the five thousand insiders in Washington who write the laws and tell the lies, and the other by the rest of us, who pay the price. That's what we can't tolerate."

Gingrich presented himself as a voice for the little guy, for the taxpayer, trying to make ends meet under the squeeze of inflation. He blamed the "special interests which dominate Congress" for sticking Americans with high inflation and charged them with "exploiting the American people." If elected, he promised to oppose "deals that cost us at the grocery store," and to reform the tax system so "everyone pays their own share . . . start by closing loopholes which allow the very rich like Nelson Rockefeller and the giant corporations to avoid taxes."

He charged that Jack Flynt was "an extremely useful watchdog for big industry." He assailed Flynt's contributions from Henry Food II, chairman of the board of the Ford Motor Company, and Benson Ford, chairman of Ford's Dealer Policy Board, saying that "two men who live in Detroit have a better chance to talk" with Flynt than did his constituents. He called the Ford land deal a "sophisticated form of laundering." When he noticed that he received much more attention in the Georgia media for bashing his opponent than for his policy papers, he stepped up the attacks.

"Name a project Jack Flynt has helped the Sixth District get in over twenty-two years in office," he said. "Name a major bill bearing his name. You can't because they don't exist."

"He used to sit around during the campaign and would say, Well, what are we gonna say today that would be outrageous enough that they'll have to cover us but not so outrageous that they'll think we're crazy and ignore us?" Lee Howell recalls.

Gingrich accused Flynt of blocking auto-pollution controls because he was doing business with Ford Motor Company. "Congressmen are not bribed anymore," he said. "They simply have a lot of friends who are willing to help them out whenever they find it necessary." And he said that he would "file at regular intervals with every public and high school library in the district" the records of his and his staff's campaign activities.

Ideologically, Gingrich offered something for everyone. Speaking to local cattlemen, he demanded the resignation of Secretary of Agriculture Earl Butz, saying that he'd been "so biased in favor of the giant corporations and the huge grain dealers that he has crippled both the small farmer and the housewife." To Republican businessmen in Atlanta and wealthy conservative white suburbanites, he was a former Nixon supporter who denounced Nelson Rockefeller. (All mention of his having worked for Rockefeller had disappeared from his biography by 1974, and, *Newsweek* reported, he even planned to send a telegram to President Ford "stating his objections" to his appointment of Rockefeller as vice president.) For

Ronald Reagan, who campaigned for him, for radical right-wing ideologues like Paul Weyrich, who founded his Committee for the Survival of a Free Congress with Joe Coors that year, and for conservative congressmen James A. McClure, Barry Goldwater, James L. Buckley, Carl T. Curtis, Jesse Helms, and Clifford P. Hansen, who wrote to district Republicans on his behalf, he was also the only Republican candidate in the state likely to win. And he was a vast improvement over Jack Flynt.

For liberal Democrats in the college community, Gingrich was an environmentalist, a conservationist who had co-founded the West Georgia chapter of the Georgia Conservancy, a former Rockefeller Republican who professed disgust for Nixon. His friends at the college saw him as an open-minded, eager reformer. He talked about a "four-point program to stop special interests from exploiting the American people," and aimed it specifically at putting the reins on the business practices of large corporations. And he was a vast improvement over Jack Flynt.

Many of Gingrich's supporters admitted they didn't see much of anything at all ideologically in his candidacy, but they liked Newt and thought it would be nice for him to get into Congress. That, anyway, was what inspired West Georgia faculty members like Lucy and James Klee, who sent Gingrich his first campaign contribution for $200 on July 16, 1973. They had supported only one Republican before—Senator Edward Brooke, the liberal Republican from Massachusetts.

"We didn't even know who he was then except that he was a friend," Lucy Klee told the *Washington Post* last year. "I don't think he had any idea what he was going to stand for."

Dr. Irving Fosberg, Gingrich's "other dad" from New Orleans, sent him a check for $300 in friendship, too.

It wasn't that Gingrich didn't have ideas. It was just that the ideas changed a bit depending on who he was talking to. And who he talked to ranged all over the political spectrum, as long as there was potential money involved. According to Bill Shipp, a veteran Georgia political observer and editor of a newsletter covering Georgia politics who first met Gingrich as the political editor of the *Atlanta Constitution,* and in the late 1970s repeatedly endorsed him as a "progressive and compassionate" politician, Gingrich was so flexible in his politics that in 1974, he at one point considered running in both the Democratic *and* the Republican primaries against Flynt—something permissible by Georgia law. But he decided not to when Republican supporters balked. Interestingly, Barry Goldwater nearly renounced his endorsement of Gingrich after he joined in with Democratic calls for opening the books on the big oil companies that year.

Gingrich collected money from Roy Richards, an arch conservative who was founder of the multinational Southwire Corporation and a major donor to politicians, including Jimmy Carter, and from his liberal circle of friends at West Georgia College. They came to Gingrich's home every weekend, thirty or forty strong, to talk reform and environmentalism and integration. They donated money, lent him money, took out second mortgages. His students gave him five and ten dollar donations. They gave their time, too, driving him all over the state to the 139 speeches he made that year.

The West Georgia crowd cheered Gingrich on in sending telegrams to President Ford urging him to abstain from granting any further pardons in the Watergate affair until the judicial system had run its course. They applauded his stands on air and water pollution, which had won him the endorsement of the League of Conservation Voters. The *Atlanta Journal* editorial page endorsed him. Chip Kahn, who had met Gingrich at a touch football game at Tulane and followed him to West Georgia College to be a graduate student and his campaign manager, wrote a check for $1,000. He saw Gingrich as a "person of destiny."

Gingrich's destiny was to lose in 1974 and finish the campaign more than $11,000 in debt. The stain of Watergate proved a greater liability than he'd anticipated. So had his Yankee name and accent. Flynt's calling him a "nice young liberal college professor" hadn't helped, either.

The defeat contained seeds of hope, however. In Democratic Georgia, Gingrich lost his first race by less than three thousand votes. He attracted the attention of such national media figures as David Broder, who called him one of the "brightest new faces" in the G.O.P. He also caught the eye of Bob Beckel, a Democrat who later managed the 1984 presidential campaign of Walter Mondale. Seeking "reform" candidates for the then bipartisan National Committee for an Effective Congress, Beckel told the *Washington Post* last year that he had visited Jack Flynt and been "appalled" by him. He then talked to Gingrich for several hours and approved of him, and passed him on to Russ Evans, a Republican strategist. Evans introduced Gingrich to Wilma Goldstein, who at that time was director of survey research at the Republican National Committee, and she began to seek backers for him in Washington. Washington money, Gingrich knew, could make all the difference in the world in the next campaign.

After election day, Gingrich returned to West Georgia College and resumed teaching. But he kept himself visible throughout 1975, meeting with potential voters, delivering speeches addressing the oil crisis and the need to develop new sources of energy, and assailing President Ford for playing too cynically upon the themes of partisan politics. Speaking out against a Ford candidacy, the future Republican Party pit bull argued, "He is preparing . . . to run a Harry Truman style of anti-Congressional campaign in the next election." He warned, "Programs will be embroiled in politics. The country can ill afford such conflict."

By the time the 1976 campaign year rolled around, he'd forgotten that kind spirit of peacemaking. It was

time to fight his own battles once again. And fight
he did.

Shortly after his reelection in 1974, Jack Flynt had
been named chairman of the House Ethics Committee—an appointment that begged campaign year outrage. Gingrich quickly pounced, pointing out that two
congressmen under investigation by the Ethics
Committee—Wayne Hays of Ohio, caught in a payroll
sex scandal, and Robert Sikes of Florida, subject of a
conflict-of-interest investigation—were both old
friends of Flynt's, and that progress on their ethics
probes was suspiciously slow. When Gingrich then
pulled out his 1974 shopping list of Flynt's ethical
lapses, Flynt counterattacked. He accused Gingrich of
"trying to disrupt the Democratic Delegate Selection
Convention in 1972 as a McGovern operative," of
having a "former McGovern worker as his campaign
director"—serious charges in a conservative district—
and, worst of all, snorted in radio spots that Gingrich
"came to Georgia recently," after an early life in
Europe and New Orleans.

The charges didn't seem to do much harm. In 1976,
Gingrich drew $135,000 in campaign contributions,
up from $85,000 in 1974. In October, the *Atlanta
Constitution* noted that he was the only challenger in
Georgia to outspend an incumbent. He was supported
by real estate developers, lawyers and restauranteurs,
a Southwire executive, a Texas housewife, Houston
oil contractors, professors, the Good Government
group of Georgia, Richard H. Kimberly, of the Kim-
berly-Clark Corporation, Life Underwriters Political
Action Committee, an art gallery owner in Houston,
the conservative Loose Group of Atlanta businessmen, Chester Roush, the Carrollton realtor, now listed
as an oil distributor, the public relations director of
Roy Richards' People's Bank in Carrollton, and two
Eastern Airlines pilots, among others.

Gingrich sought endorsements from both the liberal
National Committee for a Free and Effective Congress
and the right-wing Committee for the Survival of a

Free Congress, and was endorsed by the League of Conservation Voters (again) and by the Sierra Club. His commitment to environmental issues hadn't changed. Neither had his bombast against Congress: "I am running for Congress because I am fed up with politicians, bureaucrats, and special interests who run this country at the expense of working people," he said, announcing his candidacy in March 1976. "Those of us who work for a living are being discriminated against. The tax laws favor the rich. . . . I am running because the special interests dominate our government and have come to believe that they own it. They think you and I don't know enough to make decisions. . . . They are trying to run America at our expense."

In some ways, though, his message had changed. Gingrich was moving, slowly but surely, to the right. In a position paper he wrote that year, "Isn't It Time—A Rededication to the Declaration of 1776," he blasted welfare, blasted minimum-wage laws, blasted busing, car pooling, and big government. He called the paper "an attempt to articulate the anger of the vast majority of Americans who consider themselves without a voice in government." He was starting to hit his stride.

He overestimated the power of anger, however, in bringing local voters to the polls that year. Jimmy Carter, a Democrat, was on the presidential ballot, and Georgians were loyal down the line. Black voters turned out in large numbers to vote for Carter, and, pulling Democratic levers, ironically gave an extra wave of support to Flynt. The man who had opposed the Voting Rights Act of 1965 and worked against it again in the summer of 1975, voting with most other Georgia congressmen, including John Bircher Larry McDonald, in favor of a raft of amendments to gut the law, in large part owed his 1976 reelection to the black vote.

Gingrich lost once again by two percentage points, or about five thousand votes. He didn't take his second defeat as sanguinely as his first. He and Jackie were up to their ears in debt. He knew his prospects for tenure at West Georgia College were nil, and that if he ran for Congress again in 1978, he'd have to do so without a job to go back to.

"They were in despair, just really deep despair," Harwell says. "They didn't have any money."

Gingrich shook himself up, and in 1977 kept his mind off his troubles by leading the statewide opposition to the Panama Canal treaty, which he called symbolic of "appeasement mentality." Roy Richards' People's Bank paid him several thousand dollars to come speak to bank employees a few times about the future. That bought groceries and fed the kids for a while.

Then someone came up with a splendid plan. One of Gingrich's local supporters, realtor Chester Roush, assembled a dozen wealthy financial backers of Gingrich's previous campaigns and talked them into donating $13,000—a sum that was well over half his annual salary as an assistant professor—to pay Newt to write a novel over the summer of 1977. The deal was structured as a tax shelter, a limited partnership called Nomonhan, Limited, with Chester Roush's Dorchester Corporation, a real estate concern, and Newt Gingrich as general partners. The money paid for the Gingrich family to spend the summer in Europe. It raised the question, never adequately resolved, critics say, of whether some of the donations could really be thought of as corporate contributions, and whether the whole deal—for a book that Gingrich never finished—was in fact a slush fund for his political activities.

The genesis of the book has always remained somewhat mysterious. The research was done: Gingrich went to Fort Benning and the Pentagon and gathered information about the possibility of war in Europe. Then he went overseas and toured the NATO defenses in Germany. Although he claimed, in a newspaper interview in 1978, that the book had been "well received so far in the literary community and has a strong chance of being published," he later said that after he wrote the first three chapters and sent them to futurist Alvin Toffler, Toffler wrote back, "You are obviously better at shaking hands than writing fiction." That critique clearly hit home. In 1988, Gingrich told the *Clayton Sun* that he had never finished the book. But when a Democratic challenger raised the issue again that year, a copy turned up in the West Georgia College archive.

Last year Steve Hanser told the *Washington Post* that Newt had finished the book in 1978. "The book is not bad, it's just not good," he said.

The book is more than "not good." A copy of the three hundred-odd page manuscript is now held in the special collections department of the West Georgia College library, carefully guarded against photocopying because, as a note to college archivist Charles Beard explains, Gingrich might want to publish from the material at some point in the future.

It's not likely.

The novel is an ideological tract about the imminent dangers of American military unpreparedness, and reads like a lecture in military history, mixed with minutes from the Congressional Record. There is no character development. There is only the outline of a plot. There is some imagery—two scorpions in a bottle locked into a death embrace—and there is the start of one promising character: Lieutenant Colonel Walter Johnson, a rehabilitated army dad who's always sadly leaving his family to go off on a potentially deadly maneuver. The first chapter reads semi-fluidly. And the rest as though someone wrote it in a few nights.

The book pits a Russian premier, Vlasov, an ideological hard-liner eager to reassert dominance in Yugoslavia and unify the Soviet hold over Eastern Europe, against a weak-seeming, friendly, and naive American president who was elected on a campaign of detente. He's surrounded by a foolish and smug brain trust, which includes a CIA agent, one "Miss Sally Roberts," who drinks Dubonnet at meetings and never makes an appearance in a room without some colleague checking out her legs. Like the battle of Verdun, it's all about symbolism, pride, and politically induced human waste. It's also specifically about the dangers of allowing the defense budget to be cut ("The budgetary squeeze tightened like an economic python squeezing the vitality out of the U.S. forces in Europe") and about the treachery of the seditious press.

The book offers none of the purple prose that characterizes Gingrich's upcoming science fiction thriller, *1945,* which, according to the *New York Times,* features a purring female spy with a "lethal pout" and a White House Chief of Staff with "fur on his chest." More's the pity.

Gingrich, in a 1978 interview with the *West Georgia News,* made no bones about his first book's blatantly ideological intent: "To use a bad parallel," he said, "if *The Towering Inferno* got people interested in the safety of high buildings, I wanted to write something to increase the public's awareness of military preparedness. . . . Soviet military doctrine is very firm," he said. "You can fight a nuclear war and win."

Gingrich had other war plans on his mind, too. Spinning his wheels in the wake of his 1976 defeat had given him the time to rethink his campaign strategy. The country was moving progressively to the right. Proposition 13 had passed in California. Donald Wildmon, founder of the American Family Association, had begun his guerrilla war against the country's "liberal" mass media, and Pat Robertson's Christian soldiers were on the march. In Fayetteville, Georgia, Greg Brezina, a former star football player, had organized a church where candidates were vetted before the altar on issues dear to the religious right. It was only a matter of time before Gingrich caught the wave.

Marilu Blaney had followed her old campaign worker's career from Columbus. "After Newt lost his second race," she says. "I said to him, 'When in Rome, do as the Romans do.' You're up there in the most conservative section of Georgia. You've got to be a conservative. Other people had this conversation with him, too. And he swung around and he did it."

Thinking about himself necessarily led Gingrich to think about making history. He thought about where the Republicans were going and how he wanted to lead. He decided that it wasn't enough just to try to win an individual congressional race. He decided that the Republican Party had to take over the American political system. It would have to become a self-perpetuating political machine that allowed for no weakness and admitted no common ground with the Democrats.

In October 1977, he announced this thought at a fund-raising dinner at the Hospitality Inn in Atlanta: "I believe deeply in the need for a conservative majority government," he said. A few months later, he delivered the goods on how to achieve it.

Speaking to a group of the College Republicans at the Atlanta Airport Holiday Inn, Gingrich delivered the battle cry that would set the stage for his first winning campaign and, it could be argued, for the next two decades of his political career. He railed against the Republican Party leadership, blaming Gerald Ford's pardon of Nixon for costing him his own 1974 congressional race, and blasting both men as "pathetic."

"The great strength of the Democratic Party in my lifetime has been that it has always produced young, nasty people who had no respect for their elders," he told the crowd of teens and twenty-somethings. "And I think that one of the great problems we have in the Republican Party is that we don't encourage you to be nasty. . . .

"This party does not need another generation of cautious, prudent, careful, bland, irrelevant, quasi leaders who are willing to drift into positions because nobody else is available. What we really need are people who are tough, hardworking, energetic, willing to take risks, willing to stand up in a slug fest and match it out with their opponent. . . .

"You're fighting a war. It is a war for power . . . to build a majority capable of sustaining itself."

The speech caused an uproar. Republican Party Sixth District Congressional Chairman Bob Simpkins called on Gingrich to issue a formal apology for his "unwise and unwarranted remarks," which, he said, had violated the "integrity and morality" of the Republican Party. Gingrich's remarks about farmers— "Farmers get nine billion dollars a year to not grow food. . . . They drive their tractors to Atlanta and they stand there piously in front of a $70,000 tractor that's air conditioned with stereo and tell you they need your money so they don't go bankrupt"—brought an angry rebuke from the president of the Georgia Farm Bureau. Gingrich did not apologize.

It was the dawn of a new era for Newt Gingrich. The attack dog was on the loose. And in 1978, when Jack Flynt retired, begging off from another grueling campaign, Gingrich seized the opportunity to try out his new teeth on his new opponent, Virginia Shapard, a socially progressive, fiscally conservative Democratic state senator from rural Griffin.

As a Democrat, Shapard should have had a huge advantage over Gingrich. But she was a woman, perceived as a liberal, and she had once flouted the Democratic establishment by leading a successful and unprecedented motion to censure one of their "boys," State Senator Roscoe Dean, for allegedly cheating on his expense account. Tom Murphy, Georgia's current Speaker of the State House, who was fast becoming the state's most powerful Democrat, refused to lend her his support. She was not endorsed by organized labor, either. The AFL-CIO kept their hands off the race, its president, a key Democratic Party leader, simply not showing up once at a campaign event where he was meant to share a dais with Rosalynn Carter, and the UAW, with employees at the Hapeville Ford plant, supported Gingrich.

Shapard had other strikes against her as well: she'd been born in the North, and had married into a wealthy family that owned Spalding Knitting Mills and American Mills. She and her husband had been active on a biracial committee that had successfully and peacefully integrated their Griffin community. She'd started her career as a child welfare worker. She was clearly a tough sell for the hard-line Flynt supporters in rural Georgia. Because she was considered a long shot, she had a hard time raising money from state and national Democratic funding groups.

Gingrich, on the other hand, now looked like a sure thing. Money for his campaign poured in—$219,000 by the time of the election, with the National Republican Congressional Committee and other Republican organizations contributing about $50,000. The committee also provided him with his first professional campaign manager, Carlyle Gregory, and a consultant, Bob Weed, both of whom had helped bring about the 1976 victory of Republican Representative Paul Trible in Virginia.

The new, professional Gingrich crew crowded out the old faithful from Carrollton and moved the campaign headquarters from the Democratic college town to the Republican suburbs of Atlanta. In his new geographic locale, Gingrich moved philosophically to the right. He jumped on the national tax-cutting band wagon, and supported the Kemp-Roth bill, which proposed a thirty-three percent cut in federal income taxes. He also endorsed tax advantages for small businesses and proposed doing away with "virtually all federal red tape related to small businesses" and vowed to "keep OSHA out" of small business affairs.

Shapard, though she opposed Kemp-Roth for cutting taxes without cutting government spending, did not significantly differ from Gingrich on matters of fiscal policy. Gingrich's campaign, however, rested on painting her as an advocate of big government and high taxes.

A new media consultant, Dino Seder, whose specialty was negative campaigning, helped Gingrich devise a campaign that aimed at exploiting voters' fears of high taxes, resentment of the rich, distrust of women, and hostility to blacks.

"We found bills in the Georgia Senate with great titles like 'A Bill to Reduce Your Taxes,' " L. H. Carter, the campaign treasurer, explained to the *Washington Post* last year. "It was a terrible bill. It failed like 49 to 1, and of course Virginia voted against it. We had a voice-over saying, 'Virginia Shapard had a chance to reduce your taxes. . . . She knows how she voted. She only hopes you don't.' "

The ads showed a heavy woman's arm with an iron bracelet on it coming down and stamping a big red no in the middle of a bill.

Gingrich's symbol, on the other hand, was a grocery cart, "Newt's family is like your family," his campaign literature read. "We know what it is to choose between macaroni and cheese and hamburger at the grocery store." When Virginia Shapard held a barbecue at her stately Griffin farm and charged $50 a plate, Gingrich held a peanut butter and jelly party at his tiny house. The Gingrich camp attacked Shapard for having attended private schools. In fact, the "private school" was a private college, just like Gingrich's. Her husband grew, in Gingrich's campaign-speak, from a "textile manufacturer" to a "wealthy textile magnate."

In an election memo to supporters, Gingrich said that in October he estimated Virginia Shapard would spend $70,000 on television advertising alone. "We have $20,000 to spend on media," he said. "We can't let Mrs. Shapard buy this election."

In an era of public outrage over "welfare queens," the Gingrich campaign also sought to portray Shapard as sympathetic to welfare fraud. "If you like welfare cheaters, you'll love Virginia Shapard," a Gingrich flier read. "People like Mrs. Shapard, who was a welfare worker for five years, and Julian Bond fought together to kill [a bill to cut down on welfare cheaters]." The bill in question had been a Republican-sponsored act that would have required everyone in

the state who received AFDC to come to the office
and pick up their checks—children, the handicapped,
the blind all included, notwithstanding the very real
dangers of muggings outside the offices.

"It was mean-spirited and punitive and would not
have accomplished what it set out to do, which was
keeping people from drawing multiple checks," a
source who was familiar with the legislation says.
Shapard proposed a substitute bill that required a
home visit on the part of a case worker instead. The
Republicans rejected it.

The welfare ads also played shamelessly on Southern racial prejudices. The flier that showed Shapard
with Julian Bond, a black state senator and well-
known civil rights activist in the Atlanta area, sent
home a clear message to Flynt loyalists that Shapard
was not one of them. A television ad that showed
dollar bills being handed out and black hands reaching
up to grab them was even less subtle. Some of Shapard's campaign workers even found, while traveling
in rural districts near the Alabama line, that Gingrich's
people were telling those voters that Shapard had
met her husband when she'd come down South as a
freedom marcher—something she'd never been. At
the same time that he ran these ads, Gingrich spent a
good deal of time visiting churches and meeting places
and walking the streets of black neighborhoods in his
district. He promised that, if elected, he would establish a mobile office to serve the black community, and
he hired a black woman as his assistant campaign
manager. He was taking no chances.

The Gingrich campaign counted on back county
voters to provide the anti-woman, anti-black support
that Newt needed to win over enough of Flynt's old
Democratic supporters. The nastiest set of ads ran in
rural newspapers, aiming at just these voters. The
ads showed Gingrich and his family on one side and
Shapard alone on the other. They said, "Newt will
take his family to Washington and keep them together;
Virginia will go to Washington and leave her husband

and children in the care of a nanny." They also played
on religious prejudice. "Newt is a deacon of the First
Baptist Church of Carrollton; Virginia is a communicant of the Church of the Good Shepherd in Griffin."

"We went after every rural southern prejudice we
could think of," a campaign worker told the *Washington Post* last year. "We were appealing to the prejudice
against working women, against their not being home.
And 'communicant' sounded like a bunch of Catholics
to Georgians."

Even today these ads make former campaign workers squirm.

"We were scared to death," a former campaign
strategist says. "Newt was out of work. He had gotten
his last paycheck August 31 of 1978. He didn't have a
job, he didn't have any source of income. We were
scared, and so we started doing things I wish we
hadn't done."

Shapard denounced Gingrich's ads as "political por-
nography." Many disgusted voters in Georgia agreed.
And it seemed, for a while at least, that the nastiness
might do Gingrich in. Polls in September 1978 showed
Gingrich trailing by a considerable margin. The *Atlanta Constitution,* which had endorsed Gingrich in
his first two races, now put its considerable weight
behind Shapard, denouncing the viciousness of
Gingrich's campaign.

In the end, though, Virginia Shapard simply ran out
of money. A campaign loan that her husband had cosigned was found to be an illegal contribution by the
FEC because Georgia was not a communal property
state. In November 1978, the *Atlanta Constitution* reported that she'd borrowed $125,000 to stay afloat;
Gingrich needed to borrow only $700. Despite reports
early in the campaign year that she was outspending him
nearly two to one, by late October Gingrich had far
surpassed her. He won the election by 12,000 votes.

Gingrich went to Congress.

Shapard went home to her red brick mansion on a
hill, and took a job selling insurance to pay off her
campaign loans.

4

Traveling Light

After the 1978 election, Newt Gingrich cleaned house.

He cleared out his office at West Georgia College. He packed up his things at home. And with a brutality that shocked many of those closest to him, he walked away from his past.

It was as though he'd been set free.

An old friend and campaign worker remembers sitting at the dining table with Newt and Jackie in their small house on Howell Drive in Carrollton that December:

"Christmas cards were coming in by the sack and Jackie was opening them and we were sorting them into piles—major contributors, major political figures, family friends and relatives," he recalls. "Newt was standing by the dining room table, reading a book. Jackie opened one card and said, 'Oh, Newt, here's a nice Christmas card from your mother,' and she handed it up to him. He never stopped reading. He just took it in his right hand and turned and dropped it in the trash and went right on reading."

The friend adds, "I thought it was incredibly significant."

It was symbolic, anyway. Gingrich would discard much more of his life in the following months, including that friend, almost all of his other Carrollton friends and aides—and Jackie.

"He decided to put that whole part of his life behind him," the former friend says.

He set about putting together a new life.

He hired Dolores Adamson, Jack Flynt's former district administrator, to run his office in the district. He instructed her to teach him how to look and act like a politician. She took him to the local mall, and he practiced smiling and shaking hands. He retained Bob Weed, a campaign consultant, to put together a staff for him to take to Washington, and gave him final say on all personnel decisions. Weed looked at the motley crew of loyalists who had helped Gingrich lose two elections, and decided to make some changes. He shed the Georgia good 'ol boys, the former hippies, the Democrats, and the good-natured professors and replaced them with a shined-up group of proto-Reaganites. He turned away Lee Howell, who'd been encouraged to apply for a job by Gingrich.

"One of Newt's phrases is, 'I find this useful' or 'I don't find this useful.' People are like that to him. He's their friend as long as they're useful to him. When they're no longer useful, it's over," Howell says.

Weed prevailed upon Gingrich to get rid of Glyn Thomas, an old friend and environmental studies colleague, to whom the congressman-elect, in a fit of post-election euphoria, had offered a job in the district office.

Thomas still laughs with half-abashed glee as he tells the story: In 1978, he was a professor who'd been well to the left of McGovern, a teacher of Alternative Lifestyles who'd lived in a farm commune and advised a Georgia Tech students' group affiliated with the Students for a Democratic Society—and he'd been shocked when Gingrich had offered him a job. After searching his conscience over whether or not to take it, he'd decided to give it a shot. But by the time he'd come to talk to Gingrich about particulars, the congressman's new consultants had gotten to him.

"His mood was totally different," Thomas recalls. "He said, 'You'll have to change your lifestyle. You can't smoke pot.' And he quoted this ridiculously low salary. It was obviously just a ploy to give me the opportunity to reject it. I said I couldn't take it. And he said, 'Well, I'm sorry you can't . . . but I could probably hire two women for that anyway.'

"Everything changed once he won the election," Thomas says. "The Republican Party sent their pros in, and they just completely took over and started systematically cutting off everybody who was an adviser. Everybody got cut out of the loop."

To make it up to some of his old Carrollton friends, Gingrich formed a group called the Rural Advisory Committee, which was supposed to meet periodically to come up with ideas for constituent services in the area.

"He met with them the first time, and the second time he sent them a bottle of booze, and after that he never said anything to them, and they never said anything to him. It *died*," Thomas says.

One group of people he was sure to remain loyal to was the black community. Gingrich had been elected to Congress with one-third of the black vote. He needed that vote, and more. So he brought to Washington a black lay minister who had helped him enormously in black neighborhoods during the campaign. Gingrich put him in charge of "special projects"—acting as liaison for the people in the district who wanted grants for projects like sewers and highways and public housing.

Marc Rosenberg, then a Washington-based political consultant who'd been hired by Gingrich to prepare him for Congress, recalls the novelty of this assignment: "This was a district that started out close to Atlanta blue collar and then became redneck very quickly. Lots of rural small towns over five counties of central Georgia, every one of those towns had a local Democratic mayor—and they were not the picture of enlightenment. And yet when they came to Washington and asked their congressman for help getting Great Society money, they had to ask him by coming to a meeting with his black assistant. If you want a negative spin, you could say this was really a way of tormenting the local Democratic establishment. If you put a positive spin on it, you'd say that sent a very strong message to the black community. That at least their congressman was thinking about them."

In a few months, Gingrich had shed nearly all his old political associates. And when he was all done with that, he shed Jackie.

Stories about his infidelity—blatant and bounteous infidelity—had started circulating around the time of his 1974 campaign, when Gingrich began spending a good deal of time away from Carrollton and several of his closest associates realized that he was having an affair. A former driver recalls often dropping him off at a woman's house in the evenings and picking him up at a Waffle House (a "good Republican establishment") the next day.

"I never asked where he spent the night, and I never was told," he says.

Jackie reportedly found out about the affair. She and Newt went into marriage counseling the next year. Gingrich's alleged continued affairs were discussed in some detail in a 1984 *Mother Jones* article by David Osborne, which was later widely circulated in Washington. It is probably a good measure of Gingrich's increasing power that virtually none of the people quoted in that article, or in a subsequent 1989 article on Gingrich's ethics, would be cited by name for this book. They pleaded off on harassment, threatening phone calls, allegations of homosexuality. One moved out of state.

The stories that surround Gingrich are colorful and strange, unique fruits of the grapevine that grows in the soil of rural Georgia, where women are still called "little girls," and men are called "boys" and "fellas," and there's a lubriciousness in the air that keeps the churches full on Sundays and makes the sinners at times perhaps tend to confuse Gingrich's life story with their own.

After his first losing campaign, members of Gingrich's political staff worried that his libido might make them losers forever.

"If he had gotten out and campaigned rather than spending his time with that girl he'd probably have won in '74," says one former senior campaign staffer. "It was a problem in '74, and it was a problem in '76 and a problem in '78."

At the very least, Gingrich has confirmed that there *were* affairs: "In the 1970s, things happened— period," he told the *Washington Post* in December 1994. He also told that reporter: . . . "All I'll say is that I've led a human life."

The campaign staff came up with a rather novel solution: They'd let Gingrich commit adultery by proxy.

"We had a guy—it was his driver—who was supposed to intercept them [the women] and sleep with them so they would think they had slept with him," the former senior staffer says. "We were trying to keep Newt focused on the campaign."

The driver confirms the story.

The tactic wasn't one hundred percent successful. The 1978 campaign rested, to a large extent, on a portrayal of Gingrich's glowing family values. To that end he sprinkled Jackie's pictures liberally throughout his "shopping cart" campaign materials, and even had her write her own request for money—ostensibly in her own longhand schoolmarmish writing—to potential campaign donors, asking them to support Newt, "a good husband, a good father, and a good Christian." He was seen walking hand in hand with her through the streets of Carrollton, sending local hearts aflutter at the sight of such a long and loyal meeting of true minds.

He was also seen, at night, while Jackie was home

with the children or recovering from a bout with uterine cancer, ducking out of campaign appearances with another woman.

"Jackie was sick and she didn't go with him to many things," says a source from the Shapard campaign. "Several times on the campaign trail, we knew he was with another woman. She would wait over on the side for him, and afterward they would zip out, particularly if we were in Atlanta doing something. They'd shake everybody and get lost. We heard talk from disgruntled campaign workers from his campaign, they talked about his fooling around. . . .

"One evening as they were whisking out, we gave chase just to see where they were going, and they saw us, and he just *mashed down*—usually he had a driver. But he just *mashed* down on the accelerator, just took off. I don't know how fast he was going."

On election night 1978, by coincidence, campaign workers in *both* Newt Gingrich's office *and* Virginia Shapard's took up bets on how long his marriage would last once Gingrich got to Washington. Eighteen months was the conviction on the Shapard side. It was their best call of the election year.

In the spring of 1980, the Gingriches came to Carrollton to spend a weekend visiting friends and constituents. On the way back to the Atlanta airport, Newt told Jackie he wanted a divorce.

"Don't you want to talk about it?" she asked.

"No," he said. "I've already made my decision."

A few weeks earlier, he had called his friend and former campaign treasurer, L. H. "Kip" Carter, who was now working for Gingrich in the district office, and spoke with him about his marriage. Carter said he and other friends had been worried about Newt and Jackie.

Gingrich told him that he had good reason to worry, and that the marriage was effectively over. " 'She's not young enough or pretty enough to be the wife of a president,' " Gingrich allegedly told Carter. 'And besides, she has cancer.' It sounds harsh and hokey, but anyone who knows him knows it's perfectly consistent with the kinds of things he says," Carter told *The New York Times*.

Gingrich also had a heart-to-heart with speechwriter Lee Howell.

"What's on your mind, Newt?" Howell asked.

"I just want you to know," he said, "that I'm getting a divorce."

"Why?" Howell asked.

"We've been having some problems," Howell says Gingrich answered. "It's just like what happens when you have a pain in the neck. Eventually you're going to have to cut it off—that's the only way you can get rid of it. You just have to decide whether you can live with it or not. And when you can't live with it, cut it out."

"He gave me a traditional, mid to late seventies kind of 'I've got to be myself, I can't be free, I'm smothered,' sort of explanation," says retired dean Richard Dangle.

Jackie Gingrich, by all reports, did not share her husband's sentiments. She saw her marital problems with Newt as the sort of growing pains that all couples go through at some point in their relationship. She turned to her pastor, Brantley Harwell, for help.

"I counseled with them long-distance for a good while," Harwell says. "I encouraged them to get help and they did. But it was at that point where Newt was just not interested in opening his mind to going back to Jackie."

Jackie at first refused to believe that Newt wasn't coming back, and continued to seek Harwell's counsel.

"[My wife] and I tried to convince him to go back to Jackie," Harwell says. "Newt and I spent many, many hours talking. And I pushed him to the wall on all the challenges that I could: did he love her, was he running around on her, was he ready to give the girls up, be with them in Washington. And he had thought about all that, he had rationalized all that. And I said,

'Well, Newt, you lost two races. You won one. And it wasn't a big win, against a woman'—women weren't running much in those times. I said, 'This kind of thing could tip the scales. Are you willing to put your political career that you dream about on the line?'

"He thought a minute, and said to me, 'I've given a lot of thought to that, and it scares me. But I've just got to do what I want to do.'

"What is it I can do?" Harwell says he finally asked Newt.

"With tears in his eyes, he said, 'Please take care of Jackie and the girls.' And I said, 'I'll do my best.' "

Newt and Jackie separated in June. Gingrich went ahead and filed for a divorce in July. Jackie, by all accounts, was devastated. And when she got over her shock, and her pain, she was furious. She refused to speak to Newt, refused to discuss the terms of their settlement. The legal proceedings dragged on and on.

According to Mel Steely, Newt's friend and biographer, who was quoted in *Newsweek* in 1994, she went before the congregation at the First Baptist Church in Carrollton and said, "The Devil has taken his heart."

Harwell has no recollection of that. "She wouldn't say that to the congregation," he says. "[But] in those early days when she was so bitter and hurt, she may have said something like that to a smaller group. She was distraught."

She was also desperate for money. The support payments that Gingrich sent her were so meager that some of Jackie's friends took up a collection to help her out. In early fall she went to court, filing a motion saying that she was "unable to support herself" and her daughters on the "inadequate sums" being provided and that Gingrich had "failed and refused to voluntarily provide reasonable support sufficient to include payment of usual and normal living expenses, including drugs, water, sewage, garbage, gas, electric, and telephone service." As a result, she said, many of her bills were two or three months past due, and she'd received notices of intent to cut off gas and electricity.

She charged that Newt had not cooperated in making available any financial information, and she was forced to file a formal notice and depose him.

In response, Newt filed court papers that included an accounting of his monthly expenses. The financial statements showed that he was providing Jackie with only $400 per month, plus $40 in allowances for his daughters. But in listing his own expenses, his "food/dry cleaning, etc." alone accounted for $400 in "living expenses." The presiding judge at the hearing was Lamar Knight, known as a "hanging judge" around Carrollton for the time he had sentenced a college freshman to a year in jail for taking a rocking chair off an abandoned farmhouse porch. The judge had little patience for deadbeat dads. He ordered Gingrich to pay Jackie $300 per month in child support and $400 per month in alimony, and reimburse her for legal fees.

Harwell had set Jackie up with the best lawyer he could find, and he had helped her come up with the most substantial settlement package he could imagine: liberal alimony, child support, percentages of Gingrich's future raises, guaranteed access to his income tax returns, the girls' college tuition.

On Gingrich's next trip back to Carrollton, he called Harwell. "We have to talk," he said.

"Newt, you asked me to take care of them," Harwell said. "Jackie got you elected. I think she has a right to have some contributions from your future."

It put a bit of a chill in their friendship.

When the divorce became final, in February 1981, the court raised the child support to $400 per month and $1,000 in alimony, with increases set for the future according to pay raises that Gingrich might receive. He was made responsible for the family's medical and dental insurance, the girls' college and professional school tuitions, and for maintaining a life insurance policy of not less than $100,000. He also had to pay Jackie's legal fees.

In 1993, Jackie pulled Newt back into court, charging that he had not kept up with payments on the life insurance policy and "has failed to pay alimony on a timely basis." Newt claimed he had misunderstood what day of the month he was supposed to make payments. When asked about the charges, he asked, if he had been so negligent, "why do both of the girls end up saying I'm a good father?" *Newsweek* reported. In March 1994, he increased his alimony payments to $1,300 per month in exchange for a promise that she wouldn't drag him into court again.

"When I heard *that,* I said, 'Newt's getting ready to make some big money,' " Harwell says.

Jackie still teaches public school in Carrollton, where students even recently have been seen wearing home-made buttons that read, WE SUPPORT JACKIE. She reportedly refers to Gingrich as "the Congressman."

"To say I gave up a lot for the marriage is the understatement of the year," she told the *Washington Post* in 1985.

In August 1981, six months after the divorce became final, Newt married Marianne Ginther, an Ohio-born personnel clerk with the Secret Service who was fifteen years younger than Jackie.

To his credit, Gingrich has been strikingly candid about this less than admirable period in his life. "Even if I had been sensitive, it would've been a mess," he told the *Atlanta Constitution*.

"I had married my high school math teacher two days after I was nineteen," Gingrich explained to *Mother Jones*. "In some ways it was a wonderful relationship, particularly in the early years. . . . But we had gone through a series of problems. . . . There was an eleven-year history prior to my finally breaking down. . . ."

He said he had been "disintegrating" as a person. "I took back on it a little bit like somebody who's in Alcoholics Anonymous—it was a very, very bad period of my life, and it had been getting steadily worse. . . . I ultimately wound up at a point where probably suicide or going insane or divorce were the last three options.''

"It was a tragedy," he said in December 1994. "I wish it had not happened."

A number of close friends from Gingrich's days at Tulane say that the break-up of his marriage didn't come at all as a shock.

"I was not particularly surprised when the divorce came," one friend says. "I had always thought to myself, 'Newton would have to get rid of her if his ambitions to be president were realized.' [Jackie] looked like Brunhilde without the mask. She was overweight, a straight up and down woman, like a Wagnerian opera star. And there wasn't any way she was ever going to not look like that. Jackie didn't change to suit Newt. From that point of view, she was not a presentable political wife." Also, he added, "Jackie was a very likable person, very sweet, intelligent, a very nice person. But she was not a sophisticated person by any means. And nice people don't survive in Washington."

Another friend is also sympathetic to Gingrich: "It was a very paradoxical marriage. A very sad marriage. My belief is that he was extremely unhappy," he says. "Jackie was a very fine woman. But she was extremely domineering of him, treated him like a little boy. There's a part of Newt which is fairly socially inept, and one of the things he's always tended to do is talk a little bit too much. And it was quite common for her to say, 'All right, Newton . . .'—whenever he was in trouble, she'd call him Newton—'It's time to go home.' Right in the middle of a sentence or whatever. And then, and this is what I thought was really peculiar, whenever that would happen, they'd hold hands and be a smiling couple for a moment and he'd obey. It was almost as though he'd married an older feminine authority figure.

"I believe he tried extremely hard to make that marriage work, for eighteen years. He didn't do it, and when he ended it, he did it in a terrible way, under

conditions that nobody can justify. And yet there is
another side to the story. He did stick with her for a
long time; I believe he was happy for a long time. I
think that he probably would have liked to have made
it work, but he just realized that he could not sustain
the thing, and that something had to be done about it.
I give him a little bit of credit for that."

Gingrich has always taken a charitable approach to
his own mistakes. In fact, he's found ways to incorporate them into his sense of himself as a historical
figure. In 1980, he did not dwell on the failure of his
marriage. He was too busy building up a power base
in Washington.

Immediately after the election, in 1978, Gingrich
had hired Marc Rosenberg, a political consultant, to
"tutor" him on the ways of the House. He had spent
two months in Georgia with Rosenberg learning basic
House rules and procedures, gaining contacts, and
preparing to set up his office in Washington. The first
item of business, Rosenberg told Gingrich, was to set
strategy. Rosenberg said that, as a Republican elected
from Democratic Georgia with such a narrow victory,
Gingrich needed to make it very clear to his constituents that he was in fact going to work on things of
value to them. This meant Gingrich would have to do
work that would benefit the airport and air industry,
then the largest source of employment in the Sixth
District. It was essential, Rosenberg said, that
Gingrich get to serve on the Public Works Committee,
which had oversight of airports. But, he said, it was
a very popular committee because it also oversaw
highways, and every congressman wanted to be able
to say he provided highway money to his district. So
it would probably be necessary to strike a deal.

On Rosenberg's recommendation, Gingrich made a
rather unusual bid: He offered to serve on the House
Administration Committee, an undesirable, very low-
profile committee that dealt with the rules and running
of the House, but said that in exchange he wanted an
assignment to the Public Works Committee. The house

leadership, glad for a warm body on the Administration Committee, immediately said yes.

By seeming to take a back seat, Gingrich was actually positioning himself for rapid and secure advancement.

"The Public Works Committee satisfied his constituent service needs," Rosenberg says. "And the House Administration Committee was the place where you learned what the rules of the House were, aside from the Rules Committee, which you couldn't sit on without a lot of seniority. He was able to sit and see which committees had a lot of seniority, how much money and staff they had, and what were the rules. It was a wonderful place for him to learn about the House of Representatives."

Rosenberg saw the fruits of his labor pay off this past year when Gingrich, after being elected speaker of the House, quickly changed the structure of House operations, consolidating his power in the process.

"He was able to move as quickly as he did reorganizing the House in part because he had sat on that committee for fifteen years and had paid close attention," Rosenberg says. "There were other members who would sit there and think the purpose of the exercise was to audit the books of the other committees. Gingrich would sit there and the purpose was to learn what was *going on* in the other committees. . . .

"It's interesting to watch him because very little of what he does happens by accident," he reflects. "Activities and events that may seem unrelated eventually become pieces of a mosaic and fit into a big picture."

More than a decade later, his intimate knowledge of Congress would serve him well in bringing about the rout of Democratic incumbents through the House banking scandal.

The "big picture" was one of the first things that Rosenberg told Gingrich to attend to. Gingrich had to decide just what kind of a congressman he wanted to be.

"There are several different kinds of congressmen," Rosenberg told him. "There are the great legislators, there are pothole fixers, there are the stump orators. In order for me to give any advice on how to proceed, I need to know what kind of congressman you plan to be."

Gingrich told Rosenberg that he didn't want to be just an average congressman, authoring bills and seeing them through to law. He planned, very simply, to be Speaker of the House. This plan, coming from a freshman Republican congressman four years after Watergate, struck Rosenberg as rather curious.

"And lo and behold . . ." Rosenberg says. "I basically told him there were two different tracks he had to proceed on. To position himself as a leader of the Republican Party, and to position the Republican Party as the majority. And getting one without the other wouldn't accomplish his goal."

Gingrich took Rosenberg's advice to heart. As soon as he got to Washington, he hung up his posters of John Belushi as a senator and of Robert Redford in *The Candidate* ("a constant reminder of how quickly one can change into something he opposes and get sucked into the Washington whirl," Gingrich's official biographer, Mel Steely has explained), he met with the National Republican Congressional Committee Chairman, Representative Guy Vander Jagt of Michigan. Gingrich told Vander Jagt that the Republican party needed to shake itself up. It needed to fight to become the majority party in America—to stop making deals with the Democrats and stop them in their tracks instead.

Vander Jagt listened with interest. He'd heard talk like this from other members of Gingrich's freshman class, a particularly militant group of young Republicans stepping in to succeed the idealistic freshman Democrats who had swept into the House just after Watergate. All these young Republicans were itching to get the Democrats out of Congress and Jimmy Carter out of the White House. But he hadn't encoun-

tered anyone with so much persuasive power—or so
persuaded of his own ability to lead. He was also in
the presence of a young man with absolutely vaulting
ambition.

Gingrich not only wanted, by 1979, to bring about a
Republican majority and propel himself to the position
of speaker; he wanted to radically change the balance
of power within the United States government. "The
Congress in the long run can change the country more
dramatically than the president," he told *Congressional Quarterly* that year. "I think that's healthy.
One of my goals is to make the House the co-equal of
the White House."

Gingrich was hungry, and he was willing to fight.
After three hours of talk Vander Jagt appointed him
chairman of a task force to plan for a Republican
majority. The task force aimed not only to increase
the number of Republicans elected to Congress but to
convince as many Democrats as possible to switch
parties. To get them to do this, Gingrich felt, the
Republicans had to offer—or seem to offer—a platform that was truly distinct from the Democrats'.
Distinction would mean denigration, he decided.

So he declared a political civil war. He assailed
the Democrats' "defeatist" attitudes and called the
G.O.P. the "party of hope." He and other G.O.P.
freshmen came up with a "Budget of Hope and Opportunity," which he contrasted with the Democrats'
"Budget of Disappointment and Despair." He assailed
the "cynicism" and "defeated" air of congressmen
and called for a sixty percent turnover for the next
two or three elections.

Eschewing bipartisanship, Gingrich said, "It's not
just a matter of working out a compromise," he said.
"The two factions are fundamentally opposed." He
led the Republican fight against the Democratic budget
and had 155 of the House's 160 Republicans behind
him.

From his experience in doing battle with Jack Flynt,
Gingrich had seen the impact that ethics questions had

on the voting public. Making allegations of ethical impropiety raised voters' hackles and made the news. He decided that he couldn't go wrong staying on the ethics beat in Congress.

He turned his sights first on Representative Charles Diggs, a black Democrat from Michigan who had been found guilty in U.S. district court the previous October of eleven counts of mail fraud and eighteen counts of filing falsified congressional pay vouchers and had been sentenced to three years in prison. Diggs had been easily reelected after that decision and was appealing it. His vindication by the voters meant nothing to Gingrich. Within two weeks of his swearing-in, he denounced the "double standard of justice that permits a convicted felon to vote in Congress," and called for an investigation of Diggs. One was already ongoing, and the House leadership all but ignored him. In late February, he sent a letter to Diggs asking him not to vote on controversial legislation the following week while he was pursuing his appeals and the House Ethics Committee was looking into his case. He threatened that if Diggs voted, he would move to expell him. He also sent a letter to all congressmen asking them to "drop a note to Mr. Diggs" advising him not to vote, and made his case as well in an op-ed piece published in the *Washington Post*. The bill, the first to come to the House floor in the 96th Congress, would have raised the temporary debt limit by 38 billion to 836 billion.

The motion to expel Diggs never came to a vote. Instead, a move to refer the question to the Ethics Committee was approved by an overwhelming margin, and Diggs later resigned to serve his prison term. And, after all the fuss, Gingrich missed the close, 201 to 199 roll call vote on the debt-ceiling measure because he was having lunch with a reporter from the *Washington Post*. When questioned about this, a Gingrich aide said, according to *Congress Probe*. "I guess you could call it a case of the media influencing events."

By the time of his second campaign, in 1980,

Gingrich had both the intially suspicious G.O.P. leadership and its rank-and-file members behind him. That year, 73 of his 87 PAC donations came from out of state. In state, his major contributors included two Southwire executives, Roy Richards and Roger Schoerner, who gave $500 each. Southwire itself, for the first time in its thirty-year history, gave a $500 PAC donation to his campaign.

His Democratic opponent in 1980, Dock Davis, raised $42,546 to Gingrich's $154,875. He accused Gingrich of being "too interested in helping Roy Richards dump his waste" to worry about his constituents and accused Gingrich of being insincere in his promises that he opposed a proposed hazardous-waste dump in Heard County; Gingrich refuted these charges as demagoguery, and said Davis opposed it because it was near his farm. He won reelection easily.

After Reagan's election, Gingrich veered sharply and permanently to the right. His railings against big government now almost touched on libertarianism and often echoed the calls for total decentralization of local government concerns issued by the religious right. He suggested that Georgia consider abolishing the State Department of Education. He asked Dolores Adamson to find him a church, and after visiting a few in his district, chose to associate himself with the quasi-fundamentalist New Hope Baptist Church, whose pastor, Ike Reighard, was a rising star in the Southern Baptist convention and encouraged political activism by his parisioners. He also began surrounding himself with young Bible thumpers who dotted his speeches with references to God.

None of this particularly impressed his old pastor, Brantley Harwell.

"He saw how effective it was for Reagan, that that was the way the nation was moving, and it was easy for him to accommodate that," Harwell says.

Nor was Gingrich's transformation lost on his old speechwriter, Lee Howell.

"I was going to be a Methodist preacher once,"

Howell says. "So when I wrote speeches for Newt, I'd put in biblical allusions here and there and refer to 'God's will' or use phrases like 'God's work must be our own.' And Newt pulled me aside one time and said, 'Lee, I really don't want to use the church or use God in running for office.' The Newt Gingrich I wrote speeches for and was close to did not want to use religion for political purposes. And he freely admitted that he wasn't sure of what he believed and that sometimes he had real doubts about religion, about the church and the way it teaches."

Ronald Reagan's "Morning in America" banished all such doubt. A few years later, Jerry Falwell himself would come to Georgia and endorse Gingrich. And as Gingrich's political machine grew and diversified in the late 1980s and early 1990s, his links to figures on the religious right became more intimate and complex.

One advantage that finding God brought Gingrich was a vocabulary and system of rationalization into which to fit his adultery. It was thus in good faith, when accused of moral hypocrisy, he could in later years say:

"I am a sinner. I am a normal person. I am like everyone else I ever met. One of the reasons I got to God is that I ain't very good."

Gingrich "got" religion at about the same time that he lost most of his friends. The combination of his turn to Reagan Republicanism and his divorcing of Jackie had set many people in Carrollton against him. Everyone in Carrollton knew how Jackie had sacrificed for Newt. She'd given her time, given up her private life, lived in an extremely modest home with modest furnishings while the family's every penny had gone to Newt's campaigns.

"Jackie and Newt were always dirt poor," Harwell says.

When stories of Gingrich's deposition before Judge Knight made it into the local newspapers, the town reacted with fury. A few weeks later, on election day,

Gingrich's winning margin in Carroll County fell from 66 percent in 1978 to 51 percent.

A story that made people even more furious made it onto the national scene through *Mother Jones* in 1984. According to this story, told then by Lee Howell and confirmed again recently, Newt came to visit Jackie in the hospital where she was recovering from a second operation for uterine cancer in 1980. While there, with Jackie still groggy from the operation, he pulled out a yellow legal pad that had a list of items on it that he wanted to discuss about the divorce settlement. Jackie had refused for weeks to discuss these details. He now had a captive audience.

Gingrich calls this story a "caricature."

"It's one of those things that becomes a myth," he told *Time* in 1994. "Which, by the way, is not to say that as seen by my ex-wife, it didn't happen. It was never a question of serving papers; the question was, I always carried papers with me, and I was taking our two daughters to see her in the hospital where she was recovering from surgery, and the question is, Was there a conversation, how did the conversation evolve, and who is saying what to whom?"

Many of Gingrich's best friends at Tulane, who'd been growing steadily disenchanted with him as he moved to the right, virtually dropped him when he divorced Jackie.

"It was his selfish, self-serving way of handling almost everything," one friend from that time recalls. "We'd known that Newt uses people, that he's not somebody who has real strong principles. The straw that would break the camel's back was the divorce."

Most of Gingrich's friends from West Georgia College also felt that they'd been betrayed—personally and politically.

"We backed him because we thought he was a reasonable kind of middle-of-the-road guy on the cutting edge of environmental issues," says a former administrator of the college. "But he was a different kind of slippery fish. I thought he was a pretty strong liberal, and he's just been milking that right-wing cow for years."

"Newt was elected with liberal help," says Glyn Thomas. "Friends of mine took out money to support him, borrowed money on their homes. Signed notes for him, whatever. Guys who were very, very liberal. Because he posed as a big society kind of Republican. And he'd pushed the idea that he had worked for Rockefeller. All of these people felt duped."

Gingrich backer Lucy Klee was terribly disappointed in the person Newt Gingrich had become. "We were taken in," she explained to the *Washington Post* last year. "We were more than disappointed. We were aghast. I told Newt that I'd never vote for another Republican, and he wasn't at all upset. He said that was okay as long as I was consistent."

Hans Schmidt, a professor of his from Tulane who later went on to become a professor at the University of Virginia, wrote to him when he took up such conservative issues as school prayer because he was so upset by Gingrich's turn to the religious right.

"Dear Hans," Gingrich wrote back. "Do you realize that someone is writing me abusive letters and signing your name?"

Schmidt was disgusted. "A case like Gingrich's seems to indicate once again that the product of education is not necessarily a person of moral substance," Schmidt told the *Times-Picayune* in November 1994. "He's Machiavellian. He'll do anything to gain his end."

Bill Mankin, a Georgia environmental leader in the 1970s who had worked as Gingrich's campaign driver early in 1980 because he was so impressed by his vote for the Alaska Lands Act, broke ranks with Gingrich on the day before the election. On that day, Mankin recalled to the *Washington Post,* he approached Gingrich and said he wouldn't be coming to his victory party.

"Newt, I hope you don't mind," he said, "But I

don't think I could stand to be in a room full of people who love Ronald Reagan.''

"That's okay," Gingrich said. "I understand."

These people were expendable. He was still elect-able. He was traveling light.

By the time of Gingrich's second and third terms, it wasn't only old personal friends who were complaining that he'd changed. Staffers had noticed a change too.

"When he first was elected, Newt changed in a positive sense," a former key district aide says. "He genuinely wanted to be a statesman. But when he got a sense of that power, it surged in him so powerfully that he didn't let it go."

Kip Carter, who had been kept on as senior administrative aide in Georgia, responsible for training staff and running the district offices, was one of the first to cry foul. He saw Gingrich fly into a rage the first time he flew back to Atlanta from Washington because Carter had walked up to the gate to greet him as he always did rather than having stood and waited for him.

Later, when Kip Carter took Gingrich to task for not staying in better touch with his constituents, Newt got even more angry:

" 'Fuck you guys. I don't need any of you anymore,' " Carter told *Mother Jones* that Gingrich had said. " 'I've got the money from the political action committees. I've got the Atlanta news media right here in the palm of my hand. I don't need any of you anymore.' "

Gingrich recalls his falling-out with Carter differently. As he told the *Washington Post* in December 1994: "This is a guy I deliberately fired because we got into an argument about whether or not he had to tell me what he was doing. . . . So here's this image that on the one hand, Gingrich really sheds people, except by the way, there are people now who have worked with him for a quarter century. Now, which is true?'' (Carter says he resigned.)

Gingrich began requiring his staff to read books he deemed essential, such as Alvin Toffler's *The Third Wave*, a book describing the forthcoming era when the industrial age is supplanted by the information age. After the end of his first term, he also began to insist that his public remarks be taped. He was assembling his archives, he said, and staffers who didn't go along with it would see their pay docked $200. It wasn't an empty threat.

Dolores Adamson lost a good deal of pay before she quit her job in 1983. "I asked him, 'Don't you think that when we record your voice at every meeting you go to that you're looking like a pompous someone who wants to hear themselves talk?' " Adamson told *Mother Jones* in 1989. "He said, 'No, it's important.' . . . He thought . . . there'd probably be a museum someday where you could go and check one of those tapes out."

"I used to get on him about the fact that he'd authored no legislation," a former top aide says. "I'd say he needed to do it to be remembered in history. At first he'd say you're right. But at the end he'd say, "I'm making history anyway. I don't need to make legislation."

"He was very docile and calm during the first couple of years," the former district worker says. "Learned a lot and was very attentive. As soon as he learned the ropes and got on his feet, he went his own way as a maverick. Angry at anything that got in his way."

He was so arrogant at times that staffers found themselves constantly apologizing for, or spinning, his gaffes. Gingrich would fly back from making a speech out West with a high-ranking army colonel, then leave the man to carry his bags while he raced to catch a connecting flight to Washington. The colonel missed his flight, the last of the day, and ended up with Gingrich's bags in the district office, fuming. Damage control was thankless work. When one staff member drew Gingrich's attention to the fact that, in a speech about finding a cure for cancer in outer space, he'd repeatedly used the word freon instead of interferon, he nearly bit her head off.

"There are two Newt Gingrichs," says Howell. "One is very articulate and entertaining, and I'd like to be at a party with him. The other Newt Gingrich is a mean, vicious partisan who's just vindictive and very little. Like Nixon, when he doesn't like somebody, he labels you the Enemy. He's very thin-skinned. He can dish it out, but he can't take it."

Richard Dangle, the man who had decided not to give Newt Gingrich tenure, a former member of the ill-fated Rural Advisory Board, and a good friend of the congressman even after his divorce, finally fell out with Newt a few years into the Reagan revolution.

"I thought he was beginning to sound more and more like a politician," Dangle says. He broached the issue one weekend when Gingrich was staying over as a house guest. The two were sitting up late at night talking.

"I told him he had changed," Dangle says. "He said, no, he had grown. I said, 'It doesn't look like you've grown to me, it looks like you've become a politician.' "

Dangle knew that, just a few years back, *politician* was one of the worst words in the Newt Gingrich lexicon.

"He said, 'If you're going to be a politician, you have to be a politician,' " Dangle says.

"And we just gradually drifted apart."

5

Apogee of an Attack Dog

The 1982 midterm elections were disastrous for the Republicans. They lost 26 seats in the House, eliminating nearly the entire 33-seat gain they had made in the landslide Reagan victory of 1980. In the aftermath the Republicans and "Reagan Democrats" no longer controlled the Congress. The Reagan "revolution" appeared to be over.

The losses only made Newt Gingrich more convinced of his mission to reinvigorate the party. He didn't care whose toes he had to step on to do so. He had already, in the early fall, raised eyebrows by sending White House Chief of Staff James Baker a five-page letter reprimanding him for predicting a loss of 50 seats in the house that November. According to the *Washington Times,* Gingrich had criticized Baker for adding to the defeatist attitude that, he said, was enslaving House Republicans into a permanent minority role.

After the election, as many conservatives began to worry that Reagan was backing off from his activist agenda and that the Republicans would once again be backed into a position of compromise, Gingrich spoke out in the strongest terms.

"Ronald Reagan is like an FDR who hired Al Smith's advisers," he told the *Atlanta Constitution* in

February. "All his instincts are to create a New Deal, and all his advisers are telling him to be very cautious. You can't have a cautious reform or a cautious revolution. It won't work."

That dreary winter Newt and Marianne Gingrich traveled up to New York to meet with Richard M. Nixon. Nixon and Gingrich, it turned out, were thinking along similar lines. Both felt that the House Republicans had become so accustomed to their minority status that they'd come to embrace it, and were doing next to nothing about trying to change the status quo.

Nixon and Gingrich both felt that something had to change radically. The former president said that House Republicans had to become "more interesting, more energetic, and more idea-oriented," Gingrich recalled to the *Washington Post* in 1994.

Gingrich returned to Washington, and assembled his thoughts and his forces. He helped set up the Congressional Space Caucus and, with Democratic Senator Gary Hart of Colorado, developed the Military Reform Caucus. He polished his rhetorical skills by leading the drive to expel Representatives Gerry Studds of Massachusetts and Daniel Crane of Illinois from Congress after a House investigating committee reported that they both had had sexual relations with teenage pages: "There is no high school or college in America where exploiting, seducing, or sleeping with students, boy or girl, would be punished with a reprimand," he said. "There is a thin line between civilization and chaos. And yet, in all of us, we know that thin line is crossed . . . when authority figures exploit high school kids."

And he approached Vin Weber with an important new idea.

"What are you doing next year—and for the next ten?" he asked one day, according to the *Post*.

Weber laughed. "Nothing special," he said.

Gingrich offered a suggestion.

He would put together a group that would be brash enough, and radically conservative enough, to bring down both the Democratic House leadership and, if necessary, their own party's leaders. They would fight for majority status both in the House and the nation. As a group they would be more visible, and more powerful, than any of them could be individually.

Gingrich sought out House members who had a similar agenda and had proven track records as activists. He approached Robert S. Walker of Pennsylvania, Judd Gregg of New Hampshire, Dan Coats of Indiana, Connie Mack of Florida, Dan Lungren and Duncan Hunter of California. Soon about a dozen young Republicans had gathered to join the new group. They decided to call themselves the Conservative Opportunity Society, and to label their enemy the "liberal welfare state."

"We felt that you needed conservative solutions, and by that we meant that you needed to base more and more decision-making in the hands of individuals and you needed to move decision-making more toward localities," Walker says. "The word *opportunity* was aimed at achieving economic opportunity by reducing tax burdens, by reducing the burden of government debt and government spending on the economy. And the concept of society was one that we were seeking to build structures that were community-based and neighborhood-based rather than in the sense of a liberal welfare state where the national government had a command-and-control kind of role to play."

The liberal welfare state, on the other hand, was, according to Gingrich, "the baroque phase of liberalism: the Soviet Union as puzzling and benign, no growth, rationing."

The COS congressmen were mostly junior members from new and growing districts. They were New Right Republicans—young and ambitious activists dedicated to fighting against communism and taxes and welfare and the ERA and for prayer in the schools—who were fed up by what they saw as the complacency and moderate positions of the G.O.P. They were impatient with the conciliatory ways of their elders, like Bob

Dole in the Senate and Bob Michel in the House, and were willing to use unusually confrontational tactics to achieve their aims.

"What we did was set out to put together an activist agenda and then aggressively promote it," says Walker. "We believed that the party, if it was ever going to become the majority, had to be an activist party. It had to identify itself with the vast majority of the American people, and then had to present the opinions of that majority on the floor of the Congress in an aggressive way to contrast what we were saying against the people who were the defenders of the liberal welfare state. There were many in Congress among Republicans who believed that that was the wrong prescription, who believed that Republicans were better off negotiating with the Democrats and cutting the best possible deals, and then sharing at least a little bit in the outcome of the legislative process. They saw themselves more as legislators than as majority activists. And we just had a fundamental disagreement with what we thought the goal of the Republican Party in the House should be."

COS developed a platform: the line-item veto, a balanced budget amendment, a tougher stance on crime, war on drugs, welfare reform, "high frontier" fighting technology (Reagan's SDI space-based defense system), changing the House rules and bringing prayer to the schools. Gingrich called it "a long-wave theory of politics"—and indeed many of the ideas showed up in the Contract with America. It was made up of only "sixty-five percent" issues—issues that, like those included in the "Contract," had been proven by years of polls to have broad public support.

"This country picks COS over 'liberal welfare state' seventy-four to nineteen in polls," Gingrich explained in 1985. "We field-tested the terms just in terms of not knowing what it is, but how do you feel about it intuitively. COS even carried blacks."

The Conservative Opportunity Society members were frevent believers in supply-side economics. They said that enhancing America's economic strength would protect the country's freedom. They were committed to creating more jobs through high technology and encouraging development in areas like space and computers—an amalgam of sci-fi ideology that political writer Peter Boyer once called a kind of "New Age Reaganism."

"We had a sense of confidence that we weren't simply dealing with the issues of the next election, we were dealing with the issues of the next generation," Walker says. "We saw ourselves as doing something that was an extension of what we had all tried to accomplish individually. And that in bonding together we gave ourselves a sense of community and a sense of success."

COS members sometimes they spent whole days brainstorming together or attending lectures by outside speakers like Alvin Toffler and *Megatrends* author John Naisbitt, whose books *The Third Wave* and *Megatrends* Gingrich had put on a Conservative Opportunity Society recommended reading list, in addition to Tom Peters' and Robert Waterman's *In Search of Excellence* and Peter Drucker's *The Effective Executive*.

They also spent a morning swapping ideas with Nixon, who remained in touch with the group of congressmen over the years, and occasionally contacted them with ideas.

"When he'd write a book, he'd send us a copy of it autographed with a note saying, 'Here's my latest thinking on things.' He used that as a forum to kind of get to know some of us, and then to stay in touch for the future," Walker says.

COS members identified "wedges," issues that would divide the Democratic Party, and "magnets," which were designed to attract people to a forward-looking Republican agenda. The idea, Gingrich said, was to develop "a more positive, more open, more optimistic Republican Party." Yet what COS mostly did was highly negative. Known as the "Young

Turks,'' Gingrich loyalists began using parliamentary maneuvers to clog the Democrats' agenda, and making floor speeches assailing the ethics and values of the opposition. The main goal was to chip away at the Democrats' control of Congress by maligning their ethics and their resistance to change while building up a Republican platform that would seize the imagination of a majority of voters. Gingrich came up with a very neat way of conceptualizing this one day while eating lunch in the Members' Dining Room. He took a napkin and drew a triangle on it, labeling the sides "reality," "personal lives," and "people's values." "All successful politicians have to be inside the triangle," he explained. That thought, illustrated on paper, would soon be a staple of COS strategic thought.

In some ways Gingrich did not march in lockstep with the New Right. He was considered a moderate on civil rights, women's rights, and the environment. He paid lip service to the idea of equal pay for equal work. He continued to try to make room for blacks within his deeply conservative agenda, cultivating strong relations with Atlanta Mayor Andrew Young and, in 1985, talking Delta airlines into taking reservations for Air Atlanta, the largest black-owned airline in the country, to help it out. He then tried to sell Benjamin Elliott, Reagan's chief speechwriter, on the idea of including Air Atlanta's chairman, Michael Hollis, in Reagan's State of the Union address. He didn't support the Human Life Amendment or a return to the gold standard. He voted for the Alaska Lands Act, the largest wilderness-protection measure ever to pass Congress, and in 1983 he was one of the first congressmen to call for the resignation of the environmental blightist, Interior Secretary James C. Watt. To the consternation of many in his district, he voted for making Martin Luther King Day a national holiday, and defied those same voters, Ronald Reagan himself, and many of his political supporters to support economic sanctions against South Africa—although he did not support the idea of an immediate transition to a one-man, one-vote state in South Africa. ("[I]f we are truly conservatives and believe in freedom, we cannot believe in freedom in the Soviet Union but not care about freedom in South Africa," he told the *Atlanta Constitution*. "They're not going to go to one man, one vote in the next fifteen years, and they shouldn't," he said. "Moving from where we are to where we'd like to be may take a century.")

Gingrich was not so much a true believer in New Right dogma as he was an admirer of its tactics. But where he was perfectly in synch with New Right innovators like Richard Viguerie was in his attunement to the new potential for political activism offered by computer technology. In the late 1960s and 1970s, Viguerie had pioneered the use of direct-mail solicitation as a uniquely effective form of fund-raising. The direct-mail techniques that Viguerie perfected through his huge computer lists would change the nature, speed, and volume of lobbying.

In 1978, the same year that Viguerie raised the impressive sum of $5.2 million through direct-mail solicitation for Senator Jesse Helms of North Carolina, Congress voted to allow C-SPAN to begin transmitting the activities of the House over the open airwaves. In an almost prophetic stroke of symmetry, C-SPAN and Newt Gingrich arrived in Congress together in 1979. As a futurist and a conservative facing what he preceived as a hostile news media, Gingrich was immediately drawn to the idea of direct communication with the viewing, voting population. He called the news media "the central nervous system by which our country talks to itself." He had started cultivating the media long before he'd become a public person. While still a student at Emory, he had walked into the newsroom of the *Atlanta Constitution*, introduced himself to political writer Reg Murphy, and told him that he was "someone a reporter needed to know," a 1985 article in the *Constitution* related. According to the *Constitution*, Gingrich said that he planned then "to be a modern political boss in twenty years." At

Tulane, he'd taken to calling Mike Wallace and David Broder cold to tell them about what was going on in the student movement. He stayed in touch throughout his congressional campaigns.

The idea of using floor speeches to capture a TV audience had really started with Democrat Bill Alexander, who in 1983 had started notifying TV stations around the country when a Democrat made a speech on a timely issue. The local stations would tape the one-minute speeches and run them on their news shows. Members of the Conservative Opportunity Society complained, though, that the Democrats stifled their floor time, and that the liberal media filtered their viewpoints off the air. C-SPAN offered a way to remedy this; Robert Walker was the first congressman to figure out how. He spent hours on the House floor, trying to defend the Republicans' interests in the Congress. When he returned to his office, he would find a stack of telephone messages waiting. People were listening.

"What it told me was, there were a lot of people out there who were politically involved themselves, who were watching what was going on in the Congress, and who commented on it from the standpoint of their own prejudices. It struck me that the core audience that you were speaking to were people who were reasonably well informed and somewhat politically sophisticated," Walker says.

Brian Lamb, the Washington journalist who created C-SPAN, claimed in 1984 that eighty-five percent of C-SPAN's viewers voted. This made Gingrich sit up and take notice. Soon he was comparing C-SPAN to the journals of congressional activity that the founding fathers had said were so essential for keeping Americans informed of the goings-on in government. C-SPAN became more than a tool for self-promotion; it was a step toward a more participatory democracy.

House rules limit the length of debate over legislation. And the Democratic leadership controlled which issues came to the floor. But COS members knew there were two periods of time in the congressional day that they could control: the one-minute speeches at the beginning of the day, and the time, at the very end of the day, set aside for "special orders." The special orders time was traditionally used by congressmen to deliver speeches on matters of great importance to their constituents and to virtually no one else. In this way they went down in the *Congressional Record*—and now on C-SPAN—as having remembered where they were from without inconveniencing their colleagues. The speeches were generally delivered to a vacant House chamber and a few lost tourists in the House gallery. Now they went out to 250,000 households as well.

The implications weren't lost on Gingrich and associates. They routinely used this forum as a soapbox for their ideology and to criticize their Democratic colleagues for their positions. They spoke singly or in groups of twos and threes, bouncing their arguments back and forth with no conflicting voices to stop them.

COS members would hold meetings just before the opening of the House session and walk as a group over to the House floor and sit down and orchestrate a series of one-minute speeches on a theme they'd agreed upon for the day. They began interrupting sessions, demanding the Democrats bring up bills on their issues.

By 1984, they had their floor strategies down pat. On January 23, the day Congress reconvened from winter recess, they tried to reserve four hours a day through the rest of that legislative session for special orders. Democratic leaders said no, but the request nonetheless filled up five pages in the *Congressional Record* and won Robert Walker forty-five minutes of airtime. That same day COS members called for unanimous consent to call up bills on school prayer, a balanced budget, line-item veto, and abortion. Several Democrats objected, including Ron Coleman, a Democrat from Texas. The National Republican Congressional Committee, noting this, immediately sent a press release to newspapers in Coleman's conservative district saying that Coleman was responsible for keeping a school prayer bill from the floor. Other Democrats were similarly targeted.

To guard against future attacks on individual Democrats, House Speaker Tip O'Neill invoked a rule two days later requiring that unanimous-consent requests be cleared by the leadership in both parties—or by the speaker if the leadership failed to clear it. That put an end to the Republicans' tactic.

Gingrich called this typical of the Democrats' unfair way of doing business.

"They are systematically willing to cheat in rigging the rules in their favor," he told *Congressional Quarterly*. "The liberal leadership is hiding behind the procedures. They're trying to hide from the American public, which wants these issues to be voted on."

"They clamped more and more down on the processes of the House," Walker says. "I think that's what created the animosity, because then it affected not only us, it affected other members' rights as well. And the more they did that, it seems to me, the harsher the situation in the House became."

Walker once demanded a roll call on a routine motion to adjourn the next day for the Lincoln's Birthday recess. And in March 1984, COS members held an all-night legislative session devoted to school prayer, orchestrated by Gingrich, with pro-prayer speeches and a vigil on the Capitol steps.

One day in the spring, Gingrich went too far. In a floor speech attacking a group of Democrats who had sent a letter to Nicaraguan Sandinista leader Daniel Ortega, addressing him as "Dear Commandante" and calling for a peace settlement in Nicaragua, he accused the Democrats of being "blind to communism," said one member had placed "communist propaganda" in the speaker's lobby, and accused the Democrats of having a "pessimistic, defeatist, and skeptical view toward the American role in the world." He said that the Democrats believed that "America does nothing right and communism [only] rushes into vacuums caused by 'stupid' America and its 'rotten,' corrupt allies.'' He threatened to file charges against them for breaching the Neutrality Act. No one rose to debate him because the chamber was entirely empty.

A few days later, on May 14, before a full and emotionally charged chamber, House Speaker Tip O'Neill attacked Gingrich for questioning the patriotism of his fellow Democrats. Gingrich was nonplussed. He reiterated his views of the Democrats' Central American policy. He accused O'Neill's language of coming ''all too close to resembling a McCarthyism of the left.'' He denied that he'd called the Democrats un-American.

''It is perfectly American to be wrong,'' he said.

And he stood his ground happily, masterfully monopolizing floor time, keeping the C-SPAN cameras focused on him, while the Democrats fulminated and fumed. At last O'Neill took the floor.

''My personal opinion is this,' he shouted. ''You deliberately stood in that well before an empty House, and challenged these people, and challenged their patriotism. It is the lowest thing that I've seen in my thirty-two years in the Congress.''

Representative Trent Lott of Mississippi, Gingrich's predecessor as minority whip, jumped instantly out of his seat, demanding that the speaker's words be stricken for the record on the grounds that House members are barred from personally attacking one another on the floor.

Strictly speaking, Lott was right and, after a few minutes of tense discussion, the presiding officer ruled in his favor.

O'Neill was the first speaker since 1797 to be rebuked for his language. Gingrich made it to the network news for the first time, and got ninety seconds at the close of all three networks' news shows. All was right with the world.

''I am now a famous person,'' he crowed to the press. He was, at least, now a national figure. And he'd proved his favorite theory: the way to the heart of the news media was by creating conflict. "The number one fact about the news media is they love fights," he told a group of conservative activists after the incident. "You have to give them confrontations. When you give them confrontations, you get attention; when you get attention, you can educate."

Not long afterward, Lott was in his office changing for an evening event. He turned on his television to watch the late afternoon's "special orders." He saw Robert Walker speaking animatedly—as usual—then saw the cameras pan around the chamber, showing that his colleague was speaking his heart out to only two people. The cameras had never panned the chamber before. Lott was furious. He called C-SPAN and warned that "somebody" would pay. Then he ran to the floor and took the podium from Walker. He called it an "underhanded, sneaky, politically motivated change . . . the most patently unfair political thing that I have seen in the fifteen years I have been around here."

Tip O'Neill had ordered the change. It made the Republicans hopping mad. Gingrich ally Vin Weber, from Minnesota, soon after attacked O'Neill in a closed-door party conference as a "petty, second-class Boston politician . . . one of the cheapest, meanest politicians to occupy that office in this century," *Newsweek* reported in a story on the event. The Republicans then voted unanimously to extend camera pans both to debates and votes.

"Why shouldn't we show pictures of O'Neill and his Democrats twisting arms during votes?" Gingrich chuckled.

The atmosphere in Congress grew more and more tense. Majority Leader Jim Wright described it: "Tempers are rising, nerves are tight like a cotton clothesline after a rain." He hadn't seen anything yet. No one had any idea of just how bad things would get.

By 1984, observers on both sides of the political

spectrum were predicting that COS's negative tactics would backfire.

"They talk about things that are out of step with the mainstream of this country, and as a result, people brand them a nuisance and a fringe element of the House," said Byron Dorgan, a Democratic congressman from North Dakota, appearing on a call-in show with Gingrich. "They will, by their own publicity, deal the fatal blow to their cause."

"They're like a gang of little boys in a treehouse with a sign that reads members only," Christopher Matthews, chief aide to Speaker Tip O'Neill told the *Atlanta Constitution*. "They giggle too much."

Representative Jack Kemp, and House Minority Leader Bob Michel of Illinois, who played golf with Tip O'Neill, never became comfortable with the confrontational techniques of the Gingrich crew. "I have given them some fatherly advice," Michel said once. "Be gentlemanly and once you've made your point, get on with the business of governing."

Even some young Republicans were saying they didn't want to be associated with the group. Representative Tom Tauke of Iowa told *Congressional Quarterly*, "I am not going to engage in tactics that are perceived to be excessively partisan or obstructionist, which may stand in the way of my being effective in my committee and subcommittee."

Some members disagreed: "The country is not served by a nice, cozy, friendly feeling here all the time," Representative Dick Cheney of Wyoming told *Newsweek*. Trent Lott strongly seconded this feeling: "When you're in the minority and the rules and the committees are stacked against you, you can roll over and whimper like a dog, or you can bite somebody," he told the magazine.

Yet even some of the original members of COS came to feel they could not abide the group's aggressive tactics. "Newt's belief that to ultimately succeed you almost had to destroy the system so that you could rebuild it . . . was kind of scary stuff for some new people coming in," Don Coats told the *Washington Post* after the 1994 elections. "I ultimately came to the conclusion that the style in which COS was operating was not compatible with my own personal style, so my involvement diminished." But he added, "I'm quick to acknowledge now that we couldn't have gotten to where we are today had Newt not kept pushing it as hard as he did."

"Our tactics were tactics of people who were frozen in a minority," says Robert Walker.

Despite its plentiful detractors, the Conservative Opportunity Society remained a force to be reckoned with. It grew in membership and in clout. Although it had been founded without the backing of the House G.O.P. leadership, by 1984 it had been embraced by the National Republican Congressional Committee. It began working with the Republican Policy and Research committees on their legislative agenda after Bob Michel, sensing that the young upstarts were there to stay, asked the group to try to reach for a broader base. The National Association of Evangelicals were helping COS bring their agenda to the public. The backing of such religious right groups would prove to be, in the long run, one of COS's most potent strengths.

Gingrich's own strength was not shaping up to be as a legislator. The most memorable piece of legislation that he had introduced in his first two terms of Congress was a "Space Bill of Rights" to protect Americans in extraterrestrial colonies, something that prompted some of his critics back home to label him "Newt Skywalker." He wasn't a maker of laws, he was a maker of words—an "idea man." In 1984 he published his nonfiction book, *Window of Opportunity,* which consolidated many of his ideas. The book tied together all the futurism, Reaganism, and apocalyptic "optimism" dear to Gingrich's heart. "We stand at a crossroads between two diverse futures," Gingrich wrote. "On the one hand, we face a window of vulnerability. . . . On the other hand there is a beckoning window of opportunity."

The book was filled with the kind of abstract, abstruse, yet simplistic flights of fancy that would characterize most of what Gingrich would put to paper in his years as resident Conservative Opportunity Society intellectual. "We are on the edge of an explosion in space and biology, and in electronics we're going through a revolution in computers," Gingrich wrote. "If we are creative, we are potentially where Britain was at the beginning of the Industrial Revolution. We're on the edge of a takeoff into what Toffler called the Third Wave."

What did this mean? Any guess will do. *Window of Opportunity* envisioned a day when individuals would be able to get instant computerized analyses of their golf swing. It bemoaned the failure of the government to follow through on the 1969 moon landing, noting that by 1984 Americans could have had two space stations and a colony on the moon. It also could perhaps have made itself permanently independent of foreign or nuclear energy: "A mirror system in space could provide the light equivalent of many full moons so that there would be no need for night time lighting of the highways," Gingrich wrote. He had other hopeful predictions about greater opportunities for handicapped people in space: "In a zero-gravity environment, a paraplegic can float as easily as anyone else," he said, noting perceptively that "wheelchair-bound adults begin asking questions in an enthusiastic tone when exposed to the possibility of floating free, released from their wheelchairs."

For all its futuristic fluff, *Window of Opportunity*, whose promotion was funded by a partnership much like the group Chester Roush had pulled together for Gingrich in 1977, was at base a deeply ideological tract. It was profoundly anticommunist, fervently pro-Star Wars. Gingrich's whole idea of investing in space exploration was a kind of metaphoric elaboration of supply-side economics. In his essay, "Space: The

New Frontier," published that same year in *Future 21: Directions for America in the 21st Century,* edited by Paul Weyrich and Connaught Marshner, he elaborated upon the idea that liberals legislate limits while conservatives dream of expansion: "One of the key differences between a liberal welfare state and a conservative opportunity society is that liberals believe man is limited by resources, while a conservative opportunity society is based on the belief that man creates resources. . . . Everything we do to prove that mankind has access to a universe of resources decreases the value and power of liberalism's most important dogma. In that setting space is a dagger at the heart of the liberal welfare state. Once you accept that opportunities in space are real . . . then it is psychologically impossible to talk about the limits to growth." What more endless source of supply was there than outer space? Gingrich certainly could not think of any. In *Future 21* he argued for *privatizing* space as quickly as possible. He called for legislation to provide a tax credit to any corporation that built a permanent space station. "[I]n the not-too-distant future, we may very well see the space equivalent of the American westward migration," he wrote, anticipating "self-supporting colonies of up to ten thousand free people who harvest the resources of space, whether that is the rare minerals contained in many asteroids or building solar-power satellites to provide cheap, unlimited electrical energy to earth."

Richard Nixon had recommended to the COS members that they establish a presence at the 1984 Republican convention. Gingrich attended the convention as a member of the executive committee of the party's platform committee. *Window of Opportunity* was rushed to press and came out in print just before the platform hearings began. This meant that Gingrich went to Dallas credentialed as the major intellectual force behind the politics of the Conservative Opportunity Society. Eddie Mahe, a political consultant working with Gingrich at the time, told the *Washington*

Post in 1994 that the convention "marked the first time we took the whole concept of Newt's thinking outside of Washington to a broader audience. It was the opening, initial thrust."

Gingrich was in his element in Dallas. He'd come out of his party platform hearings cocky with victory after having fought until "Conservative Opportunity Society" was inserted into the platform. His fellow young turks, with the support of presidential hopeful Jack Kemp, had succeeded in rewriting sections of the party platform calling for school prayer and opposing any new tax increases. It was a victory for the congressional upstarts—and also for the far-right wing of the Republican Party. Indeed, summing up the mood, the minister who delivered the benediction at the convention, Reverend W. A. Criswell, told CBS the next day: "There is no such thing as separation of church and state. It is merely a figment in the imagination of infidels."

The 1984 Republican platform was anti-abortion, anti-tax increases, anti-communist, pro-free enterprise. It expressed a willingness to consider returning to the gold standard. Many Republicans, including the Reagan White House, were uncomfortable with the final platform document. But members of the new right were thrilled. Richard Viguerie, Howard Phillips, chairman of the Conservative Caucus, and Paul Weyrich, director of the National Committee for the Survival of a Free Congress, held daily press conferences. One was entitled, "Are Liberals Soft on Communism?" and featured a discussion of Senator John Warner of Virginia, a conservative Republican, as an example of a politician who had been "softened up by Communists."

Viguerie said at the time that he considered Gingrich "the single most important conservative in the House of Representatives."

At the Republican convention, he certainly was among the most visible. Before Gingrich had arrived in Dallas, a *Los Angeles Times* survey had shown that most delegates didn't know enough about Gingrich to be able to offer an opinion of him. They quickly learned. COS members pushed Gingrich's thinking into the spotlight at the convention. They handed out COS bumper stickers on the convention floor and held conferences to explain what COS stood for. Gingrich talked about Toffler and space and optimism, playing professor, bragging to the *New York Times,* with a gesture toward the crowded convention floor, "This is my campus. And I'm teaching seminars."

He was mobbed by reporters, tourists, and admirers. One Republican at the convention called him "a walking media event." Supporters grabbed him, shook his hand. Reagan Youths looked up to him in awe. He was so busy that he turned down an interview with CBS News anchorman Dan Rather and gave it to C-SPAN instead. "I owe C-SPAN. I don't owe CBS," he explained.

"I was young once too. But I got over it," Senator Howard Baker joked.

His joviality was not shared by the majority of delegates on the floor. Although they had ratified and would publicly cheer for the very conservative Republican platform, polls conducted by news organizations found that many delegates disagreed with the key provisions and the conservative rhetoric coming down from the key speakers. Polls showed that "significant majorities" of delegates supported a freeze on nuclear weapons production and opposed legislation prohibiting abortions, the *New York Times* reported. Indeed, half the delegates thought the deficits incurred during Reagan's first term represented the worst problem facing the country.

They kept those thoughts to themselves, though. Dissension from the left and the center wasn't encouraged on the floor that year. As a writer for the *New York Times Magazine* noted, when an alternate delegate from Iowa walked across the floor in a red, white, and blue button that read REPUBLICAN MAINSTREAM COMMITTEE, conservatives hissed: "Why don't you just get out of here?'' An abstaining delegate, Paul Zimmerman of Pennsylvania, told the *Times,* "You get the whiff of fascism.''

Gingrich was inspiring plenty of strong reactions, too—many of them negative. After his victory at the platform hearings, he'd written a op-ed piece for the *New York Times* in which he pulled no punches about his feelings toward the Republican establishment. "As I see it, the new Republican Party should argue aggressively with the decaying welfare state establishment—both the Republican and the Democratic side of that establishment. . . . We must move beyond the old, passive, and reactive Republican Party, encouraging the energy, aggressiveness, and combativeness of the party's newcomers. The welfare-state Republican Party must be willing to give way to the opportunity-society Republican Party."

He then derided the party's old-style moderates, House Minority Leader Bob Michel and Senator Bob Dole, in an interview with the *Times* during the convention: "They have compromised for fifty years with the liberal welfare state that I'm trying to do away with," he said. "In compromising, they are defeated. . . . The pragmatists are the tax collectors of the welfare state."

Dole countered by calling Gingrich and his COS fellows "the young hypocrites."

"They think they can peddle the idea that they've taken over the party," he said. "Well, they aren't the Republican Party, and they aren't going to be. . . . Tough, tough times are coming," he warned.

Tough times *were* coming, though not for the Republicans.

In 1984, Ronald Reagan won reelection in a landslide, sweeping 49 states. The G.O.P. gained 300 state legislative seats, and House Republican candidates won the largest number of votes since 1952. A Gallup poll found that 35% of the nation's voters called themselves Republicans—up from only 24% in 1980. And

in Congress, the Conservative Opportunity Society
had grown to include more than 40 members.

Newt Gingrich was not above taking some personal
credit for all of this. After Reagan included the phrase
"American opportunity society" in his second inaugural address, he brimmed with self-congratulatory
pride:

"I have an enormous personal ambition. I want to
shift the entire planet. And I'm doing it," he told
the *Washington Post* after Reagan's speech. "Ronald
Reagan just used the term 'opportunity society' and
that didn't exist four years ago. I just had breakfast
with [Richard] Darman and [David] Stockman because
I'm unavoidable. I represent real power."

The *Post* wrote, "Newt Gingrich may be just about
the most disliked member of Congress." The *Atlanta
Constitution* called him "the House version of John
McEnroe."

Having tasted the glory of war so triumphantly at
the Republican National Convention, Gingrich lost no
time in inserting himself back into the line of fire.
Right after the election, he told Reagan's budget director, David Stockman, "You're becoming the greatest
obstacle to a successful revolution from the liberal
welfare state to an opportunity society."

He accused House Democrats of playing around
with the Constitution when they refused to seat a
Republican, James McIntyre, in favor of seating his
opponent, Democratic incumbent Frank McCloskey,
in the wake of a still-contested Indiana House race.

There was speculation in the *Washington Times* that
he might have been gunning for National Republican
Congressional Committee chair Guy Vander Jagt's
job.

Then, just when his rising tide of righteous indigna-
tion might have been expected to overflow, he suddenly quieted down. In 1985, he was said to have
"gone underground." His associates were reported to
be spending time lecturing him on how to get along
with people. He spent time reading about President

Dwight D. Eisenhower, who, he said, in a strikingly open interview with the *Atlanta Constitution*, "was very successful at getting along with people who despised him."

Newt Gingrich's latest campaign seemed to be a battle to overhaul himself. It seemed that he was trying to groom himself for the responsibilities of leadership.

"There's no question that he wants to be an insider now," Vin Weber told the *Constitution*. "The question is what price is he willing to pay?"

"Think of me as a back bencher who used to work very hard trying to figure out how can I articulate something in a flashy enough way so the press can pick it up," Gingrich explained. "Now all of a sudden I have this microphone, and when I yell, it comes across like a painful noise because the system is now geared to carry me.

"That's requiring that I change my style. I will be somewhat less abrasive in the future because I am no longer the person I once was. A Newt Gingrich press conference or interview is now potentially a real news story. That means I can be much quieter, much more positive. And so I'll change. And it will take two to five years for my reputation to catch up and in some ways it never will. There are scars I have made in the last two or three years that will be with me through the rest of my career."

Perhaps Gingrich's words were sincere at the moment that he uttered them. Or perhaps he was simply trying a new tactic—the good-cop/bad-cop routine he would play with the press throughout the next decade. In any case, by 1987 the "kinder, gentler" Newt Gingrich was getting antsy. Ronald Reagan was seeming less and less engaged in his presidency, and the Democrats in Congress were growing more powerful. It was time to throw a bomb again. A big bomb. His self-confidence bolstered by the honor of having been named one of the twenty-six most influential members of the House by *The Almanac of American Politics* in 1986—this despite the fact that he held no committee chair or leadership position in the party—Gingrich did the almost unimaginable: he decided to bring down Speaker of the House Jim Wright.

Wright had represented the state of Texas in Congress since 1955. He had become speaker of the House in 1987, and had quickly established himself as a particularly effective roadblock to the Reagan agenda. He was able to assemble his Democratic forces well enough to override the vetoes of their popular president, was true to his values, and led with a strong, if isolating, sense of personal conviction. He made enemies quickly: ideological ones on the Republican side, jealous and disgruntled ones on the Democratic side. He was a major impediment to the Conservative Opportunity Society's plan of dividing and conquering the Democrats.

As John M. Barry, author of the encyclopedic account of the Wright affair, *The Ambition and the Power: The Fall of Jim Wright,* reports, Gingrich admired Wright, in his way. "As a technician of power," Barry quotes Gingrich as saying, "Wright gets an A-plus."

In May 1987, Gingrich decided to try to topple Jim Wright. He assigned an aide, Karen Van Brocklin, to dig up whatever dirt—personal, political, or financial—that she could. Van Brocklin began spending days in newspaper morgues and found that, as Wright grew stronger and Reagan appeared weaker, more and more Republicans were willing to come forward with what information they had or had heard of. She began calling newspaper reporters and asking if they'd like to swap information.

By June, Gingrich had enough material to begin an assault. He accused Wright of having converted $100,000 in campaign funds for his personal use (Barry points out that this was true, but not illegal at the time); of having lobbied Anwar Sadat on behalf of a powerful Texas oil man; of having pressured the Carter administration to help an oil company in which he had invested (untrue, Barry says); and of having

"Big Newt" McPherson left for the Navy after hitting wife Kit one too many times. (*John Zeedick, courtesy Randy McPherson*)

Married at sixteen, Kit McPherson was divorced within the year. "The only good thing was I had Newtie." (*John Zeedick, courtesy Kathleen Gingrich*)

Lt. Colonel Robert Gingrich, Kit's strong, silent, second husband, adopted Newt immediately. "I wanted him to have a sense of belonging." (*John Zeedick, courtesy of Kathleen Gingrich.*)

Kit wanted to go to war—but balked when told that she'd have to give up her "Newtie" for adoption. (*John Zeedick, courtesy Kathleen Gingrich*)

As a boy, Newt loved John Wayne almost as much as he loved animals. (*John Zeedick, courtesy Kathleen Gingrich*)

In elementary school, young Newt lobbied the mayor of Harrisburg, Pa., to build a town zoo and printed his views in a local newspaper. (*John Zeedick, courtesy Kathleen Gingrich*)

Birth of a politician: After a 1957 trip to Verdun, Newt (*left*) swore he'd use politics to put an end to senseless misery. (*John Zeedick, courtesy Kathleen Gingrich*)

Miss Jackie Battley taught Newt high school math—and married him. (*Courtesy Kathleen Gingrich*)

While other kids raced to drive-ins and necked in cars, Newt read— and read. (*Courtesy Kathleen Gingrich*)

Newt was voted "Most Intellectual" by his high school senior class. (*Courtesy Kathleen Gingrich*)

During his 1976 run for Georgia's 6th district congressional seat, Newt got some campaign help from an old pro, Senator Barry Goldwater. He lost. (*AP/Wide World Photos*)

Slugging it out on Central America, Gingrich challenged some Democrats' patriotism. Speaker Tip O'Neill called it "the lowest thing I've ever seen in my 32 years in Congress." (*AP/Wide World Photos*)

Gingrich made himself the Republicans' darling and the Democrats' nemesis when he assailed Speaker Jim Wright's ethics. (*AP/Wide World Photos*)

When Democrats struck back, attacking Gingrich's ethics in a 1984 book deal, second wife, Marianne, came to his defense. (*AP/Wide World Photos*)

Past differences forgotten, a triumphant Gingrich is congratulated by House Minority Leader Bob Michel after being elected Minority Whip in 1989. (*AP/Wide World Photos*)

Senator Phil Gramm and Gingrich compare guns, as
Clayton County, Georgia, Police Chief Ronnie Clackum
looks on in 1990. (*AP/Wide World Photos*)

Speaker Tom Foley, President George Bush, and Minority
Whip Gingrich during a 1991 discussion of interest rates
in the Cabinet Room of the White House. Newt's stealth
attack on Bush's "No new taxes" reversal helped
destroy his presidency. (*AP/Wide World Photos*)

After letting the world know (via Connie Chung) that Newt thought Hillary Rodham Clinton was a "bitch," mother and son went to the White House to make nice with the First Lady. (*AP/Wide World Photos*)

Speaker Gingrich leaving the White House after meeting with President Clinton on the soundness of the Mexican economy. (*AP/Wide World Photos*)

House Speaker-in-waiting and incoming Senate Majority Leader Bob Dole meet with reporters on Capitol Hill after election day. Gingrich once called Dole a "tax collector for the welfare state."
(*AP/Wide World Photos*)

Gingrich takes a break from bashing the United Nations and receives fresh makeup during the taping of *Meet the Press*.
(*AP/Wide World Photos*)

brought home $11.8 million in grants to Fort Worth, Texas, that, he falsely said, primarily benefited "people who are Jim Wright's personal business partners."

He began to militate for a House ethics investigation of Jim Wright. At first it was a lonely crusade. Even after stories began to circulate about Wright's possibly shady connections to some Texas savings and loans, he couldn't find a G.O.P. colleague to join him. Colleagues criticized him for being trigger-happy. Then the *Washington Post* reported that Wright had received an unheard-of 55 percent royalty deal and had made $62,000 on his book, *Reflections of a Public Man,* which had been published by a Texas political ally. He wrote to Fred Wertheimer, president of Common Cause, a nonpartisan group that monitors Congress. He received no response.

He began to unleash a litany of complaint against the Speaker: "Jim Wright has reached a point psychologically in his ego where there are no boundaries left."

"Jim Wright is the least ethical speaker of the twentieth century."

His explosive rhetoric, as always, got attention.

Soon the content of his quotes mattered less than their volume, and the volume of newspaper clips that they generated. He embarked upon a brilliant media campaign. He assembled the press clippings that Van Brocklin had amassed and sent them around to opinion-makers like Meg Greenfield at the *Washington Post*. Then he began planting seeds in local media outlets. Whenever he traveled to make a speech, he told his audiences to write letters to the editor of their local paper, to call in on talk shows, to write their congressmen about Jim Wright. He cultivated local reporters and editors and gave them his packet of clippings and told them about Jim Wright. "I'm trying to create a resonance out there," he explained, as Barry reports in an article on his smear tactics in a 1989 issue of *Esquire*. "When something moves on the wire, there will be echoes." He also said: "We worked on the assumption that if enough newspapers said there should be an investigation, Common Cause would have to say it. Then members would say it. It would happen.''

Jim Wright turned whatever few sympathetic souls there might have been on the Republican side of the aisle against him in October 1987 when, by playing with a technicality in the House rules, he brought a tax bill to the floor and, through a series of parliamentary loopholes, pushed it through to passage even after it had been once defeated by the Republicans. He also infuriated conservatives by trying to work with Nicaraguan President Daniel Ortega on reaching a peace settlement. After Wright had held a Veteran's Day meeting with Ortega, Gingrich attacked Wright on the House floor for having committed "the most destructive undermining of U.S. foreign policy by a speaker in our country's history."

Gingrich had something of a personal grudge against the Nicaraguan government ever since, in 1985, he'd been snubbed at a debate on U.S. involvement in Central America at Oxford University by Nicaraguan Vice President Sergio Ramirez Mercado, who read a statement and then left the Oxford Union without debating Gingrich because he felt "they were not of comparable standing." Lacking an opponent, Gingrich essentially debated students and an empty chair—and the judges at Oxford ruled him the loser, anyway. But his fervent anti-communism was shared by many of his colleagues in Congress.

By December, with Gingrich and Van Brocklin's help, the *Washington Post, Los Angeles Times, Business Week, Newsweek, New York Times,* NBC, *Wall Street Journal,* and a number of regional papers were all preparing stories on Wright. Gingrich stepped up the pressure on Wertheimer, but to no avail. He put together a complaint, and, at Bob Michel's urging, showed it to Republican congressman Robert Livingston and James Sensenbrenner, both attorneys. They and three other lawyers told Gingrich that he had no case. In response, Gingrich stepped up his investigation, even checking out parking spaces reserved for Wright's friends in a Fort Worth garage built with federal funds, Barry reports. The atmosphere on the Hill was so thick that when fire broke out in Jim Wright's office one evening, the joke was that people were checking for Gingrich's whereabouts.

Only after the *Wall Street Journal,* followed by scores of other newspapers, had called for an investigation of Wright did Common Cause follow suit. Wright was quite isolated now. His giving in to public pressures and backing away from supporting a congressional pay raise much desired by Democrats and Republicans alike had left him with virtually no allies when Gingrich formally filed his complaint against him in May 1988.

Eleven months later, after an investigation that cost taxpayers well over a million dollars, the House Ethics Committee found that it had "reason to believe" that Wright had committed sixty-nine violations of House rules. It charged him with possibly having violated House rules by taking gifts from someone with a "direct interest" in legislation and failing to report them as gifts and with seeking to avoid House limits on honoraria for speeches by receiving royalties from bulk sales of his book, chiefly to lobbyists. (Book royalties are not subject to any limit.) Wright and his wife were accused of having formed a sham company with wealthy friends who had an interest in legislation and who funneled the Wrights' money through the company in the form of a salary and benefits for Mrs. Wright, a Cadillac, and use of an apartment.

Not long after the charges were disclosed, the *Washington Post* published a story saying that Wright's top aide, John Mack, had brutally beaten a woman sixteen years earlier and left her for dead, and that Wright had helped Mack, whose brother was married to Wright's daughter, win parole by offering him a job as a file clerk. Mack resigned, but not before the story had added a sordid stain to Wright's already sorry affairs.

The Wright affair, by all accounts, took the backbiting partisanship that had become all too common in the House to new lows. Gingrich admitted as much—in his way—but defended his actions in Wright's case. "I'm so deeply frightened by the nature of the corrupt left-wing machine in the House that it would have been worse to do nothing," he told the *New York Times*.

In Georgia, most of Gingrich's constitutents knew a very different man than the attack dog they now saw quoted almost daily in the news. They knew a man who wrote homey "Notes on Self-Government" for the *Cedartown Standard,* where they ran on the page next to "Dear Abby"—bromides on George Washington, a dressing-down for Washington's cherry trees: "Our Georgia azaleas and dogwoods create a much more beautiful and breathtaking spring than do the famed Japanese cherry blossoms along the Potomac River and the Tidal Basin"; thoughts "on being thankful"; a tale of "Three Afternoons," when Gingrich visited some state parks and monuments. Even at their most ideological, the "notes" managed to sound like something typed by a contented man out on the back porch on a Sunday afternoon after dinner: "My grandchildren should plan for a reasonable retirement in a society that encourages saving all their life," he mused a few years before he proposed gutting Social Security. "My grandchildren should live in the light of God, knowing that He looks over us and that ultimately all we are or can be is to do His will."

Gingrich's longtime political aides knew a different man than moral crusader, too—but for entirely different reasons. Many of those who watched the Wright affair from Georgia did so with some sense of irony. For they knew that, in the district offices, Gingrich had a longstanding reputation for being indifferent to the fine points of ethics.

"I think the ethics policy that congressional members had to adhere to came as sort of a surprise to Newt," a senior staffer who worked for Gingrich from

1978 and 1984 says. "He had been used to doing things whenever he wanted to and felt like it. He was using government property and government employees. . . . Once he found that he couldn't use those funds, he possibly set up all these foundations so that he could cover for that."

Gingrich had hired Dolores Adamson with orders to keep him in line on ethical matters. "If I ever get out of line, call me down," he had told her in his first year as a congressman. But soon he wouldn't listen. An extremely conscientious woman, Adamson took Gingrich to an ethics seminar and read to him from the congressional manual. But Gingrich, she told *Mother Jones,* persisted in using congressional staff and office space and equipment for campaign work.

"It would always amaze me how insignificant Newt thought all of that was," she said. "Because to me it was significant."

Adamson quit after she returned from a week's vacation and learned that despite her admonitions Gingrich had been using the district staff to edit and copy early drafts of *Window of Opportunity.* Dot Crews, Gingrich's scheduler from that time, said that after Adamson left Gingrich, his staff began to "blur the line of separation between congressional and campaign work." She said of Gingrich, "He's not interested in ethics as an issue; he's interested in ethics as a tool to complete his agenda."

Bob Cooley, a GOP political activist and airline mechanic had stories of woe, too. Cooley had broken with Gingrich in 1987 for the way one of his staffers had compelled a delegate to vote for the candidate of Gingrich's choice at a state Republican convention. As Cooley has told it, the staffer grabbed a man with cerebral palsy and "drug him across the room because the little guy was going to vote for a state party chairman other than the one Newt wanted. And I interceded and had a few words with him."

Cooley, who worked on Gingrich's 1986 reelection campaign, often hosted meetings for campaign workers in his home. Two weeks before the election that year, someone broke into his home and wrote NEWT SUCKS in toothpaste and lipstick on the walls and mirrors. Cooley always suspected that the prank had been pulled by people working on Gingrich's side to cast aspersion on the opposition.

And, not long after Jim Wright's resignation, reports would emerge that Gingrich had taken members of his congressional staff off the payroll to work on his campaigns in 1986 and 1988 and then gave them large, temporary raises when they returned to Washington. If, as critics alleged and could never definitively prove, those pay raises, derived from taxpayer money, were in fact compensation for campaign work, they would have been illegal.

David Worley, a Jonesboro, Georgia, lawyer and moderate Democrat, tried to bring the differences between Gingrich appearances and realities to the fore when he challenged Gingrich for the Sixth District congressional seat in 1988. He accused Gingrich of waiting to unveil plans to do away with Social Security until the day of his 1986 election. He attacked Gingrich's plan that proposed abolishing the fourteen percent FICA payroll tax and requiring workers under forty to set aside ten percent of their wages in a mandatory IRA that would completely replace Social Security for them *while* paying a new value-added tax on consumer goods so that people over forty could *keep* their Social Security. He recited a litany of ethical abuses carried out by Gingrich, including his book deals, his alleged abuse of franking privileges, and his use of informational town meetings with constituents for campaigning purposes. To illustrate his points, Worley appeared at campaign stops with a mockup of a book titled, "What I Did on My Summer Vacation" by Newt Gingrich, with blank pages and a $13,000 price tag. Worley lost, with 41 percent of the vote.

* * *

Rather than face a drawn-out, painful hearing, Jim Wright resigned from his office on June 6, 1989. With his wife, Betty, weeping in the visitors' gallery, he spent an hour speaking in his defense. "Are there things I would do differently? Oh, boy . . ." he whispered. Finally he said, "Let me give you back this job you gave me."

Many Democrats now say wistfully that their failure to stand up and defend Jim Wright, who they watched fall like gawkers at a gory car crash, would haunt them for the rest of their political careers. Some think that if they had done something in Wright's defense, Gingrich might not be where he is today. And maybe more of them still would be in the Congress.

In the months to come, Majority Whip Tony Coelho would resign rather than face his own ethics investigation into an improper junk bond deal. Shortly afterward, Pennsylvania Congressman William Gray, the leading contender to replace Coelho, would have to ask Attorney General Dick Thornburgh to investigate the source of an unfounded rumor that the FBI was checking out whether he had a no-show employee on his payroll. Tom Foley, the majority leader who became Wright's successor, would be asked by a group of conservative Democrats for assurances that nothing in his background would trouble them.

The atmosphere in the House chamber had become scornful and angry.

As Wright drew near the close of his remarks, he clenched his fists and roared, "Both political parties must resolve to bring this period of mindless cannibalism to an end." The Democrats rose to their feet and applauded. The Republicans sat in silence. Gingrich was seen by reporters later in the day whistling cheerfully on his way to a party caucus.

6

"Mindless Cannibal"

The fight with Jim Wright had brought Gingrich's name to the fore, and in April 1989, he felt emboldened to set his sights on a higher goal: the position of House Minority Whip. As whip, Gingrich would be the second in command of the minority party in the House of Representatives and a strong contender for the post of speaker of the House should the Republicans ever win a majority. The position involved surveying the 176 Republicans in the House and cajoling them into abiding by the party program. It also involved coordinating these efforts with House Minority Leader Bob Michel and the Republican-held White House.

Gingrich's mentor in the House, Trent Lott of Mississippi, had vacated the post in 1988 to go over to the Senate. But in March 1989, his successor as House Whip, Representative Dick Cheney of Wyoming, was nominated to be President George Bush's Secretary of Defense after the diminutive reprobate Texan John G. Tower failed to be confirmed for the cabinet post by the Senate. Although Edward R. Madigan of Illinois was the favorite of Bob Michel and other Republican leaders, as well as President Bush, Gingrich had his finger on the pulse of other Republican House

members who were tired of being bullied by majority
Democrats. Sure of their support, he pounced.

Bush tapped Cheney on a Friday. Gingrich pon-
dered his candidacy over the weekend, making over
ninety phone calls to fellow law-makers.

"There was just a group of us who spent the weekend on the phone calling." Representative Robert S.
Walker of Pennsylvania told the *Washington Post*. "By
Monday morning, we had sixty people committed to
vote for Newt for whip. . . . The last thirty or thirty-
five votes came real hard."

Gingrich personally telephoned Representatives
Nancy L. Johnson of Connecticut and Steve Gunderson of Wisconsin, both of whom agreed to give support. Gunderson then began lobbying other moderate
Republicans on Gingrich's behalf. "I said, 'Don't
commit to anyone else until we have a chance to tell
you why we think this is important to the future of
the party,' " Gunderson told the *Post*. Johnson also
lobbied hard for Gingrich, extolling him to her colleagues as a "leader who has the vision to build a
majority party and the strength and charisma to do it."

For the mostly young, moderate Republicans, the
elevation of Gingrich to the whip position represented
an opportunity to emerge from their underdog status
as the least influential members of the House minority
party. Even as Gingrich had been building the Conservative Opportunity Society since 1983, the moderates
had created a group of their own, the 92 Group. For
more than a year before the whip race, the moderates
of the 92 Group and Gingrich's Young Turks had been
meeting on Wednesday mornings to try to hammer out
a common agenda. While many of the moderates had
their qualms about Gingrich's controversial tactics, in
the end they decided to endorse him in order to break
free from the stifling yoke of the older Republican
leadership, which they felt was too complacent toward
their Democratic counterparts. In a House where the
Democrats outnumbered Republicans 258 to 174, the
Republicans felt they needed a whip who would stand

up to the other side of the aisle, as Gingrich had proven he was willing to do during the Wright affair.

"Most of us see minority status for a long time to come if we keep doing things the same old way," Representative Sherwood Boehlert of New York, co-chairman of the 92 Group told *Atlanta Journal and Constitution* columnist Donald Lambro. "A vote for Madigan would have ensured continuation of the same old thing."

Gingrich called the whip race a choice between the "timid" manner of old House Republicans such as Madigan and the more assertive, confrontational style he favored. "I would be bipartisan when we get our share, confrontational when necessary, and ruthless when there are unethical actions involved," he said. He promised to revitalize the House Republicans and bring them a majority by 1992. He convinced the young Republicans that he could bring the gains the G.O.P. had earned in the past three presidential elections to the Congress and state legislatures.

But Gingrich still needed to woo the House right-wing Republicans.

"It was a tough choice for me," says William E. Dannemeyer, a former representative from California known as an arch conservative who at the time was a member of the Health and Environment Subcommittee. "The only person who was senior to me was the chairman, Ed Madigan. And Madigan came to me and said 'Dannemeyer, if I win, you win. If I lose, you lose,' meaning that if he, Madigan, was elected whip, he would leave the chairman's seat, which means that I would have been the ranking member of the subcommittee.

"But I voted for Newt and it was the right thing to do. Madigan was a good man but not the activist that Newt is and we needed an activist to grapple with the institution. . . . When you are in the minority, you don't need somebody whose strong suit is concilia-tion. You need a tireless fighter. And Newt, I think, exhibited that," Dannemeyer says.

The vote was so close that Madigan offered to send an airplane to bring back the only absent Republican lawmaker, Representative Jim Courter of New Jersey, who he believed to be a supporter of his. Gingrich finally won the election by two votes.

The Democrats exulted in Gingrich's election. They knew that George Bush needed to appeal constantly to bipartisanship to get anything done in the Democratic-held Congress, and that Gingrich's radicalism would make Bush's job more difficult.

"They may not be able to control Newt; they never had in the past," Tony Coelho, the House Democratic whip, told the *New York Times* after the minority whip election. "And the more Newt is going to cause trouble, the more they're going to have to work to solidify their relationship with us."

Democratic Majority Leader Tom Foley echoed the warning. "If it's pikes, guns, and grenades on the House floor, it would not be good for the President," he said.

Indeed, being a senior statesman and a team player didn't come easily for Gingrich at first. Never known for his attention to legislation, he said the whip post was "probably regarded as the most technically legislative job in leadership."

Bob Michel had supported Madigan for the whip position but had to come to his own modus vivendi with Gingrich. "From time to time, you have to go with the flow," he said philosophically after Gingrich won. And Gingrich, upon becoming whip, said he knew he had to tone down his confrontational tactics. "I need to be careful in what I say," he told a press breakfast shortly after his elevation to the post.

But only three months later, Michel reprimanded Gingrich before the Republican House leadership team for speaking out on his own on campaign finance and ethics reform, and Gingrich was forced to apologize. He had learned that he was no longer simply a lone bomb thrower, but was expected to be a spokesman for the entire party.

"If you look at the clippings, I was very open in saying . . . 'Michel chastised me because I was wrong,' " Gingrich told *Atlanta* magazine in 1990. "And it really helped our relationship because . . . if I am wrong, I have to say I am wrong."

He even went so far as to say that rather than always being on the offensive, as whip he might even consider apologizing once in a while. "If I am going to be a public player, which I am, then I have to say publicly occasionally, 'Well, that was a mistake.' Then the rest of the team relaxes. They say, 'Well, if Newt is going to be a big enough guy to admit he's wrong, how can you complain?' "

At forty-five and in his sixth term in Congress, this "kinder, gentler" persona was a tactical adjustment for him. "If you are standing in the back of the room, trying to communicate with an audience, you have to raise your voice," he told *Atlanta*. "If you are standing in the front of the room, you may have to lower your voice."

In August 1989, Gingrich proved that he could shed his maverick firebrand role and adapt to his new position as coach of the Republican congressional team and even, if necessary, defer to Michel.

On the morning of an important vote on a savings and loan bill opposed by the White House, Michel informed Gingrich that he would vote for the bill because he felt the White House hadn't briefed him sufficiently on the administration's objections to it. Gingrich decided he wouldn't follow the White House line, either, and would also support the bill. He told a White House staffer to inform the President's staff of his and Michel's decision.

"You had better go back and tell John [Sununu] that he has neither Gingrich nor Michel, and if the President wants this to work, *they* have a big problem, we don't," Gingrich told the White House staffer, according to *Atlanta* magazine.

An outraged response from the White House was not long in coming. An hour later, Sununu "called me screaming for about ninety seconds. He went through this long tirade and then he said, 'There. Now I feel better.' " In response Gingrich explained that Michel felt that he hadn't been sufficiently briefed on the White House's objections to the bill.

"Unless the three of you [Sununu, Bush, Secretary of the Treasury Nicholas Brady] make peace with Michel," Gingrich admonished Sununu, "you are going to lose. . . . You three call Michel, and I'll be glad to whip the organization. But I ain't moving until Bob Michel is satisfied."

Thirty minutes later, Minority Leader Michel walked into Gingrich's office. "I guess we're going to help them," he said.

It was then that Gingrich fully realized the centrality of his new position. "It is pretty hard if you get called by the Secretary of the Treasury, the chief of staff and the President. You sorta go, 'Well, this is reasonably good transactional stuff. I'm on board.' So then we went to work, and in four hours we turned the party around. Because we were able to communicate a rational strategy that had a real purpose on behalf of the President of the United States," he said, recalling that heady day.

In no small part thanks to the new minority whip, the bill was defeated. Gingrich's transformation didn't go unnoticed.

"Once you are in leadership, you have to mute your approach, be more diplomatic, be a little more bipartisan in some matters and less confrontational," Representative Jon Kyl of Arizona, then chair of the Conservative Opportunity Society, told *Atlanta*. "Newt has undergone that subtle transformation since his election. [But] he has maintained his idealistic leadership among the rank and file. He is leaving a lot of fighting to the troops."

Gingrich's new found civility notwithstanding, the Democrats didn't wait long to counterattack. On April 11, 1989, Representative Bill Alexander of Arkansas filed a complaint with the House Ethics Committee, asking it to determine whether it was necessary to launch a full-scale probe of the Conservative Opportunity Society partnership formed in 1984 to promote Gingrich's book, *Window of Opportunity*.

In return for their investment in the book's promotion, the COS partners were promised half of the publisher's profits. The book hadn't sold well, however, and the losses on the deal by the twenty-one partners, who each invested $5,000, were later turned into tax write-offs. Fifteen of the investors in the book project, including Georgia real estate developer Joel Cowan, textile magnate Roger Milliken, James Richards, son of Southwire founder Roy Richards, and Howard "Bo" Callaway, were contributors to Gingrich's political campaigns. Though Gingrich himself was not an investor, his wife, a co-author, was paid more than $10,000 for running the operation. Also, the Gingriches received $24,036 in royalties. The book sold only 12,000 copies.

In essence, the complaint suggested that the partnership had been set up to disguise campaign contributions and gifts to Gingrich. It charged that the royalty payments, along with the share in the partnership that Marianne Gingrich received, could, if tabulated as outside income, a gift, or a campaign contribution, put Gingrich over the House limit of $1,000 for such items. It also suggested that some of the investors could have an interest in legislation before the House or might benefit from federal programs or contracts.

Gingrich denied that the book deal was improper in any way, saying that he believed "there was a reasonable chance that it might make money." In addition, several of the investors came forward to say that they had invested in the partnership because they were sympathetic to the conservative ideas contained in the book and wished to see them disseminated.

Gingrich recognized that his book deal was "as weird as Wright's." But, he said, unlike Wright's deal, "we wrote a real book for a real company that was sold in real bookstores and sold to real people for a realistic standard royalty."

And it is also true that at least three of the companies represented by the investors, McClain International, Southwire Company, and Milliken and Company, had in the past received federal grants and projects. In addition, another contributor, Flowers Industries, stood to benefit from pending House legislation. Gingrich denied helping Southwire in its dealings with the government when it obtained a $1.5 million contract from the Tennessee Valley Authority but, in published reports, admitted to having once intervened in a Customs dispute to win the release of some materials Southwire was seeking. He argued that it was part of his job as a congressman to help the wire producer, which was one of the largest employers of his district. "I would be derelict in my duties if I did not do so," he said.

In October 1989, Alexander added more complaints to the ethics charges against Gingrich, even as the House Ethics Committee was still considering whether to launch an investigation of the initial charges. In the new complaint Alexander charged that in 1986 Gingrich had failed to report the purchase of a house from a political supporter. In a financial disclosure form Gingrich hadn't stated that he had cosigned a $77,800 mortgage on a house in Fulton County that he and his daughter Linda Kathleen had bought from Patricia Grunden, the wife of a longstanding political supporter, John Grunden, in 1986.

At the time, Gingrich said he was "incensed that the fact that I helped my daughter by cosigning or signing the note, or whatever one calls it, gets drug out and becomes a story." He added that the new complaint "carries politics in the House to a new low level. I mean, it just strikes me as madness."

Alexander's new complaint also charged that Gingrich lobbied federal agencies on behalf of Chester Roush, a Georgia real estate developer who had supported and raised funds for Gingrich since 1974 and had spearheaded his 1977 book partnership. The complaint charged that Gingrich had intervened with federal authorities on Roush's behalf on several occasions but that he had refused to intervene similarly on behalf of another one of his constituents who had not contributed to Gingrich's projects.

An article from the *Atlanta Business Chronicle* that was included in the complaint showed, however, that the two occasions when Gingrich had intervened on Roush's behalf had failed to yield any tangible results. Roush received more than $12 million in federal subsidies during the period between 1978 and 1989, which coincides with the period between Gingrich's arrival in Washington and the time of the complaint. But the article also indicates that on the two documented occasions Gingrich appealed on Roush's behalf—once to the Farmers Home Administration, a division of the Department of Agriculture that subsidizes rental housing for the rural poor, and once directly to Reagan Administration Department of Housing and Urban Development (HUD) Secretary Samuel Pierce—he failed to obtain favors for his supporter. In a letter to Pierce in 1986, Gingrich asked the secretary to reconsider an application Roush had made to receive federal help in building a housing project in Villa Rica, Georgia, which HUD had previously rejected on the grounds that the local housing market was too soft to justify the project. In the letter, Gingrich said that "after studying the . . . application and the reasons given [for the application's rejection by HUD] . . . I believe there is cause for reconsideration of this project. If there is a reallocation of recaptured grant funds, I'd like you to take another look at this application to see if it qualifies."

Despite Gingrich's letter, Roush's grant application was never approved by HUD. Gingrich denied that he had ever helped Roush in any way.

None of this would have been unusual if Gingrich hadn't, only a few months before, told another constituent, the administrator of an existing low-income housing project for the elderly, that the government needed to curb its spending on subsidized housing, and for that reason he would be voting against a bill to override Ronald Reagan's deferral of $2.3 billion in housing funds that had been previously appropriated by Congress. Gingrich said his decision to vote against the override was in perfect accordance with principles he had long held.

In addition, in 1989 Gingrich joined the clamor deploring the corruption and mismanagement at HUD during the Reagan years that was then being uncovered. He told the Associated Press that he was "absolutely appalled at what we are learning about how HUD was run." Attributing the travails of a department run by a Reagan nominee to the usual liberal/Democrat suspects, he said, "This fits exactly the model I was describing of the corrupt liberal welfare state."

Alexander's amended complaint also charged that a Gingrich PAC, the Conservative Hope and Opportunity Political Action Committee (CHOPAC) had solicited by mail more than $217,000 to support conservative candidates, but had actually only donated $900 to campaigns. The rest of the money, the complaint charged, had been spent on direct mailings, consultant fees, and travel for Gingrich. The complaint charged that CHOPAC continued to solicit money for campaigns when the treasurer of the PAC knew that it couldn't pay longstanding debts and thus would be unable to disburse the money to candidates.

The violence of the attacks shocked Gingrich. No one else was surprised.

"I was shocked that he was shocked," former colleague Vin Weber, one of Gingrich's close allies, told *The Atlantic* in 1993. "He had charged into the enemy camp and killed the king's pig. And he wondered why the king's solders were gathering with their swords drawn."

Gingrich had essentially attacked Jim Wright for laundering excess earnings through his own book deal.

Now Democrats charged that the unusual promotional deal paid for by a group of conservative political supporters amounted to basically the same thing. Wright himself tweaked Gingrich on the book deal, sending him a copy of his own controversial book, *Reflections of a Public Man,* with the dedication "For Newt, who likes books too" on the flyleaf.

Gingrich was outraged by the comparison to Wright. In April, he released several hundred pages of documents pertaining to the book deal and held a highly emotional press conference to defend himself against Alexander's charges. Marianne Gingrich stalked out of the press briefing in tears after a reporter asked if Newt's 1984 book deal wasn't similar to the type of dubious transaction that had brought down Jim Wright.

Adding to Gingrich's woes, in September 1989, two former Gingrich House staffers charged that Gingrich had used his congressional staff and office space for work on his reelection campaign as well as on *Window of Opportunity.* One of the women, Dot Crews, said that in 1983 Gingrich had enlisted his House staffers to edit, copy, and collate the book. The other staffer, Dolores Adamson, said that Gingrich would often conduct campaign work from his congressional office with the assistance of his House staff. Federal and House laws prohibit congressional employees from doing campaign or personal work while being paid with tax money. Gingrich admitted to using his staff for the book but said that the practice was common on Capitol Hill and that the Ethics Committee had not charged Wright with a similar violation even though the former speaker had used his staff for his book. Besides, Gingrich said, the practice of using staffers is legitimate if it involves the drafting of a public policy document.

"You're clearly allowed to write a public policy document if you want to, and I think if you read *Window of Opportunity,* it's clearly a public policy document, precisely within the limits of House rules,"

Gingrich said. These charges were never added to the complaint before the Ethics Committee.

On March 3, 1990, the committee, on the recommendation of independent counsel Joseph Phelan—who ironically had previously been retained by the panel to investigate the Wright affair—cleared Gingrich of any wrongdoing in the publishing partnerships, and declined to proceed with charges. The committee did, however, admonish Gingrich for not disclosing that he had cosigned his daughter's mortgage and for the improper use of House stationery to promote a senior citizens' cruise being organized by a travel agency, Marathon Travel Company. The panel also noted in its report that several of the charges filed by Representative Alexander were outside its jurisdiction.

The analysis of the allegations by Phelan, however, noted that in three instances, investors in the book deal were reported to have received federal benefits "several years after the time of their investment," though it did not imply that there had been any wrongdoing on Gingrich's part. Joel Cowan, the real estate developer, it said, "received preliminary approval in 1988 for a $200,000 low-income housing project grant from the Department of Housing and Urban Development, but dropped out of the project prior to disbursement of funds." It also noted that Cowan had purchased a "troubled thrift" in 1984: Habersham Savings and Loan in Cornelia, Georgia, which had benefited, as had all thrifts, from a vote Gingrich had cast against a plan to increase funding to the Federal Savings and Loan Insurance Corporation proposed by President Reagan. Gingrich denied intervening on behalf of Cowan, the report said, but "admitted that he once was instrumental in getting a $7.6 million grant to help expand the Peachtree City, Georgia, airport in Mr. Cowan's community."

The investigation exonerated Gingrich. It left taxpayers footing a $1,115,851.20 bill. And it left Gingrich burning for revenge. Immediately after the conclusion of the Wright affair, he said, "If we get rid of Wright but keep ninety-nine percent of the other Democrats, we've accomplished nothing. I'm ready for more action."

He didn't wait long to start getting back at the Democrats. He moved into his new whip's office, a grand place with a picture-postcard view of the Washington Monument out one window, of the dome of the Capitol out another, with nineteenth-century furnishings, a red carpet, and a great gilt mirror above a marble fireplace, all illuminated by an enormous crystal chandelier—and he turned it into a den of intrigue. The door of Room 219, known simply as "219" in House whispers, located just a few steps from the House chamber, took on the look of the Gates of Hell to the Democrats. If Gingrich had been a thorn in their side during the Wright affair, as minority whip he had become perhaps the most hated man in Congress.

By the time of the Gulf War the jokes were flying fast and thick in the Democratic cloakroom, where a poster mounted during the 1990 campaign year read, "Newt-free Congress."

"You find yourself alone in a room with Saddam Hussein and Newt Gingrich and you have two bullets in your gun," one joke went, "what do you do? Shoot Newt twice."

The very day following Wright's resignation speech, a rumor began to circulate in the House that the new House Speaker, Tom Foley, a venerable Democrat from Washington state, was a homosexual and a pedophile. Democratic outrage at the rumor reached a crescendo when the Republican National Committee issued a memo calling on the speaker to come "out of the liberal closet," and compared his voting record with that of Barney Frank, who is gay, thus echoing, albeit not so subtly, the imputation of homosexuality that hovered over the Speaker.

A firestorm ensued and Republican National Committee Chairman Lee Atwater, of Willie Horton fame, was forced to apologize to Foley and fired the aide who had written the memo. It became apparent, however, that the person who had originally circulated the rumor, which had only been echoed by the RNC aide, was none other than Karen Van Brocklin, the Gingrich staffer responsible for helping to bring down former House Speaker Jim Wright. *New York Daily News* columnist Lars-Erik Nelson reported that on June 5, 1989, only twenty-four hours after Wright's resignation, Van Brocklin had quipped: "I hear it's little boys." Gingrich condemned Van Brocklin's actions but refused to fire her. "I would have given any person with that track record one major mistake," he told *Mother Jones.*

In the first of many incidents involving Gingrich and the Republicans' use of homosexuality as a political weapon, Barney Frank, an openly gay Democratic congressman from Massachusetts, says he contributed greatly to stopping the Republican assault on Foley by threatening to give them a taste of their own medicine.

"I threatened to expose gay Republicans," he recalls. "It was Gingrich and the Republican National Committee using Tom Foley's potentially being gay as a weapon against him, and I said if they don't stop this, I'd *start."* The threat apparently worked because the attacks stopped, even though today Frank isn't sure he would have carried out his threat. "I had no idea what I would have done if they hadn't stopped," he says, adding, "but they stopped."

Or at least they stopped attacking Foley. In the fall of 1989, there was growing speculation that Barney Frank might resign after it was disclosed that one of his aides had operated a male prostitution ring out of the congressman's Washington apartment. An investigation was taken up by the House Ethics Committee, which determined that Frank had not known that his aide was using his apartment for illegal purposes. In 1990, a congressional panel recommended that Frank be reprimanded but not censured or expelled from the House, as had desired some Republicans such as Dannemeyer.

Since he was also under investigation by the Ethics Committee for his 1984 book deal, Gingrich had at first reacted cautiously to calls for censure, saying that he would prefer it if Frank quietly resigned. But later on, when it appeared certain that Frank would emerge with just a slap on the wrist, Frank says Gingrich became more vindictive.

"He did move that I be censured," Frank says. "By the way, totally inaccurately. I mean, it was not that he thought that I was being inappropriately punished for the things I was charged with. He claimed that I was guilty of things that the Ethics Committee had said, 'No, those charges are not true.' In fact, in his speech [Gingrich] said I had lied to a parole officer to protect a felon. Steve Gobie [the male prostitute] had charged that, and in fact the Ethics Committee found that that was not true."

But Dannemeyer recalls things differently, even expressing puzzlement at what he perceives as Gingrich's excessive tolerance for homosexuality.

"I made the motion to expel Barney Frank from the House. Guess who led the Republican effort against my motion to expel: Gingrich. He went out of his way to make that effort," Dannemeyer recalls, adding cryptically, "In Newt's mind, his reason for doing what he did is the same reason he has sought continually, and seeks the support, of someone like [Steve] Gunderson [a gay Republican]." Throughout his years in Congress and beyond, Dannemeyer has taken strong and controversial positions on the subject of homosexuality, which he believes is a treatable disease. He is particularly well-known for his declaration in 1985, during a discussion of AIDS, that "God's plan for man was Adam and Eve, not Adam and Steve."

While some Republicans had rejoiced in the incidents, the party's elder statesmen felt Gingrich might have gone too far. At a meeting of the Republican National Committee around the time of the Foley affair, the new whip was greeted as a conquering hero by a revitalized party, but senior statesmen such as Bob Dole, the Senate minority leader, showed less enthusiasm. The vicious turn politics had taken of late was a "tragedy for John Tower, Robert Bork [both of whose nominations as, respectively, secretary of Defense and Supreme Court justice had recently been scuttled] and yes, for Tom Foley," said Dole. "I love politics. I know it's rough and tough. I know we can have our differences. And I know we want to win. But it's got to be based on wanting to win for some good reason."

There were midterm elections coming up, and Gingrich knew that if the Republicans were ever to obtain a majority in the House, they needed a plan. And so he spent eighteen days in August holed up in a cabin without electricity or telephone at the Crested Butte resort in Colorado, which had been lent to him by GOPAC contributor and former congressman Howard "Bo" Callaway. There he met with sympathetic strategists and GOPAC contributors in groups of four, for three days at a time, to discuss how to move the country toward the rule of a conservative majority. He would later say that the 1994 victory grew out of those rustic conversations.

Discussions at the cabin centered on how to redesign the G.O.P.'s agenda in the wake of the Cold War. As Jeffrey A. Eisenach told the *Washington Post:* "Since the New Deal, Republicans had been against things. The idea was 'What are we for?' "

Toward the end of 1989, Gingrich showed that when it suited his purposes, he could play ball with the Democrats as well as anyone. He supported a bill awarding representatives a pay raise of more than thirty-five percent over two years to compensate for a reduction in the amount of honoraria they could receive. Democrats and Republicans alike justified the pay raise by presenting it as an ethics issue. At the time, having earned $111,474 since 1983, Gingrich ranked eighteenth among House members in the amount of honoraria received. The elimination of honoraria, he and others argued, would reduce the amount of money members of Congress received from outside groups.

Knowing that voting themselves a pay raise in the middle of a recession could make them subject to a great deal of voter resentment. Democrats and Republicans decided to put their differences aside momentarily and signed a "non-aggression pact" that stipulated that the pay raise would not be used as a campaign issue. Gingrich was an early supporter of the pact. According to *Roll Call,* he appeared before the Democratic Caucus to plead for support for the pact before it had even been approved by Republican National Committee chairman Lee Atwater.

The amity between former enemies was such that House Speaker Foley even went so far as to say that the Democratic Congressional Campaign Committee would refuse support to any Democratic candidate who attacked a Republican incumbent on the pay-raise issue. This was of particular interest to Gingrich, since, on the day of the vote, David Worley, his Democratic challenger, had sent out a letter promising to make the pay raise a central issue of his campaign. At the time there were reports that the DCCC would refuse to support Worley and that, as a result, Gingrich had been removed from the committee's target list.

In the election, despite favorable polling data, the Democrats refused to support Worley, who lost to Gingrich by a one percent margin, after having been outspent five to one.

Gingrich had his first major run-in with the White House as whip the following January, when he said that he was in favor of overriding President Bush's veto of a bill that would have allowed Chinese students to extend their stay in the United States after their visas ran out. In the wake of the Tianamen Square massacre, the House had unanimously adopted a bill that would have allowed Chinese students in the U.S.

universities to stay beyond their visa's expiration date, as many had participated in pro-democracy activities in the U.S. and feared for their lives if they returned to China.

George Bush, fearing a deterioration in U.S. relations with China, had vetoed the measure but had drafted instead an executive order protecting the students' status in the United States under existing laws. When Congress reconvened, Democrats and Republicans alike were determined to override his veto of the bill. Gingrich delivered the bad news to the White House on behalf of the Republicans. "I told them, 'Accept the loss . . . it's not a big deal,' " he told reporters at the time.

"I think the President made a mistake," Gingrich told the *Washington Post*. "I cannot for the life of me understand what their strategy is. . . . I do not believe you gain anything in the long run by letting the Chinese dictatorship believe that you value their friendship enough that you will tolerate brutality and repression."

Although the Bush administration had cited the recent lifting of martial law in China as evidence that its policy of appeasement was working, Gingrich remained unconvinced. "The country doesn't understand what [Bush] is doing," Gingrich continued. "The Congress doesn't understand what he's doing."

Gingrich was feeling his oats. As 1990 began, the prospects for the fall elections were very dim for the Republican party, and rumors began to swirl that Gingrich would be making a play for Michel's House Minority post if Michel decided to retire.

He began more and more frequently to assert that if the Republicans ever hoped to reconquer the House, they would have to push aside the collegial manner of the likes of Michel and the bipartisan compromising of the Bush White House. Instead, Gingrich said, the G.O.P. should undertake an all-out assault on the Democrats and their "welfare state," and should show voters that the Republicans stood for entrepreneurship, high technology, and tax cuts. This, of course, was the same message he had been trumpeting since his political beginnings, but as minority whip he had a far greater audience.

In an interview with *Business Week* in February 1990, he stopped just short of advocating an all-out rebellion against the President's conciliatory manner. "The President can't take the kind of radical gambles that an opposition party can take," he said. "That shouldn't prevent the rest of us from inventing an absolute explosion of reform ideas, throwing them into the hopper and letting them ferment."

In the wake of the Cold War, the Republicans were rethinking their ideology. On the far right, Pat Buchanan was probing an "America First" isolationist policy, calling for the withdrawal of U.S. troops from abroad. George Bush, an old-school Republican, could not escape from the Cold War culture he had been raised in. Republicans of Bush's vintage had been conditioned to see the primary mission of the United States as one of defending the world from communism. With the Soviet Union in disarray, and the Iron Curtain drawn, Bush continued to focus his energy on foreign policy. Despite some striking successes, however, he was unable to appear victorious because the political gold now was to be panned at home, not abroad. Having to walk a tightrope between the majority Democrats and the increasingly combative Republicans in the House made the President's position particularly difficult. Bush seemed lost, unable to chart a new course.

America's mood was not lost on Gingrich, though. He sensed an opportunity to redirect the G.O.P.'s energies to the home front and began trumpeting the social policy he had been formulating for so long. Calling this new Republican attention to social matters a "new reform movement," he began expounding a message that "applying common sense will lead to a more prosperous America." The message was not so different from the points contained in the "Contract with America." He drew a lot of attention in the summer of 1990 when he said that he would offer poor third-graders in his district two dollars for every book they read, as an example of how local government initiatives could replace the federal "bureaucratic state." Some liberals smirked that by focusing on social policy, Gingrich and other Republicans were beginning to sound a lot like the Democrats. History would show that Gingrich's concept, if not his explicit message, was the way to voters' hearts—as was amply proven by Bill Clinton's victory over Bush in 1992 on a "Putting People First" program.

All of this did nothing to endear Gingrich in the eyes of the Bush White House, but it wasn't until the summer of 1990 that relations between the two would hit their lowest point. Gingrich found that having conquered attackers on his left, he would still have to fight for his political life—but this time fending off enemies in his own camp.

President Bush had supported his rival for the whip position, Edward Madigan, and by summer the White House and its supporters in Congress were extremely distrustful of Gingrich. Nonetheless, they never expected him to actually rebel against a president of his own party. They underestimated him.

As whip, Gingrich was part of negotiations between White House officials and congressional leaders from both parties over the 1990 budget. And it was with dismay that, after months of negotiations, he watched Bush agree to a budget that broke his "no new taxes" pledge of "read my lips" fame. At the time, Gingrich said he saw defending the G.O.P.'s anti-taxes stance as integral to the life of the party. History was to prove him right.

He sat at the table while Democrats and Republicans negotiated and attempted to work out a five-year, deficit-reducing budget deal. The deal would have reduced the federal deficit by $40 billion in 1991 and by $500 billion over five years—mainly by raising taxes on gasoline, tobacco, and alcohol, and by cutting

Medicare spending. While the others worked, Gingrich read pulp novels. For once, uncharacteristically, he stayed silent. But saying nothing is not the same thing as endorsing the plan, and Republicans were stunned when, on the morning the congressmen gathered in the Cabinet Room of the White House to present the package to Bush, Gingrich raised his voice.

"I can't support this," he announced to the enraged group. He explained that since the package raised taxes without including "economics growth measures," such as a cut in the capital gains tax that he desired, he had to fight it.

Later, Gingrich was to say that during the negotiations he had tried very hard to find a reason to support the plan, but in the end just couldn't find it in himself to go along. "There got to be a point . . . that I was beginning to listen carefully to liberal Democratic arguments and tried to figure out how I could agree with them," he told the *New York Times*. "When I got home I realized, in fact, that that was not why I got hired. I suddenly realized how real the Stockholm syndrome is—when you are captured by a terrorist and start identifying with the kidnappers."

His eleventh-hour disruption caught the politicians off guard. There was nothing that they could do. As Bush and the rest of the negotiating team paraded out to the Rose Garden on September 30, 1990, to present their deal to the press, Gingrich left by another door, drove up to Capitol Hill, and began politicking to destroy the deal he'd been supposed to cement.

Some ranking Republicans contend that Gingrich had pledged implicitly to endorse the plan. In his defense, though, he had made it clear throughout the negotiating process that he had grave reservations about a deal that failed to include a capital gains tax cut.

Dannemeyer remembers that a few months before the scene in the Rose Garden, a number of conservative Republicans opposed to any tax hike had called

Gingrich into the office of Illinois Representative Phil M. Crane and "reminded him who elected him and who he was."

"In the early summer of 1990, we began to pick up rumors that the budget summiteers were using whatever pretense they could to pressure for a tax increase, and we were uncertain as to how committed Newt was to our position—the majority G.O.P. position—to oppose any tax increase and focus on the spending side of the budget," recalls Dannemeyer.

"We made clear to Newt that we had just elected him whip, and that he had won the race by one vote. I think we impressed upon him that we helped him win his position because we were committed to a no-new-tax position," says Dannemeyer. "The sense of our chat that day was that he needed to hang tough. I don't know that I would call it pulling him into the woodshed because he hadn't done anything yet. It was more in the spirit of 'get on the right road.'

"I think we were successful in shoring up his position," Dannemeyer adds gleefully. "His vote speaks."

Republican critics of Gingrich's defection say, however, that on July 19, Gingrich had told Democratic budget negotiators that he was "prepared to sponsor and support" a tax increase to reduce the deficit. His critics also point to a memorandum Gingrich sent to White House Chief of Staff John H. Sununu and Office of Management and Budget Director Richard C. Darman only days before the agreement was presented to Bush in which Gingrich concluded: "With a good agreement and full partnership in the decision process on the other items, the Republican leadership will work hard."

Richard Darman has said that, for him, the memo represented a clear endorsement of the budget plan. "[Gingrich] never led people to believe he might bolt," Darman reportedly said at the time.

But Gingrich's lack of enthusiasm for the budget proposal was evident even to Democrats who observed him during the negotiations at Andrews Air Force Base, where he would sit each day, silent, with piles of unrelated reading material before him. "He sat there and read," one Democrat who was present told the *Washington Post*. "He walked from the guy [Bush] even during it."

Gingrich has said that Alan Drury's novel, *Advise and Consent,* which tracks a lurid scandal regarding a president's nominee for secretary of state and won the 1960 Pulitzer Prize for fiction, helped prepare him for the fight with Bush. Ironically, this book was cited by Barbara Bush as one of her favorites in 1989. "I loved that whole series," she said of Drury's Washington novels, "but then he got, so, sort of far right."

While it is clear that he sent mixed signals, Gingrich's contention that he had never promised to support Bush's tax plan appears to be bolstered by an argument over the budget between Gingrich and Nick Calio, Bush's congressional lobbyist, that occurred on Labor Day of 1990, a short time before the deal was unveiled and the fight became public.

Gingrich's argument, an eyewitness said, "was that whatever his role in the leadership, he had a responsibility to his members and a responsibility to his principles."

For some Republicans, the sense that Gingrich had betrayed them was compounded by his having defected so publicly, drawing inordinate attention to Bush's backtracking on his "no new taxes" pledge. Had Gingrich held his peace that day in the Rose Garden, and had the bill sailed through Congress quietly the first time around, it is entirely conceivable that the non-sequitur "read my lips" might never have become a staple of Democratic political rhetoric during the 1992 presidential campaign. Adding insult to injury, the version of the budget bill that did pass— which Bush had to beg Democrats to endorse to make up for Republican defections—contained new compromise provisions that were more distasteful to

Republicans than those contained in the initial bill scuttled by Gingrich.

No other action caused him so much ill will. President Bush felt profoundly betrayed, and moderate Republicans felt that Gingrich was betraying his role as party leader.

"I don't know if [Bush] felt betrayed or not . . ." Gingrich recalled in a 1992 interview. "Others have said he does not trust me. But I think that's reasonable. I think in their world, it was so inconceivable: (a) that I would walk and (b) that I would fight actively and (c) that I would fight publicly. . . . [the Bush White House] just go, 'That son of a bitch.' "

In the midst of the budget battle, Gingrich attended a fund-raiser with his wife, and a photographer suggested a picture of the couple with George Bush. The two men approached. As Gingrich later recalled to the *Washington Post,* he said, "I'm really sorry that this is happening."

"You are killing us, you are just killing us," the President answered.

The budget bill passed, but not without serious repercussions for the Republicans. It led the way to George Bush's defeat in 1992 by Bill Clinton, who found a handy weapon in the broken pledge. Even Bush associates later admitted that Gingrich, in opposing his own president and risking ostracism from his own party, had seen the handwriting on the wall.

"He thought [the budget deal] was going to be a disaster for the Republicans," Nick Calio, Bush's congressional lobbyist, told the *Washington Post* in recalling those heady days. "And you know what, he turned out to be right."

Some Republicans were less admiring of his prescience, however. Budget Director Richard Darman later described Gingrich's perceived about-face as a "stab in the back."

To Newt Gingrich, the tax fight with Bush was necessary. It also allowed him to hone the type of politics he would use in unifying the Republicans be-

hind him in 1994 with the "Contract with America."
"The number one thing we had to prove in the fall of
'90," he told the *Washington Post* in 1992, "was that
if you explicitly decided to govern from the center
then we could make it so unbelievably expensive you.
couldn't sustain it."

Bush never forgave Gingrich. When, in 1991, Bob
Michel began once again to talk about retiring—
leaving the road open for Gingrich to become the
leading Republican in the House—Bush called the
House minority leader and appealed to him to stay on.
The Democrats would not forgive and forget, either.
On September 18, 1990, the Democratic Congressional
Campaign Committee filed a complaint alleging that
GOPAC had been active in federal elections without
being registered as a federal PAC—charges that less
than a year later, on May 8, 1991, the FEC decided to
investigate. GOPAC registered as a federal PAC one
day after the investigation was announced.

As the 1990 elections loomed, there was trouble on
the home front, too. A strike in his district by Eastern
Airlines had given Gingrich a new set of problems to
deal with. His congressional district had the greatest
number of airline employees in the country. A third
of them were striking Eastern Airlines workers. In
addition, the district included twenty thousand union
members, six thousand of whom worked for Eastern.
Yet Gingrich had impoliticly sided with George Bush
against the Eastern Airlines unions. He had declined
to support a House measure asking Bush to convene
an emergency board to arbitrate the dispute. His constituents were furious. In 1989, picketers had clogged
the entrance to his annual $250 a head fund-raiser in
Atlanta, and as John Sununu, then Bush's chief of
staff, looked on, interrupted the proceedings screaming, "Boot Newt! . . . Boot Newt!"

The airline workers claimed that Gingrich was two-
faced, first assuring help for the out of work, then
saying their plight was hopeless. They accused him of
ignoring the strike while he had served as ranking

minority member of the Aviation Subcommittee of the House Public Works and Transportation Committee, a post he resigned when he became whip. He also aroused their ire by accepting campaign contributions amounting to $2,000 from a Texas Air PAC, when Texas Air was another one of Eastern Airlines Chairman Frank Lorenzo's companies.

And it didn't help Gingrich's image any when a district employee, during the strike, took a call from the machinists' union and told them that the congressman didn't have time to meet with them because "he was going to Miami to get a campaign contribution from Frank Lorenzo and she couldn't be sending him over to talk to them," a witness to the conversation recalls.

Under Lorenzo's stewardship, Eastern Airlines later filed for bankruptcy.

Steve Hanser, who observed the strike and was privy to Gingrich's thoughts about it at the time, says that the machinists union's strategy was to "go out on strike even though the company was near bankruptcy. They would then ask the President, under special powers dating back to World War II which were designed to deal with the railroads, to declare the strike an emergency, at which point Congress can then, in effect, decide the outcome of the strike and deal with it."

But there was one critical element of the strikers' strategy that hadn't been thought through, according to Hanser, who has always had strong pro-union sentiments. "They never asked the President about it," Hanser says. "So, when they went out on strike, the President announced that he wasn't going to do it. They then asked Newt—because the airport was in his district—to convince the President to change his mind. But Newt said, '(a) the President is not going to change his mind; and (b) I don't think he should. This act was designed for a shutdown of the entire country; this is just shutting down one airline, and it's not what the act was designed to do.' "

An airline mechanic from Gingrich's district agreed: "The employees were not going to cooperate with Frank Lorenzo no matter what. It would have been a futile attempt if he had tried to do anything. I know several of the employees that worked there and were affected by it, and some of them said they would run the company out of business before they would accept the terms that Frank Lorenzo wanted them to accept. And if they were going to destroy the company themselves. I don't see how anybody else could have come in and tried to save it."

Largely as a result of his handling of the strike and his support for a 1989 bill authorizing a pay raise for congressmen, in the 1990 election Gingrich held on to his seat by just 974 votes, a margin so small that federal election regulations mandated a recount.

Hanser says the wrath of Gingrich's union constituents was unjustified. "He despised Lorenzo, and said so at the time. And all of his sympathies were with the workers. But it was not a strike they could win."

In addition to the ire of his union constituents, Gingrich faced a demographic shift in his district: the Democratic-voting black population had increased substantially. Bill Shipp, the editor of a newsletter covering Georgia politics and a longtime Gingrich-watcher, said that as the 1990 elections rolled around, "Gingrich looked ripe for defeat."

His Democratic opponent, David Worley, a thirty-two-year-old Harvard-educated moderate, was able to make political hay out of Gingrich's approach to the airline strike. "Not only has Gingrich taken money from Lorenzo's PAC and failed to support federal efforts to end the Eastern strike," Worley told the *Journal of Labor* in 1989, "now Gingrich has abandoned his constituents in their hour of greatest need by giving up his position on the House Aviation Sub-committee." When he quit, Gingrich had retained a seat on the House Administration Committee, which, among other things, allocates parking spaces to Congressmen. The irony wasn't lost on Worley. "Thirty thousand jobs are generated by the Atlanta airport, and Newt Gingrich puts parking ahead of people. His contempt for working Americans is clear.''

Worley also attacked Gingrich on his voting record on issues pertaining to the savings and loan industry. It had recently been reported that bailing out the federally insured thrifts was likely to cost taxpayers more than $500 billion. Much of the blame for the S&L fiasco was attributed to rampant deregulation of the industry throughout the 1980s. Gingrich, Worley pointed out, had consistently supported legislation that favored S&L operators, beginning in 1980 with the Depository Institutions Deregulation and Monetary Control Act, which raised the amount of federally insured deposits to $100,000. Over the next ten years Gingrich consistently supported laws that allowed the S&L's to proceed unhindered and consistently voted against laws that sought to regulate the industry. "At every step on the road to this fiscal holocaust, Gingrich acted to let savings and loan executives do their worst to the American taxpayer," Worley said somewhat hyperbolically.

In addition, Common Cause, a Washington watchdog group, showed that in that same period, Gingrich had accepted more than $8,600 in S&L PAC contributions. In Gingrich's defense it must be said that the Common Cause report on S&L PAC contributions showed that Gingrich ranked 132nd out of 148 in the list of S&L PAC House beneficiaries. His $8,600 in contributions pales in comparison to the six-figure amounts received by some members of the Senate.

Worley also raised the issue of the $5,000 invested by Joel Cowan, the operator of a failed Georgia S&L, in the *Window of Opportunity* partnership. In a highly public gesture, Worley signed over a $650 contribution of S&L PAC money—including $500 from Cowan—that his campaign had received in 1988 to the Resolution Trust Corporation and urged Gingrich to do the same with his S&L campaign money.

Worley did himself in, though, in pointing out that

Gingrich had opposed an increase in the minimum wage while voting along with the rest of Congress for the thirty-five percent pay increase—thus violating the sacred House non-aggression treaty. When he approached the Democratic party for funds, pointing out that polls showed that Gingrich was in trouble and could be defeated, the party leaders turned him down. Writing in the *Atlanta Business Chronicle* after the 1994 elections, Michael Hinkelman pointed out that "the pettiness of [the House Democrats'] decision not to bankroll Worley set the stage for" the Republican landslide of 1994. With only a little more money, he argued, Worley might have been able to remove Gingrich from Congress forever.

Worley says he was outspent five to one by Gingrich, who spent more than a million dollars in the campaign. Worley spent $266,837 and never ran a television commercial.

On election night that year Gingrich said his narrow victory had taught him a lesson. "The voters do feel they are not getting their voices heard," he said. "We were very fortunate that while they sent us a message, they gave us a chance to live out that message in the next two years."

Gingrich realized that if he was to build a Republican majority in Congress in 1992, as he had often stated he would, he was going to have to first make sure he won at home. It was a lesson that he would never have to apply, however. Redistricting, in 1991, would cause the Sixth Congressional District to be redrawn, giving Gingrich an entirely new pool of constituents.

After his first two years as whip, "chameleon" was the word now applied to Newt Gingrich in Congress. There was the Bush budget deal, for one thing. There was also the fact that, although Newt had for years been caroling for a radical overhaul of the Social Security system, he had become the system's greatest champion when Democrats had begun looking for a cut in the Social Security payroll tax earlier in the year.

In January 1990, Senator Daniel Patrick Moynihan had proposed cutting the Social Security payroll tax by $50 billion a year, a plan that the Bush White House called a tax hike in disguise and immediately denounced as a "charade." Gingrich saw an opportunity to turn the tables on the Democrats and backed, but never explicitly endorsed, a substitute plan proposed by Representative John Edward Porter, a Republican from Illinois, which would gradually have privatized the system by using its surplus to establish individual retirement accounts for taxpayers—but would not have resulted in an immediate reduction in taxes like the Moynihan plan. The *Wall Street Journal* said that by opposing the possible tax cut offered by the Moynihan plan, Gingrich and the Republicans had "turned conventional politics on its head."

Where most people saw only confusion, Gingrich saw political benefit for the Republicans. He began distributing buttons that read, "Save Social Security. Vote Republican."

"Having Republicans defending the elderly from a liberal Democrat's proposal that might cut benefits is wonderful," said Gingrich. "We owe Mr. Moynihan a debt." Gingrich said the Moynihan proposal, which in fact would not have cut benefits, was a unique opportunity for the Republicans to be seen protecting "the system from the Democratic Party."

Bush played his cards close to his chest, saying that he found the Republican plan "interesting" but that he was "not prepared to endorse" it.

The plan never got off the ground. In the future, as he had in the past, Gingrich would again play political football with the sacred middle-class entitlement. The game goes on to this day.

7

Cracking the Whip

In becoming House whip, Gingrich made the great leap from outside rabble-rouser to ultimate insider. He hired an image consultant; he got a better haircut and more flattering suits. He was working all the time, calling aides and friends at six-thirty in the morning and eleven-thirty at night, never resting, never relaxing, drinking Slim-Fast shakes and eternally faxing.

"He never smiles, he never tells jokes, he's the most joyless man I've ever dealt with," one congressional aide complained at the time. "He's constantly trying to convert you."

He began every day at six with an oft-photographed inspirational walk from Capitol Hill to the Lincoln Monument or the Washington Monument.

Perhaps this manic activity helps to explain why even as Gingrich's fame and political stature were growing, his personal life was suffering. In 1989, Marianne Gingrich had admitted their marriage had been "off and on for some time."

"You marry to get married, not because you want to 'change the world,' " she is reported to have said. "We can do that without being married."

"Marianne has no interest in being married to The Whip," Gingrich told *Atlanta* magazine in 1990. "She'd like to be married to Newt. And sometimes we have a very difficult time transitioning back and forth." He explained, "You acquire a rhythm and a drive and a focus to do this job well, which makes it hard to unwind. . . . My wife, and I think this would be true of any spouse, has no interest in dealing with the level of intensity that is appropriate if you are trying to change 435 members."

Newt and Marianne began seeing a marriage counselor. In one article at the time, Newt estimated that their marriage had only a 53 percent chance of surviving. He ascribed the difficulties to the challenges of his unusually time-demanding life.

Though they tried to keep it a secret, it has been confirmed that he and Marianne separated.

"It was funny," Kathleen Gingrich says. "Susan came back from a trip to see them and said, 'Marianne has the prettiest pink couch you've ever seen.' Next time I came down to Atlanta, for one of Newt's fundraisers or something, I looked for that pink couch and I couldn't find it. I said, 'Marianne, when do I get to see the pink couch?' She said, 'Pretty soon.'

"I got back and told Susan and she said, 'Mother, they have a pink couch. They have!'

"The next time Bob took me there, I said, 'Marianne, I still haven't seen your pink couch yet.' And she and Newt started laughing. Earlier, she had left him. And she took the pink couch with her."

During the period described by Gingrich's mother, Marianne had returned to her native Ohio, where she took an apartment near her mother.

Rumors of the instability of the Gingrich marriage have continued through the 1990s—and have been reported repeatedly in the mainstream press. In fact, immediately before the 1994 election, a rumor circulated that Gingrich was leaving Marianne for another woman. There were also rumors that she had told a friend that she might be leaving him.

"People will tell you that before the election Marianne told people she was leaving him after November.

Now, she didn't expect he'd be speaker, and he didn't
know anything about a four and a half million dollar
book deal," an observer says. "So, she's a smart
enough woman to wait for that to get signed!"

His marital problems notwithstanding, Gingrich
continued to target 1992 as the year that Republicans
would gain control of the House. He had begun planning for the 1992 elections shortly after Bush's election as president, during his closed-door sessions in
the cabin at Crested Butte. The main strategy that
emerged from that time was to attack the Democratic
majority in Congress. It was a strategy he believed
was working. By 1991, he was estimating there was a
"one in three chance" that a Republican majority
could overcome its 103-seat deficit and take over the
House in 1992.

"Harry Truman picked up 76 seats in 1948," he
mused to a reporter from the *Los Angeles Times* in
1991. "The [Gulf War's] been won, and quickly. Assume the recession is clearly over in the fall, and you
get the Democratic presidential candidates you are
likely to get. . . . They're going to have a convention
in New York City—as it collapses—of AIDS activists,
left-wing environmentalists, ultra-feminists, unilateral
disarmers, and random professional politicians, with a
mixture of union bosses thrown in. You tell me, which
party will be on the winning side of history?"

Gingrich seized upon the House banking scandal as
an issue that was sure to unseat Democratic incumbents. In 1991, an audit of the House bank showed
that some members were allowed to maintain nearly
permanent and unlimited overdrafts in their accounts.
Since overdrawing was a bipartisan and time-honored
institution, most members were willing to let the matter slide and had opposed the release of names except
in the case of the worst offenders. Some Republicans,
led by Gingrich, called for full disclosure, hoping to
capitalize on the fact that the majority of check bounc-
ers were Democrats.

When the results of the audit were disclosed in 1991,

Gingrich began conspiring with a group of freshmen Republicans who called themselves the "Gang of Seven" to press Foley to close the bank and initiate an investigation by the House Ethics Committee. While House Minority Leader Bob Michel would have preferred to settle the matter quietly and collegially, Gingrich began to protest increasingly loudly and embarrassed a majority of Democratic representatives into pressing for full disclosure of the names of the members who had overdrafts.

"He seized the moment," Representative Jim Nussle, freshman Republican of Iowa told the *New York Times*. "He came to his leadership role by being a grenade thrower. Unlike Bob Michel, he can be part of the leadership one moment and be a freshman back bencher the next."

On the House floor, where he was greeted with catcalls, his attacks became increasingly virulent. They culminated when he said the newly appointed House sergeant-at-arms "may have been involved in actions stopping the Capitol police from investigating cocaine selling in the post office," and that Foley was covering up the bank scandal—allegations for which he offered no evidence.

On April 16, 1992, the House Ethics Committee released the names of 325 former and current members who had overdrawn their checking accounts at the House bank. No rules were broken because there were virtually no rules to be broken. Members insisted that it was their understanding that they could overdraw as long as the amount didn't exceed their next month's salary.

On that same day Gingrich, who had previously admitted to three checks "with problems," released a statement explaining his twenty-two overdrafts, including a $9,463 check to the Internal Revenue Services to pay his federal taxes in 1990. "I regret the errors with my checking account and apologize for them," he said. "But one thing I do not apologize for is leading the fight for disclosure of all names. Last year and last month the Democratic leadership tried to suppress the facts. I fought for disclosure even though I knew I would be opening myself to public embarrassment.''

Gingrich also released a letter from his accountant stating that none of the overdrafts were "associated with personal investments or with campaign funding." Gingrich said that there was a difference between perk abusers and people like him who were merely "sloppy."

The Democrats gloated.

"While Newt Gingrich was lining up a partisan firing squad, what he saw instead was Republicans standing up in a circle and shooting themselves in the Cabinet," said House Majority Whip David E. Bonior of Michigan.

Why did Gingrich throw himself into an issue that, in the long run, was certain to embarrass him and cause damage to his party? In an interview with the *New York Times,* he said that he saw his role as similar to those played by dissidents in the Eastern Bloc in the collapse of communism. "I'm going to the Gdansk shipyards," he said, in an allusion to Lech Walesa of Poland. "I can't tell you when we will win. Every year is a make-or-break moment until the system collapses. We'll know that when it happens." He said he hoped the Congress would collapse, allowing the Republicans to "replace the welfare state and install an honest Congress responsive to the American people."

Despite his own indiscretions, Newt continued to work with the freshmen molded by GOPAC to direct the national spotlight on the overdrafts at the House bank, threw his weight behind the term-limitation movement as a way to get the Democratic incumbents out, and backed a measure allowing incumbents to keep their accumulated campaign war chests—but only if they retired in 1992.

But instead of being the undoing of the Democrats, as Gingrich had hoped, the House bank issue threatened to undo Gingrich himself—and his colleagues within the Republican party. At a campaign rally in Georgia, someone posted a bumper sticker that read BOUNCE NEWT to his car. The House banking scandal caused House Republican Mickey Edwards of Oklahoma (386 overdrafts) to lose his primary, and forced some Republican members to not seek reelection, including Gingrich's old friend Vin Weber of Minnesota. Weber, with 125 overdrafts, retired rather than campaign against his own fiscal irresponsibility.

Anticipating a deluge of open seats, Gingrich used GOPAC to recruit and train a "farm team" of Republican congressional candidates. While the House banking scandal raged in the corridors of Congress, a future army of Newt Gingrich acolytes listened to tapes of his speeches in their cars and watched his videocassette in their homes. They learned to think like an attacking army. They learned to speak like Newt.

GOPAC educated them. "As you know, one of the key points in the GOPAC tapes is that 'language matters.'" GOPAC political director Tom Morgan wrote to the faithful in "Language, a Key Mechanism of Control," a document that he had drafted and which Gingrich sent to candidates in 1990. "Language," Morgan wrote, is "a key mechanism of control used by a majority party, along with Agenda, Rules, Attitude, and Learning. As the tapes have been used in training sessions across the country and mailed to candidates, we have heard a plaintive plea: *'I wish I could speak like Newt.'*

"That takes years of practice. But we believe that you could have a significant impact on your campaign and the way you communicate if we help a little. That is why we have created this list of words and phrases."

The list of 133 words—for use in "speeches, direct mail, brochures, flyers, newspaper ads, electronic advertising, news releases, door to door campaigning"—was divided into two sections: "Optimistic Positive Governing Words," i.e., "your message," and "Contrasting Words" to "help you clearly define the policies and record of your opponent and the Democratic party." The good words included: liberty, peace, change, commitment, rights, opportunity, legacy, unique, proud/pride, duty, control, preserve, truth, pro-(flag, children, environment), reform, workfare, prosperity, crusade, success, choice, activist, we/us/our, hard work, conflict, pristine, dream, and freedom. And the bad words included: decay, endanger, failure, coercion, welfare, collapse, hypocrisy, corrupt, radical, selfish, threaten, urgent, devour, status quo, mandate, sick, pathetic, permissive attitude, they/them, self-serving, unionized, bureaucracy, ideological, machine bosses, anti- (flag, family, child, jobs), shallow, traitors, intolerant, red tape, and criminal rights.

"Read them," the GOPAC materials said. "Memorize as many as possible. And remember that like any tool, these words will not help if they are not used."

After news of the mailing came to light in the national press after the 1994 election, Senate Majority Leader Bob Dole criticized the GOPAC mailing on NBC's *Meet the Press* as an impediment to bipartisanship. The *New York Times* called it "The Politics of Slash and Burn."

Gingrich & Co. were unrepentant. They were optimistic. And they had every reason to be: Redistricting in 1991, after the 1990 census, shifted nineteen House seats from slow-growth states in the Northeast and Midwest to fast-growing states, mostly in the conservative-voting South and West, and seemed to offer the Republicans a plum in the 1992 elections. As the election approached, Newt traveled across the country campaigning for Republican candidates and sponsored press conferences to promote Republican legislative proposals. GOPAC worked hard to convince wealthy businessmen that supporting Republican candidates was a worthwhile investment.

While Gingrich was tearing around the country denouncing the values of liberals, he at first didn't worry too much about his own House race. He had been one of the great beneficiaries of redistricting. In the reapportionment of Georgia's congressional districts, a Republican paradise had been created for Gingrich: the renamed Sixth District, which demographers call the "second most Republican district in the nation." The new district stretched across five suburban counties, including prosperous Cobb County, to the north of Atlanta. Moving from Jonesboro to Marietta, Gingrich left his old district, now filled with disgruntled blue-collar workers—including a good number from Eastern Airlines—the Democratic-voting blacks, and settled in the "chic Republican sprawl of East Cobb County." The mostly white Cobb County, with its average income of $55,000, has earned the nickname of "the platinum triangle."

The state Democratic leadership, which oversaw the redistricting, Georgia political observer Bill Shipp says, had thought of configuring the district so that Gingrich would have to face a popular Democratic incumbent: Buddy Darden. But Darden had protested and Gingrich received a district without an incumbent challenger. Nonetheless, he almost lost his primary against Herman Clark—even though Gingrich outspent him eight to one and Clark's campaign consisted mostly of standing at busy intersections with a cardboard sign.

Campaign ads by Clark drawing attention to Gingrich's own twenty-two overdrafts from the House bank, including the infamous check to the IRS for $9,463, badly dented his already tarnished image in his district, still hurting from the recession and job losses after the failed Eastern Airlines strike. Clark also attacked his use of a government-provided Lincoln Town Car and driver. Phone calls to Clark's office were answered, "Clark for Congress. Our checks are good."

Perhaps Clark's most devastating piece of agit-prop was a sixty-second radio spot to the tune of "Old MacDonald Had a Farm."

Congressman Newt Gingrich bounced twenty-two checks,
For more than twenty-six grand.

With a bounced check here and pay raise there.
Here a check. There a check. Everywhere a bounced
   check.

The *Atlanta Journal-Constitution* chimed in as well
in an editorial that criticized Gingrich for a perceived
excessive use of congressional perks. "You can't
preach the evils of the entrenched political elite from
the backseat of a chauffeur-driven Lincoln," the editorial, which ran during the Easter recess, read.
Gingrich was also damaged by a report from the
Center for Responsive Politics, a nonpartisan research
group in Washington, which found that he, more than
any other member of the House, had failed to identify
fully the source of his campaign contributions.

Perhaps unwisely, Gingrich counterattacked with
campaign material that listed the benefits he had
brought home from Washington: federal help to control noise at the Atlanta airport, an increase in veteran
benefits, aid for the cleanup of toxic waste sites,
reading programs for youngsters, and a new rhinoc-
eros for the Atlanta zoo. In the final week of the
campaign against Clark, Gingrich spent about
$100,000 on television commercials, almost as much
as Clark spent in the entire campaign. Gingrich also
mailed out 100,000 pieces of direct mail. In the end,
he squeaked by with less than a thousand vote margin,
partly because Georgia election laws allow Democrats
to cross over and vote in a Republican primary.

The Georgia Democrats were gunning hard to bring
Gingrich down. In the general election, his Democratic opponent, Tony Center, ran a television advertisement that said Gingrich had "delivered divorce
papers to his wife the day after her cancer operation,"
and that Newt had "left his wife and child penniless"
while profiting from his position as minority whip
using a Lincoln Continental limousine and driver.

In reaction to the commercial, Gingrich's younger
daughter, Jackie Gingrich Zyla, was moved to make
her own advertisement: "My dad has always stood

behind and supported me and my sister in everything we have done," she said. "We care about our father and he cares about us."

Gingrich's other daughter, Kathy Gingrich Lubbers, issued her own challenge to Newt immediately before the 1992 Republican National Convention. Joining with the National Republican Coalition for Choice, she urged the Republican party to drop its anti-abortion stance. She said her father and she had been having a running dialogue on the issue for some time and that he probably wouldn't be surprised by her announcement. He had always, she said, encouraged her to "speak her mind." She said, "I don't think this is much of a blip in his embarrassment meter. He's got his own battles to fight."

Gingrich said he found Center's campaign attacks so abhorrent that he considered quitting the race.

"This filth is so sickening," he told the *New York Times* during the campaign. "If survival in public life means this level of degradation, I don't want to be part of it."

He did, however, announce that he would give up his Lincoln Town Car and his highly paid chauffeur, who happened also to be a detective who carried a gun and worked as his bodyguard. "Newt's a physical coward," a former top campaign aide says. "He's always afraid someone's going to hurt him."

Having finally learned a lesson from their lack of action in the 1990 election, the Democratic party of Georgia milked Gingrich's insider status for all it was worth. They mass-mailed a glossy brochure deliberately designed to look like a credit card advertisement, and which on its cover had a photograph of an elegantly set table bearing the caption "Membership has its privileges." As the reader opened the brochure, across two pages the large print went on, ". . . and Newt Gingrich took every one of them." The brochure lambasted Gingrich for his House-provided car and driver, his $3,000 living-expenses tax deduction, and said that while he lived high on the hog at the taxpayers' expense, he was blocking legislation that would have assisted "people like you. People who have to drive *themselves* to work."

Meanwhile, Gingrich's campaign materials took a softer approach. "Is he perfect?" they asked. "Clearly not." But, they added, he had learned from his mistakes, a Bill Clinton-esque mantra that had served him well before.

In all, Newt spent $1.96 million on his campaign—$6.91 for each of the 274,817 votes cast in the election—the fifth highest amount spent by a candidate for the House that year. Gingrich also accepted $654,000 in PAC donations, the tenth highest amount received by a House candidate.

Toward the end of the election, he used his incumbent status in one final push. In the last four months of 1992, he sent out more than a dozen press releases announcing new federal grants or contracts in his district. In the end, he had to resort to bringing home the pork he had so derided to win. "If you had the choice between the number two-ranking Republican in the House or you can have a freshman who doesn't have any idea who the Cabinet members are, has never met any of them, and has never worked with the President, which one do you think can do more for Cobb County!" he told constituents.

Gingrich had won again. But the apathy of his new constituents was evident when only thirteen people attended one of his first highly hyped town hall meetings in this district in January.

In a sense, on the national level, the Republicans' anti-incumbent theme worked. Voting yes on the "throw the bums out" ticket, Americans decided to boot the reigning party out of the White House, not Congress, where the Republicans gained only ten seats, leaving the Democrats with a 258-to-176 majority and Bill Clinton in the White House.

In June, Gingrich had sent a warning to George Bush urging him to change his ways if he wanted to be reelected to the White House. In a memorandum to Bush-Quayle campaign advisers and to top White House officials, he'd described the particularities of the 1992 election with its added ingredients of Ross Perot and overwhelming voter discontent.

"If the President is ever to recover from the current situation and win," the memo said, "he had better start dealing with . . . how unique this year is, how frightened and angry the American people are, and how deeply the American people believe the current situation . . . justifies the radical gamble of a third candidate."

But Gingrich was blind to the threat posed by Clinton and urged Bush to focus on Perot instead. "The voters willing to leave the Democrats to insure Bush loses could combine with independents and anti-Bush Republicans to give Perot a ceiling of 45 percent in his support," he wrote. "A 45 percent Perot, 30 percent Bush, 25 percent Clinton race is very plausible." By this time Bush was widely seen as out of touch, and his campaign appearances, such as the one where he wondered at a supermarket scanner, were only reinforcing this perception. "We keep trying to force 1992 into a modern model. . . . Normal, traditional consultants keep applying their knowledge of the normal in a year that is unique," Gingrich said.

Rather than heeding the bad tidings, which were valid insofar as Bush had badly misjudged the degree of dissatisfaction abroad in the land, the White House decided to shoot the messenger.

"I got another [memo] from Newt this morning," White House Press Secretary Marlin Fitzwater told the press, his voice coming with sarcasm, causing reporters to break up in laughter. "This man is a kind of modern Plato, you know, he just thinks all the time. . . . He came in last week and gave me four or five [memos], and we appreciate all of them . . . and this man is brilliant. . . . Everybody just reads Newt's memos."

Two days later, at a session with congressional

leaders, Bush himself went on the offensive. "I never criticize the Republican leadership [in Congress]," he said, "and I would appreciate it if you don't criticize me. If you have to criticize me, go right to me, not through Ann Devroy [the *Washington Post* reporter who broke the story]."

But Bush hadn't always been so dismissive of advice from the Gingrich camp. In his State of the Union address, he had borrowed a phrase from Jeff Eisenach, a long-time Gingrich associate who was the head of GOPAC, which was supposed to symbolize both Bush's international achievement and his newly found commitment to domestic policy. "If we can change the world, we can change America," he said. Unfortunately, he hadn't heeded his own words. America had already changed while he was looking abroad.

A Republican National Convention in Houston, which *Newsweek* described as "wall-to-wall ugly," sealed Bush's fate.

The convention had been hijacked by the more rightward elements in the Republican Party, and instead of focusing on the economy or other issues that polarized the electorate, the platform was one of family values.

The tone was set when Patrick Buchanan, a conservative columnist and presidential aspirant, declared before a prime-time television audience, "There is a religious war going on in this country. It is a cultural war as critical to the kind of nation we shall be as the Cold War itself—for this war is for the soul of America. And in that struggle for the soul of America, Clinton and [Hillary] Clinton are on the other side; and George Bush is on our side."

Not to be outdone, Gingrich let loose as well. In his speech, he said the Democratic Party "despises the values of the American people" and indulges a "multicultural, nihilistic hedonism that is inherently destructive of a healthy society."

As the G.O.P. House Conference regrouped after the election, many conservatives began to call for censuring those members who had supported Bush's 1990 budget deal. Gingrich, however, spoke against that. And since most of the newcomers to Congress were former GOPAC students, his word carried the day. Perhaps he had a premonition that he would find reason to be grateful to the Bush budget deal someday. Recently Gingrich said that "it is a grand irony of history" that if Bush had been reelected, the Republicans probably wouldn't have won control of the House in 1994.

Gingrich took a philosophical approach to the Republican loss of the White House after so many years of control. He even found a way to steer blame for the defeat away from his own party.

"We were faced with a system that was corrupt," he told the *New York Times* in 1994. "We adopted a series of positions that were very popular in the country—a balanced-budget amendment, a line-item veto, no tax increases—and the corrupt Democratic machine . . . remained rigid and stuck in place. It then won an accidental election for president with forty-three percent of the vote."

In truth, he knew that the Republican defeat was going to offer him a tactical advantage. It offered him the chance to *reculer pour mieux sauter*. His strength had never been in bipartisanship and conciliation—being in the opposition was going to play to his strengths, especially when the opponent was a liberal whom he thought he could push even further to the left. President Bill Clinton wouldn't disappoint.

In 1994, Gingrich recalled that the Clinton administration, "instead of moving to the center, which would have required analyzing the Perot vote, which was anti-government and for cutting spending—an amazing populist rebellion—it moved to the left. What you got was Dukakis with a Southern accent."

In his analysis, Clinton's perceived leftward shift had inevitably brought the Gingrich Republicans to power. The 1994 elections, he believed, would be a necessary correction in the course of world history.

"Faced with that reality, whether it's the collapse of the Japanese system, the collapse of the Italian system, the collapse of the Russian system, the collapse of the Canadian governing party last year, we are the natural result," he said in 1994. "We are reformers. We are prepared to say bluntly what the machine is. And we're prepared to offer policies that are very popular in the country and very unpopular in [Washington]. And that's fine with us. Our power base isn't in this city."

The "kulturkampf" of the past summer's convention in Houston and the campaign in general took its toll on the Republican Party, however.

In January 1993, on the day before the 103rd Congress convened, Representative Steve Gunderson of Wisconsin, an openly gay member of Congress, resigned as chief deputy whip, saying he could no longer stomach Gingrich's style of leadership. Representative Fred Upton of Michigan quit as deputy whip the following week for similar reasons.

Kevin Kennedy, a press secretary for Gunderson, says the congressman decided to resign because "the party had moved to the right. It was less an affront to Newt than out of the feeling the party was not representing the broad interest" of the party and the nation. "It was to make the statement: things have gone too far."

"Newt was consulted before the decision," Kennedy says. And Gingrich encouraged Gunderson "to organize moderate G.O.P. members." Kennedy said, "They have maintained a good, public friendship. There is no rift. Gunderson's decision to give up [the leadership post] was merely a statement."

Kennedy said that while Gingrich's "public persona may seem harsh, he's rather tolerant in private."

Candace Gingrich, Newt's openly gay twenty-eight-year-old sister, commented this past January on Gingrich's concept of "toleration": "A leaky faucet is something you tolerate. When your dog barks, that's something you tolerate," she told the *Washington*

Blade, in response to an interview Newt had given the *New York Times* saying that the G.O.P.'s stance on homosexuality should be "toleration. It should not be promotion, and it should not be condemnation." Over the years he had made pronouncements comparing homosexuality to alcoholism.

On the opening day of the new Congress, Bob Michel promised that mutual respect and goodwill would set the tone for business in the House. A few hours later, however, Gingrich was already attacking the Democrats. The furniture had barely been arranged in the Clintons' new living quarters before Newt was once more on the offensive. In January 1993, only days after Clinton's inauguration, Gingrich publicly announced that Clinton should withdraw Zoe Baird's nomination for attorney general because she employed an undocumented Peruvian housekeeper. "Clearly, she has crossed the line. You can't have a person who ought to be prosecuted serving in the Cabinet." he said.

He then savaged Clinton's plan to drop the ban on homosexuals in the military. Although he had at first said that he had "no strong position" on lifting the ban, when it became a raging public issue, Gingrich said he consulted with the Joint Chiefs of Staff and decided to support the ban.

"Unlike the commander-in-chief, who has changed his position somewhat, I am sticking with my military advisers," he announced.

Under Gingrich's leadership, the G.O.P. minority derailed Clinton's crime bill in a procedural vote. Eleven Republicans, however, broke ranks and said they were willing to work with Clinton to rework a passable bill. This cooperation set off a fury among conservative Republicans nationwide. The Alaska state party voted to expel the eleven peacemakers. The *Wall Street Journal* editorial page called them "Clinton Republicans," and some major political backers vowed never to give money to G.O.P. candidates again.

Even though Gingrich opposed the bill—mostly because it included a ban on assault weapons—he held his tongue, and, surprising many, accompanied the eleven dissenters to the White House to meet with President Clinton. He assigned his experts on crime to serve as technical advisers to the group that was meeting to renegotiate the bill. Clinton eventually agreed to a series of changes, which included trimming the package by $3 billion. At that point, almost forty Republican congressmen joined their Democratic colleagues to pass the crime bill.

Gingrich, however, did continue to play hardball when necessary. From the beginning of the Clinton administration he had served notice to lobbies and special-interest groups that the rules of the game were changed now that the Republicans no longer held the White House and woe betide he who dared support the new president. And he kept his word. When Clinton presented his economic package during his first State of the Union address, Gingrich criticized the U.S. Chamber of Commerce because it had dared to grant the President some faint praise. In July, he led a boycott of an event sponsored by the Chamber at which one hundred House Republicans were supposed to be honored.

"While we understand the value and importance of this kind of award, it is equally important that we do not act as props for an organization that has opposed us in our fight against the higher taxes of the President's budget," he wrote to the intended recipients of the awards. Only twelve Republicans came to the award gala, and they were honored with more than a plaque. They also received a letter from the chamber's president explicitly opposing Clinton's plan, or whatever version of it might emerge from Congress.

When the budget finally reached the House floor, the Republicans voted unanimously to derail it. It passed nonetheless.

In the House, Gingrich consolidated his power, already preparing to depose Michel as House minority leader in the event the G.O.P. failed to obtain a majority, or as House speaker if, as he hoped, the Republicans became the majority party.

Preparing for the final push, Gingrich began placing his allies in key positions. According to the *Washington Post,* in 1992 Gingrich arranged for the number three Republican in the House, Representative Jerry Lewis of California, to be replaced as conference chairman by Richard K. Armey of Texas, a longstanding Gingrich ally. "There aren't many people who walk around with war generals' books under their arms." Lewis told the *Post* without rancor, "There's little question that Newt felt if there was a competitor on the leadership ladder who might be in the way, it was probably me. So early on I was moved out of the way."

Throughout his tenure as whip Gingrich had to defer to Michel, whose congenial, gentlemanly style was antithetical to his, causing more than a little friction. Some, however, say that Gingrich looked up to Michel as a father figure.

"I found his relationship with Michel was more complicated than people thought," Vin Weber once told the *New York Times.* "Newt challenged him and made life tough for him, but I felt he wanted Michel to like him, at times more than I thought was appropriate. Newt was bending over backward to try to get his approval. I think that is related somehow to something that was missing before."

It is not clear, however, that any affection flowing from Gingrich to Michel was ever reciprocated. In their first joint news conference after Gingrich was made whip, Michel's epidermal dislike of Newt was made clear when he mispronounced Gingrich's first name as "Nit."

And Michel was not alone. Foes and supporters alike agreed that, under Gingrich's influence, Congress had become a meaner and harsher place. Fellow Republican Jim Leach concurred, "I shudder at the thought that people judge the Republican Party by

him.'' ''Some days, you think of hiring a food taster,''
Michel told the *Los Angeles Times* in 1991. Michel,
the ultimate technical and collegial legislator, could
have little in common with Gingrich the bomb thrower,
who had sponsored only 31 measures in a decade in
the House, of which only one had actually passed.

The tensions between Gingrich and Michel were
never more evident than when, on election night 1992,
Michel's staff was tracking the returns in Michel's
office and it was announced that Gingrich could be
losing.

They cheered.

Gingrich never made a secret of his desire to attain
the speakership, and had Michel not retired in 1994,
Gingrich would certainly have challenged him for it.
''He basically drove Michel out,'' Ed Rollins told the
Washington Post.

In October 1993, Michel announced that he would
not be seeking reelection. Gingrich sprang into action
immediately and began lobbying support, even, according to the *Boston Globe,* tracking down one freshman representative, Peter Blute, in his home district.

Only days later, as sixty Republicans chanted,
''Newt! Newt!'' Gingrich triumphantly announced
that he had enough votes to win the election to succeed Michel—fourteen months in the future. Positioning himself for the role he was to play in 1994, Gingrich
said he represented a new generation of conservatives.
''We know the welfare state has failed . . . our generation must replace the welfare state with an opportunity
society,'' he said.

The Democrats were terrified, but he appeased them
briefly in November when he mustered 132 Republican
votes for the North American Free Trade Agreement—more than half of the votes received by the
treaty on which the credibility of Clinton's presidency
was then resting. For a brief moment all was peace
and love. Gingrich had done for Clinton what the
Democrats wouldn't. ''He did a terrific job,'' George
Stephanopoulos told *USA Today*. ''It shows us we can

come together across party lines," he added with the overoptimism of youth.

Gingrich, however, warned the White House against interpreting his gesture as a sign of things to come. "When the President is wrong, I'm going to take him head-on," Gingrich said, basking in his power. "That doesn't mean I don't like him. It doesn't mean I'm not trying to cooperate. But when he tries to raise taxes again, which he inevitably will, I'm going to oppose him." He was as good as his word. He continued the scorched-earth strategy he had developed over the years, and time after time rallied the Republicans to defeat Clinton's proposals.

His tactic was simple: constant offensive and death by a thousand cuts. He was tireless. In May 1994, for example, Gingrich displayed a photograph from the Frederick, Maryland, *News-Post* that showed senior White House aides boarding a helicopter at a golf course in Maryland. The national press picked up the story and showed that it costs $2,380 an hour to operate the helicopter. At first the White House said the aides were scouting the course for a possible trip by the president. Later, Dee Dee Myers said one of the aides, David Watkins, the White House director of administration, had resigned and the taxpayers would be reimbursed for the junket.

These were all sideshows to the main event. Early on Gingrich had found the single issue that he knew was going to help him administer the coup de grace to the Clinton administration and vault him to his long-held dream of the speakership.

Only days after the White House presented its health care plan and began looking for one hundred sponsors to introduce it to the House, Gingrich launched an all-out assault.

"The Clinton health plan is culturally alien to America," he declared in December 1993 to an audience at the Empower America think tank. It consists of "1,300 pages of red tape," he added. Gingrich compared the plan to the kind of "central planning" that might have been concocted in the old days of the Soviets, saying, "Bill Clinton is doing almost precisely the same thing we are telling Boris Yeltsin to stop doing."

Gingrich had in fact once had some ideas of his own about health care reform. In a 1986 position paper entitled *Creating a Learning Society for America's 21st Century,* he'd suggested six steps toward an affordable health care system, including the creation of "Jonas Salk Invention Centers" which, he said, could develop innovations such as "a self-dialysis kit to replace the $2 billion a year professional dialysis centers," and the "Life-Line," a "wristwatch that dials emergency help at the push of a button, to allow older Americans to live longer in their own homes instead of nursing homes."

The paper also contains several ideas for reforming health care that Gingrich probably would not have endorsed had they been suggested by the Clinton administration only eight years later. The paper advocates the development of preventive care vouchers to "be issued to cover the cost of local public health prenatal care," as well as vouchers covering the cost of preventive-care breast exams for women. It also discusses the "creation of a systems approach to the AIDS epidemic," saying that AIDS is "a real crisis which in our lifetime could affect virtually every family in America." It continues in a vein that many of his more conservative colleagues might find distasteful. One passage is worth quoting in full. "We need to communicate in clear, explicit terms how to avoid AIDS," he writes. "We should talk openly about the use of condoms. We must explore public health education opportunities in both our schools and in the media. If we don't start talking openly and honestly soon, this epidemic is going to be out of hand and we're going to lose a million people in the 1990s." This stands in strong contrast to the ideas of Gingrich ally Paul Weyrich, who during the same period was advocating such tough measures as national screening and "mandatory reporting of all intercourse contacts" by male homosexuals and permitting insurance companies to deny coverage to AIDS carriers.

In his position paper, Gingrich also advocates the creation of some type of catastrophic health insurance that "would help families face illness without the additional burden of bankruptcy." It is interesting to imagine that, had Gingrich followed through on some of these ideas, and had not, by the late 1980s, come to espouse such free market placebos as tax credits for doctors who choose to treat poor people, the explosion of the health care crisis, which he predicted, might never have occurred. Another enticing scenario would be to imagine if Gingrich had joined forces with Hillary Clinton and Ira Magaziner in the creation of the aborted national health care plan of 1994.

Now, in an effort to seize upon the health care issue, the Republicans unveiled their own health plan, co-sponsored by Gingrich, which they said would contain insurance costs and allow workers to retain coverage if they left their jobs, but didn't require employers to provide insurance for workers. They sensed fairly quickly, though, that health care reform was a dangerous business with few chances for success, and so ceased plugging their bill, preferring instead to concentrate on knocking down Clinton's.

The Republicans also realized that by dragging out the health care debate, they could dilute health care's potency as an issue. This brilliant stroke of strategy was laid out in a four-page memo from William Kristol, Dan Quayle's former chief of staff and now head of the Project for the Republican Future, a conservative think tank. Kristol's message was, simply put, "there is no health care crisis."

Gingrich took it from there. During his campaign Clinton had promised to deliver a health care plan covering every American within the first one hundred days. In his first few days in office, he had asked Hillary Rodham Clinton to draw up the plan, and she put together a task force of five hundred advisors, met with thousands of individuals across the country and, in closed-door meetings, drew up the 1,342-page bill.

It wasn't until September 1993 that Clinton outlined the proposal before a joint session of Congress. It was finally introduced in November 20. More than a year had passed since the election, and Americans were distracted by foreign policy crises in Somalia, Haiti, and Bosnia and the revelations on Whitewater, Hillary's commodities deals, and the president's sex life. In the nation's consciousness, health care had moved off the front burner, not least because of a recovering economy.

Interest-group activists then kicked in, spending $120 million to kill the plan. Gingrich as well as many other legislators of both parties, had a long track of involvement with groups with a vested interest in defeating the health care bill. Since 1979 he had accepted $79,935 in contributions from insurance companies and medical groups. The CEO of one company, J. Patrick Rooney of the Golden Rule Insurance Company of Indianapolis, had given $95,150 to GOPAC from 1991 to 1993. In lobbying to defeat the health plan, the anti-reform groups pulled out all the stops. The Health Insurance Association of America spent $15 million on the Harry and Louise television campaign alone. By this time the plan was as good as dead, and Gingrich had found the issue that was going to ensure Republican control of the House in 1994.

Gingrich made sure health care stayed dead. By June it was clear the Republicans wanted to scuttle any effort on health care reform proposed by Clinton. Sensing total victory, Gingrich told Republicans to oppose any amendments to the bill that might make it more palatable to legislators or the public and give it a chance of passing. The Republicans adopted a tactic of pointing out that the health care plan mostly benefited the fifteen percent of Americans with no health insurance at all, and that the remaining eighty-five percent, who had some form of health insurance, stood to lose.

The strategy worked. In September, Senate Majority Leader George Mitchell, the administration's point man on the issue, announced that there would be no health care bill in the 103rd Congress, and Clinton admitted that the plan would have to be deferred until 1995.

In an interview with the *New York Times* in July, Gingrich said that he had known all along that the President's bill was doomed. Clinton's plan, he said, "goes to the core of the difference between Democrats and Republicans. I suggested to Hillary a year and a half ago—I said, 'I would not ever try to change fourteen percent of the national economy in one bill.' I said they should bring in a bill a year, and they should do five good things a year and minimum damage. I said: 'You can't write a comprehensive bill. Nobody is smart enough to write a comprehensive bill.'"

The man who wanted to move the world was urging moderation.

The Clinton presidency had been critically wounded, and the House Republicans under Gingrich's stewardship had emerged triumphant.

Gingrich could taste a majority and the long-awaited speakership.

8

The Member From "Madderthanhell"

On November 9, 1994, the Republicans won control of Congress, winning fifty-two new seats and paving the way for Newt Gingrich to realize his ambition of becoming the first Republican speaker of the House in forty years.

Two days after the landslide, the *Wall Street Journal*'s lead editorial was headlined THE REST OF HIM, a reference to Ronald Reagan's famous line in the film *King's Row* in which he wakes up to find his legs amputated and says: "Where's the rest of me?" The implication was that, finally, the elections had brought forth a new day that would allow the Republicans to finish the Reagan revolution, which had been left unfinished and, in fact, derailed by the "obstructionist" Democratic Congress.

"Ronald Reagan has been reelected, not once but hundreds of times," said Edwin J. Fuelner, Jr., president of the Heritage Foundation, at a celebratory meeting after the election. "American voters sent to Washington and the statehouses and legislatures of America an army of soldiers who will fight to finish the revolution President Reagan began."

Whereas before the elections the Republicans had been outnumbered 178 to 256 in the House, they now had 230 seats. They also gained a 53–47 majority in the Senate. It would be the first time since 1954 that the Republicans would control both Houses. They also grabbed 11 governorships.

The Democratic rout was so complete that such luminaries as Tom Foley of Washington, the Democratic House speaker, lost his seat, becoming the first speaker to do so since the Civil War. Sitting speakers don't generally lose elections because their position gives them unparalleled power to "bring home the bacon."

Former Secretary of Education, author, and potential Republican presidential candidate William Bennett said: "It was if the angel of the Lord did go House to House, and seeing a Republican incumbent inside, he moved on."

The Democrats were stunned. In the days after the election, the White House, struggling for a way to rationalize the defeat, ultimately came up with the rather lame explanation that the vote was not "anti-Democrat but anti-incumbent." To a certain extent the spin doctors were right. Two-thirds of Republican candidates ran as challengers or were seeking open seats.

The pundits, though, were still puzzled. Some said that the victory was an accident. Others that the Republicans owed their good fortune to Bill Clinton's waffling, bungling and big-government policies. Still others attributed the Republican victory to the inchoate mood of discontent sweeping the nation. All of that may be true. It's also true, though, that all these factors merely presented an opportune time for one man to implement a plan he had been building step by step, battle by battle, coalition by coalition, slur by slur, for years. It was Newt Gingrich's election, and it was no accident.

"For a number of years now, the country has been much more aligned with Republicans philosophically than it has with Democrats," says former Republican Representative Mickey Edwards. "But we had been unsuccessful in putting together the kind of a campaign operation that could win a majority in Congress, and so, even though the public generally was sympathetic with Republican views, Republicans didn't call the shots. And Gingrich, more than anybody else, played a big role in changing that.''

In 1994, Gingrich was clearly a kingmaker. GOPAC set the agenda for the election by orchestrating the writing and signing of the Republican "Contract with America," and gave House candidates around the country marching orders, declaring that if the election was to be won on a large scale, their campaigns would have to turn not on local issues, as congressional campaigns normally do, but national issues, particularly Bill Clinton's ineptitude as president.

Gingrich himself was tireless, traveling around the country, stumping on a vision of imminent, welfare-induced, apocalypse: "If we are not careful, our children could inherit a dark and bloody planet in the twenty-first century," he intoned to a crowd of two hundred at American Legion hall in Tullahoma, Tennessee. His speech drew cheers and cries of "Amen!"

Gingrich was everywhere, making people pay for the privilege of meeting and eating with the likely future speaker of the House. Bill Paxon, head of the Republican National Campaign Committee, said Gingrich raised between $10,000 and $100,000 every time he spoke. By election day he is said to have personally raised $3 million.

In all, he visited 125 districts, and in each place he made sure his basic message got through: he and the Republicans were the last bulwark against absolute barbarism. "It is impossible to maintain a civilization with twelve-year-olds killing each other, seventeen-year-olds dying of AIDS, and eighteen-year-olds getting diplomas they can't read," he said time after time.

By October, Gingrich was certain of victory. On the campaign trail people were addressing him as "Mr. Speaker."

He quipped to the *Washington Post* that soon the Democrats would be contemplating measures similar to those taken two years before by Boris Yeltsin, when right-wing parliamentarians took over the Congress and threatened to topple him. "Based on their [the Democrats'] recent hysteria, [Chief of Staff] Leon [Panetta] will be asking Yeltsin, 'Well, exactly how did you do this?' " He added that George Stephanopoulos and Panetta would soon be looking for "dachas."

Election week, he received the supreme accolade, gracing the cover of *Time* with the caption: "Mad As Hell." His stepfather was so impressed by the picture of his son's grimacing face that he had the picture framed. Even Bob Dole, "the tax collector for the welfare state," had now made a peace of sorts with him. In a thirty-second commercial for the foundation he is affiliated with, the Better America Foundation, Dole featured himself with former Presidents Reagan and Bush and, inevitably, Newt Gingrich.

Gingrich made sure he was never far from the spotlight. He found a political twist to every issue to grab the nation's imagination. In the closing days of the campaign, he said Susan Smith, the South Carolina woman accused of killing her two children and then stealing the headlines, showed the sickness of the Democrats.

In desperation the Democrats tried hitting below the belt, faxing out anti-Gingrich materials so continuously that journalist David Remnick quipped in *The New Yorker*, "The Democratic Party has taken upon itself the research duties and the faxing of raw materials to a press finally grown bored with hammering nails into the President of the United States: the Gingrich divorce papers must be in the hands of every reporter from here to Maui." And Ben Jones, Gingrich's Democratic opponent, was saying things like, "Newt Gingrich represents the secret right-wing cabal aligned with Jerry Falwell and Pat Robertson and others—who have contributed millions [to GO-PAC] that have been concealed from the voters of the district." But it was to no avail.

For one thing, Jones' attack on Gingrich's links to

the religious right had little effect in a district filled with fundamentalist activists, many of whom, like Gingrich, had come to settle in Georgia from other states because the political climate there was so promising. Jones, better known as "Cooter" in the television series *The Dukes of Hazzard*, got more attention when he showed up at Gingrich campaign rallies with bloodhounds to show how little the "fugitive congressman" was available at home because Gingrich was so often out on the stump for other candidates. Gingrich countered that Jones could attend his rallies if he bought a ticket, "and the dogs can come for half price."

In the end, Jones claimed he was resorting to following Gingrich to out-of-state appearances as far afield as Connecticut and Alabama in order to attempt to debate him.

In the very last days of the campaign, however, Gingrich reappeared in his district, and immediately claimed a thirty-one-point lead in the polls. Jones disagreed. "The fact is, this is a dead heat," he said optimistically in early November, "and the question is, can he spend a half million dollars in the last four days of this race and salvage his career?"

Even though Gingrich knew he had the election basically sewn up, he hedged his bets. At a campaign stop, sounding just like the old-time pork barrel politicians he'd spent a career deriding, he told voters that they should reelect him because ". . . one thing's for sure, the Speaker of the House will be able to bring home a lot more bacon than a freshman."

The voters rallied to him. He won the election with sixty-four percent of the vote.

Gingrich had a lot more on his mind, though, than bringing home the bacon to suburban Marietta.

From his very first year in Congress, in 1979, Gingrich had not only wanted to bring about a Republican majority and propel himself to the position of Speaker; he had also wanted to radically change the balance of power within the United States government. "The Congress in the long run can change the country more dramatically than the President," he told *Congressional Quarterly* in 1979. "I think that's healthy. One of my goals is to make the House the co-equal of the White House."

Ironically, with the election of Bill Clinton, the first Democratic President in twelve years, Gingrich had been handed a golden opportunity to do just that. It was easy to delegitimize the indecisive and unpopular Clinton White House—especially with conservative talk-show hosts whipping their mass audiences into a feeding frenzy day after day, and a rabid *Wall Street Journal* editorial page inflaming the anti-Clinton ulcers of the financial elite. In a kind of trickle-down effect, innuendoes and half truths relayed by the newspaper's prestigious editorial page (suggestions that Clinton White House Counsel Vince Foster had been murdered and his body transferred from the murder site to the park where it was found; a story that a reporter investigating Hillary Clinton's former law firm was assaulted and beaten unconscious in his hotel room) were picked up by mass-market ideologues like Rush Limbaugh, who were able then to pass them off as fact. It is impossible to overestimate the effect the *Wall Street Journal* editorial page had in the midterm elections, and it will fall to a historian someday to write an account of the Clinton years, focusing particularly on the role played by the *Journal* in discrediting his administration, five days a week, to two million of the country's most powerful readers.

By September, Clinton's disapproval rating was at 51%, according to *USA Today*, and the G.O.P. was favored 48% to 45% in the congressional elections. By October, certain Democratic candidates were refusing Clinton's offers to come campaign for them. Some even ran campaign advertisements in which they criticized his policies.

At the same time that Clinton was going down, Gingrich's star was rising; paradoxically, by bringing down Congress as well. The Perot moment had taught

Gingrich that there was political gold to be mined in an anti-politics politics. By blocking legislation and perpetuating the Congress's appearance of gridlock, inefficiency, and imperial disdain for "normal Americans," Gingrich demolished the credibility of the very institution he sought to lead as a counter-power to the executive branch. He exploited the sense, already well honed, that the government took much but gave little of value in return—a popular sentiment that commentator Kevin Phillips had called the "politics of frustration."

The 103rd Congress was for him a permanent campaign event, and every Democratic bill he derailed or defeated supported his goal of showing the Democratic-controlled Congress as a hopelessly inefficient place incapable of reforming itself.

"Gridlock plays into his hands," Senator Carl M. Levin, the chief sponsor of a key lobbying-reform bill introduced in October, said before the Senate failed to silence the Republican filibusters and proceed with a vote. "If Gingrich can stop this from passing, it fits his political agenda. People will get mad at incumbents, and the minority party will benefit."

With Gingrich's help, the lobbying-reform bill never even got to a vote in the Senate.

From long experience as a bomb thrower, Gingrich knew, however, that it wasn't enough to be simply against the establishment; that alone, after all, had never gotten him his majority in Congress. He knew that he couldn't win without at least giving the appearance of being *for* something. He needed a pro-active platform as well. "Clinton is in such trouble with the American people that our job is to go out and offer a clear, positive alternative," he stated.

Thus was born the "Contract with America."

In January 1994, Gingrich had instructed Republican pollster Frank Luntz to conduct focus groups every ten days to sound out voters. What came from these discussions was the conviction that five issues were of greatest concern to Americans: debt, welfare, bureaucracy, taxes, and spending. With these results in hand, Representative Dick Armey of Texas and Gingrich set out to draft a specific program. The idea of the program was to include issues that would satisfy the demands of right-wing Republicans without scaring off moderates or creating division within the party at the moment it most needed to be unified.

As the drafting of the Contract entered its final stages in September 1994, Gingrich began raising funds for GOPAC by offering contributors a chance to influence the Republicans' congressional agenda. A fund-raising letter from that period signed by Gingrich asks, "Will you help me draft the Republican legislative agenda for the 104th Congress?" Although Gingrich asked the potential donors to complete a "Republican Legislative Survey" and return it with their checks, it is clear that by then Gingrich already knew what the legislative agenda would be. On September 27, Gingrich rallied more than three hundred G.O.P. candidates around the finished contract, which he billed as a revolutionary document. The Republican candidates, sitting members of Congress and challengers alike, participated in an elaborate ceremony in which the Contract was signed on the steps of the Capitol. The ceremony included a prayer, a recitation of the Pledge of Allegiance, candidates holding flags, a marching band, and red, white, and blue bunting. The men wore dark suits, the women predominately wore blue or red. Designed to resemble a *tableau vivant* of a historic moment, the ceremony bore the fingerprints of a professor of history fully aware of the weight of myth and iconography. It was perfectly stage-managed from start to finish to resonate with the appearance of a seminal and solemn moment in history, equivalent in significance to the launching of the New Deal or Washington crossing the Delaware. Newt Gingrich rose to the occasion.

"The point is to say to the American people: 'We want you to hold us accountable,'" he said at the ceremony.

"Today on these steps we offer this contract as a first step toward renewing American civilization. If America fails, our children will live on a dark and bloody planet.

"It may be a heroic dream," Gingrich said. "But isn't that what America is all about . . . the right to dream those heroic dreams," he added, echoing Ronald Reagan.

"If the American people accept this contract," vowed Gingrich, "we will have begun the journey to renew American civilization. Together we can renew America. Together we can help every American fulfill their unalienable right to pursue happiness and to seek the American dream. Together we can help every human across the planet seek freedom, prosperity, safety, and the rule of law. That is what is at stake."

Michael Kelly described the scene in *The New Yorker*. "If American life had not vaulted beyond parody some time back, the scene would have seemed a joke, of sorts: a hundred and fifty members of Congress and some two hundred people who would very much like to be members of Congress standing in front of the institution they served, or wished to serve, in order to rail against it, as if they were the Free Silverites or Dust Bowl farmers come to smite the corruption of Washington."

One hundred-fifty of the signatories to the document were incumbent lawmakers, but they, too, had no qualms about presenting themselves as outsiders seeking to reform a decaying institution. Even Bob Michel, who had been in Congress thirty-seven years and was retiring, denounced the "decades of neglect and mismanagement."

Like the Ten Commandments, or the Bill of Rights, the Contract contains ten essential points.

The pledge, which was subsequently published as an advertisement in *TV Guide,* promised that on the first day of the new congressional session the Republican majority would pass a series of reforms changing the way Congress operates: requiring that all laws that apply to the rest of the country apply to the Congress, guaranteeing a "comprehensive" audit of the Congress by an independent auditing firm; reducing the number of House committees and reducing their staffs by one-third; setting term limits for committee chairs; forbidding members to cast proxy votes in committees, opening committee meetings to the public, requiring a three-fifths majority vote to pass tax increases, and implementing "zero base-line budgeting."

The contract also promised: "Within the first 100 days of the 104th Congress, we shall bring to the House floor the following bills, each to be given full and open debate, each to be given a clear and fair vote and each to be immediately available this day for public inspection and scrutiny."

The bills were:

The Fiscal Responsibility Act, calling for a Constitutional amendment to balance the budget and a line-item veto to "restore fiscal responsibility to an out-of-control Congress."

The Taking Back Our Streets Act, calling for stronger truth-in-sentencing, "good faith" exclusionary rule exemptions, permitting evidence obtained in warrantless searches to be admitted in court, reducing prisoners' abilities to bring lawsuits, permitting the deportation of illegal aliens who commit aggravated felonies, tougher death penalty laws, and cutting crime prevention programs in the Clinton crime bill in favor of more funds for prison construction and police.

The Personal Responsibility Act, advocating refusing welfare benefits to mothers under age 18 and refusing additional Aid to Families with Dependent Children [AFDC] benefits to women who have children while on welfare, reducing welfare spending, requiring mothers to identify their children's fathers in order to receive AFDC benefits, limiting benefits to two years, and instituting workfare requirements.

The Family Reinforcement Act, strengthening child support enforcement laws, providing a refundable tax credit for adoption expenses, "strengthening the rights of parents in their children's education," and advocating tax credits for families taking care of dependent older parents.

The American Dream Restoration Act, which promises a $500-per-child tax credit, aims to reduce the tax burden on married couples, and calls for tax-deferred IRA's that can be used for the purchase of a first home or for education expenses, as well as for retirement.

The National Security Restoration Act, calling for the removal of all U.S. troops from U.N. command and staving off further decreases in military spending.

The Senior Citizens Fairness Act, raising the salary threshold for social security recipients, lowering taxes on Social Security benefits, and giving tax incentives to senior citizens to purchase health insurance.

The Job Creation and Wage Enhancement Act, calling for a 50 percent cut in the capital gains rate, giving a series of incentives to small businesses, requiring Congress to issue cost analyses on all mandates to state and local governments.

The Common Sense Legal Reform Act, with "loser pays" rules, uniform product liability laws limiting some damages, controls on attorneys who work on contingency fees.

The Citizen Legislature Act, setting term limits for representatives and senators.

That night, the Republicans feted themselves at a $5,000 per table fund-raiser that netted $500,000 in donations.

Interestingly, the contract says that the Republican majority will *try to introduce* legislation aimed at implementing these ten points, but offers no guarantees that any legislation will in fact be passed. The Republicans say that if they fail, their constituents can opt not to reelect them—an option, one would presume, they had from the start. Right from the start the contract leaves open the possibility that the "liberal welfare state" may cause its defeat. Meaning that, in 1996, the

Republicans will have a powerful platform one way or the other.

After the signing, the Democrats, led by House Majority Leader Richard Gephardt, immediately went on the offensive, saying "the contract would blow a hole in the federal budget of roughly $1 trillion." They called it the "Contract *on* America." Democratic National Committee chairman David Wilhelm dismissed it as "voodoo part two, the son of Reaganomics." Even some Republicans had their doubts. Two weeks before the contract was formally presented to the public, Gingrich held a dinner at the Republican Capitol Hill Club with G.O.P. intellectuals who expressed skepticism with his platform.

The Democrats thought that the contract would allow them to shift the focus of the election away from personal attacks on Clinton to specific issues; they thought they could convince voters that the ideas of the Republicans were bad. Suddenly, instead of having to defend Clinton, they, too, could go on the offensive. They pointed out that the only way to fulfill the contract would be to dramatically reduce Social Security or Medicare, since the two huge sacred cows of middle-class entitlement were expected to account for half of the budget in fiscal year 2002.

At a press briefing on October 7, President Clinton himself seized on this theme: "Do they really want this contract, which is a trillion dollars of unfunded promises, a contract which certainly will lead to higher deficits, cuts in Medicare and throwing us back to the years of the eighties when we lost jobs and weakened our country? Or do we want to face up to the challenges and use the next Congress to keep the economic growth going, to pass health care reform, to pass political reform, to deal with these environmental issues?"

Gingrich shrugged off these objections.

"If all you wanted to worry about was how do you maximize public anger and minimize your own risk, no contract would have been a safer stand," he said when asked by *Time* about the perceived flaws Democrats were pointing out in the contract. ''It also would have been worse for America. In the long run, the party that stands for something and is willing to live by what it stands for has an enormous edge over the party that is cynical and negative and has only smear campaigns and attack advertising.'' The truth was, he knew these objections didn't really matter.

Democrats and various experts said that $700 billion would have to be cut from the budget in the next seven years to keep the deficit from exploding. Before the election, Gingrich said he hoped to balance the budget by eliminating waste, fraud, and abuse—the same promise Ronald Reagan was unable to keep in his eight years in the White House. But that didn't matter either.

The truth was, the Democrats were barking up the wrong tree.

Pundits and politicians have debated the Contract in every conceivable way. They have discussed balanced budgets, unfunded mandates, dynamic scoring. For the time being, no one seems to be able to say whether some of the more ambitious items in the manifesto are actually viable. But the truth is, as far as the elections were concerned, it didn't matter. In an election year no one really needed to prove whether those particular policies were implementable because no one really cared. The Republicans swept the elections—and the contract had virtually nothing to do with it.

Polls conducted after the election showed that the specifics of the proposed legislation were seldom a factor in the decisions of voters about candidates and that, in truth, the content of the contract had an almost negligible impact on the choices Americans made at the voting booth. In fact, a poll taken after the election showed that seventy-two percent of respondents, presumably a group made up of a representative cross-section of Americans, said they had never heard of the contract. And sixty-five percent said they didn't know enough about Gingrich to have an opinion of him.

What they did know, however, was that they were angry—and they had been angry for some time. And they knew that in the form, if not in the content, of their presentation the Republicans somehow were echoing that anger. As has been said many times before, while the United States' GNP had doubled since 1970, the incomes of middle-class Americans had stagnated, if not declined. Manufacturing jobs, as many have pointed out, had been disappearing and the "symbolic processing" jobs promised by Democrats such as Secretary of Labor Robert Reich had been slow to appear. In addition, many Americans felt there was something unmistakably wrong with America's social and political institutions.

The Democrats made a fatal error in whipping out their calculators with glee and analyzing the specifics of the contract. In doing so, they only increased their perception among the public as an out-of-touch "wonkdom" running the country into the ground. They should have realized that it was the spirit and not the letter of the contract that mattered.

The Contract merely existed to reiterate for the few stragglers who hadn't gotten the message already that the Republicans were fully attuned to their resentments over welfare, affirmative action, and the social pathologies of the underclass—as well as those of the media and political "elites." Gingrich applied the Perot method of addressing intricate problems ("I'm just an ordinary guy like you with commonsense solutions") for a population that was fed up.

The Contract articulated what had been Gingrich's strategy all along: to nationalize the midterm elections. It shifted the issues from the local concerns that are normally the focus of congressional campaigns to the future of the country as a whole.

In *The New Yorker*, Michael Kelly referred to Gingrich as the member from "Madderthanhell—a state that in this election autumn has become the most powerful in the union." The inhabitants of "Madderthanhell" are the so-called "angry white males" to whom many analysts have attributed the Republican landslide. "That group of people is tired of being an epithet . . . and civil rights laws are an intrusive form of regulation . . . that has hurt them very directly and very personally," said David Frum, the author of *Dead Right,* at a post-election victory bash organized by former Quayle Chief of Staff William Kristol's Project for the Republican Future.

It could be argued, though, that the "angry white males" were not the most important factor in the 1994 elections. Angry white males didn't slap themselves on the back in late November, congratulating themselves on getting out the vote. The Christian Coalition, however, did. After the election the coalition described a "surge in participation by white evangelical born-again voters." Arthur J. Kropp, president of People for the American Way, a watchdog group that monitors the religious right, agreed: "The biggest story in Washington, D.C., isn't the Republican Party takeover of Congress," he said in January. "It's the ascendancy of a political movement that was once considered to be 'political exotica' and which now, amazingly, commands the loyalty of the leaders of both houses of Congress."

Exit polls in November found that fully thirty-three percent of all voters were self-identified evangelicals—the largest turnout in history, according to Ralph Reed, executive director of Pat Robertson's Christian Coalition. That number was nearly double the number that religious conservatives represented in the 1988 presidential race, and well beyond the fifteen percent of the voting population that the Christian Coalition has long said it must secure in order to form a voting bloc with real and recognizable power.

The evangelicals supported Republican House candidates 69 percent of the time, Senate Republicans 68 percent of the time, and Republican gubernatorial candidates 71 percent of the time. People for the American Way says that candidates supported by the Christian right won 60 percent of the races they entered. In Pennsylvania alone, the Christian Coalition distributed 2.4 million voter guides highlighting Senate-candidate Rick Santorum's "pro-life and pro-family" views. According to the conservative weekly *Human Events*, 38 of the new Republican House seats went "to candidates who either stoutly embraced religious conservatism or who welcomed to their ranks religious conservative activists."

In the South, whose suburbanites now form one of the country's most significant voting blocks, the Christian Coalition regularly makes or breaks races. The Republicans, says Ben Jones, "cannot win without the [Christian Coalition]. That's how they got so many blue-collar white folks in the South." Indeed, according to Georgia political observer Bill Shipp, Democratic incumbent Congressman Buddy Darden was defeated in the Seventh District in 1994 "principally because of the Christian Coalition."

One of the more curious aspects of the 1994 Republican landslide is that despite the huge evangelical turnout, the moral and cultural issues that had so shaken the 1992 elections were almost completely absent, at least overtly. Abortion and school prayer were not mentioned at all in the "Contract with America," a decision that Gingrich made over the objections of Dick Armey. Gingrich "felt it would be a red flag that would be focused on by the liberal media to characterize our effort as radical right-wing," Armey told the *Washington Post*.

Does this mean that the Gingrich Republicans have in fact backed away from these hot-button social issues?

"People of faith know better," says the Christian Coalition's Ralph Reed, who was described once by the *Wall Street Journal*'s Paul A. Gigot as someone who "looks like a cherub but thinks like Machiavelli." What the "people of faith" know is that the evangelical turnout for the Republicans, which was so strong despite the absence of school prayer and abortion in the contract, was part of a concerted strategy elaborated long before the election.

In an article entitled "Casting a Wider Net," published in *Policy Review*, the journal of the Heritage Foundation, in the summer of 1993, Reed wrote that the "pro-family movement . . . [t]hough blessed with talented leadership, strong grassroots support, and enormous financial resources, has not yet connected its agenda with average voters" and "still has limited appeal even among the forty million voters who attend church frequently, identify themselves as evangelicals or orthodox Roman Catholics, and consider themselves traditionalists on cultural issues."

To approach these voters, Reed wrote, the Christian Coalition had to downplay its moral and cultural message and focus instead on "policies that personally benefit voters—such as tax cuts, education vouchers, higher wages, or retirement benefits. Without specific policies designed to benefit families and children, appeals to family values or America's Judeo-Christian heritage will fall on deaf ears." To win "at the ballot box and in the court of public opinion," he said, "the pro-family movement must speak to the concerns of average voters in the areas of taxes, crime, government waste, health care, and financial security."

The "Contract with America" was Newt Gingrich's way to "cast a wider net," and insure a broad coalition of people whose interests, in the long run, may not coincide: like wealthy Northern, urban, *Wall Street Journal* editorial page readers and Southern fundamentalists. As Reed says, "If religious and economic conservatives can cooperate where possible and remain civil in disagreement, they will accomplish far more together than separately."

The potential effect that the Christian Coalition could have on reordering American life and culture cannot be underestimated. Evangelicals have long called for dismantling the Department of Education, decentralizing the schools in the goal of allowing local communities to monitor more thoroughly their curricula and, presumably, make religion central to them. And the Christian Coalition represents the "liberal" end of the fundamentalist political movement. In Cobb County, the spiritual and financial heart of Gingrich's congressional district, one resident and political observer says, "The Christian Coalition are considered mainstream centrists—probably a little too liberal for some folks. The Reconstructionists—people who believe in the absolute literal word of the Bible, who believe that the penalty for being homosexual should not be just death but death by stoning, are closer to what most of the religious conservatives in this district believe."

Never one to mince words, after the election Jesse Jackson said that a force resembling the Christian Coalition "was a strong force in Germany. It laid down a suitable, scientific, theological rationale for the tragedy in Germany. The Christian Coalition was very much in evidence there."

There is no doubt that the Republican landslide of 1994 owes a lot of its strength to "stealth" campaigns by groups on the political right, including the Christian Coalition. According to Democratic analysts, last fall the coalition handed out voter guides that, while in appearance seemed nonpartisan and factual, contained covert endorsements of Republican candidates. *Time* magazine noted that one such voter guide, handed out for "educational reference" in Oklahoma, contained a description of the Democratic candidate for Senate, Representative Dave McCurdy, as a supporter of "banning ownership of legal firearms." The statement was based on McCurdy's vote for the 1994 crime bill, which included a ban on nineteen types of assault weapons but not on all legal firearms, as the voter guide suggested.

In other states, "non-partisan" voter education advertisements would often be aired immediately before advertisements for Republican candidates and would replicate the exact tone and message of the candidate's own campaign ads—often going so far as to use the same jingle. The Democratic Congressional Campaign Committee has filed complaints with the Federal Election Commission alleging that the Christian Coalition, along with a group called Americans for Tax Reform, led by Grover Norquist, have broken the "expressed advocacy" rule, which prohibits groups doing voter education from endorsing a specific candidate. Voter guides and voter education campaigns are a particularly powerful form of support for candidates, for the groups that sponsor them are under no obligation to disclose the amount of money they spend in an election to the Federal Election Commission. Nor are they required to disclose the sources of their own funding. Democratic Party sources said that if these "educational" efforts were tallied up and counted as partisan campaign spending, Democratic candidates were often outspent five to one in 1994.

Newt Gingrich has a long association with the religious right dating back to the Reagan revolution, and some have speculated that his election strategies were frequently developed in cooperation with the Christian Coalition.

Beginning in 1982, Gingrich strongly supported an amendment to the Constitution proposed by Ronald Reagan to allow voluntary prayer in schools. "Nothing in this Constitution shall be construed to prohibit individual or group prayer in public institutions," the amendment read. "No persons shall be required by the United States or by any state to participate in prayer."

"This is a well-drafted amendment," Gingrich said. "It makes it unconstitutional to force children to pray, but lets the children who want to pray participate in a voluntary prayer session. . . . It would get the Supreme Court out of the business of deciding if our children can pray."

In 1986, Gingrich was endorsed by fundamentalist preacher Jerry Falwell. By 1987 he was holding "town hall meetings," open community meetings that he had generally held in city halls and county courthouses in churches, usually Baptist. That year he applauded the work of Protestant fundamentalist missionaries in Central America: "America's missionaries may be more powerful than anything else America does in the long run," he told the *Atlanta Journal and Constitution.* "People who come to believe in religious salvation—particularly first-generation religious fundamentalists—have the enthusiasm and the energy to compete head-to-head with communists."

In 1988, Pat Robertson's "invisible army" swamped Republican Party meetings in Georgia and, through stealth maneuvers, ultimately won control of the state's delegation to the Republican National Convention. That year Gingrich sided with the Moral Majority's Falwell in opposing a civil rights restoration bill, which required federal funds to be cut off to institutions that discriminated against minorities, women, the elderly, or the handicapped because, he said, it endorsed a "secular, left-wing value system." Falwell had charged that loopholes in the bill could require religious institutions to hire atheists or teach about homosexuality. In the course of the debate on the bill, which was vetoed by Ronald Reagan and overridden by Congress, Gingrich said he and other conservative congressmen were drafting a "religious Bill of Rights" that would protect religious institutions from values imposed by the government.

Some Christian activists felt betrayed by the lack of positions on social and cultural issues in the "Contract with America." They were somewhat mollified after the election, though, when Gingrich promised to introduce an amendment on school prayer.

"It was significant that the contract failed to include these [social] items. But I think the error was corrected by Newt when he came out very strongly supporting voluntary prayer in schools," says former Congressman William Dannemeyer, who is active in support of an amendment to the Constitution allowing voluntary prayer in schools.

Dannemeyer makes it clear, though, that Gingrich

will have to strengthen his allegiance to the religious right if he hopes to hold onto his power base in the coming years. "I think drafting those ten points and not including the social items reflects the desire on the part of Newt to pacify, to keep going down the same road as Representatives Nancy Johnson of Connecticut and Steve Gunderson of Wisconsin. These are activist liberals on the Republican side. And I think Newt makes a serious mistake in accommodating those small minority members the way he has. Those members I have identified—and there are others—are totally out of sync with the vast majority of the new clout of freshmen coming to the House. They're gut conservatives. They want not only the economic issues but also the social issues."

Even Ralph Reed's plan to hold his troops together behind the banner of economic issues has already failed the test of time. In February 1995 he announced that the Christian Coalition would refuse to support any candidate who did not have an explicit anti-abortion stance. At a Conservative Political Action conference on February 10, he said that "pro-life and pro-family voters, a third of the electorate, will not support a party that retreats from its noble and historic defense of traditional values and which has a national ticket or a platform that does not share Ronald Reagan's belief in the sanctity of innocent human life."

"The coalition is a three-legged stool," he said then to the *Wall Street Journal*, describing a structure made up of economic free-marketeers, anti-government Perot supporters, and believers in conservative "family values." "To win in 1996, Republicans need to remain steadfastly loyal to each of those three issue clusters."

Newt Gingrich, in his own way, keeps the faith.

He wasn't supposed to attend the "Georgia Salute to Newt" celebration held in his honor on the night after his swearing-in. He had sworn to keep the House in session until all hours of the night, and not take any breaks until the work was done. He couldn't keep away, though. At about ten o'clock, during a floor vote, he showed up on the stage at the party, and, catching Lee Greenwood about two-thirds of the way through a rendition of "Georgia on My Mind," called for a moment of silence. There were just two or three things that he wanted to say, he told the crowd, *Pray for Georgia*, he said. *Pray for the House of Representatives. Pray for the Senate. Pray for the President. Pray for Newt Gingrich*, in all the work he had ahead of him. Many in the crowd were enthralled.

Brantley Harwell, Gingrich's former pastor and close friend from Carrollton, says, "I pray for Newt regularly. I believe God changes people. And I pray for Newt, that he will become what I think is inside him, a statesman. I just believe that if Newt could get the dark side out of himself, the mean side, the caustic side, and could let his lighter, brighter side come out, let his statesmanship come out, he could do this country an awful lot of good. But do it in a kind, sweet spirit."

9

Newt, Inc.

One afternoon in early October 1994, seemingly on a whim, Newt Gingrich abandoned his schedule, raced from his second-floor office to the House floor, and in five minutes blasted the last drops of life out of the already drooping Democratic-sponsored lobbying-reform bill, a bill he had previously supported. The bill required groups giving more than $2,500 to a congressman to register as a lobby and report the sources of their funding. It also prohibited members of Congress from accepting gifts such as meals, entertainment, or travel. Singling out one minor clause that required greater disclosure of grass-roots lobbying and third-party lobbying reimbursement, Gingrich said, incorrectly, that it was "designed to kill pressure from back home that has been so effective in this Congress."

Gingrich had written to House Speaker Tom Foley in March 1994 asking that those very provisions be included in the bill, which would merely have required lawmakers to disclose financial backers. Now he was claiming that it would force groups to disclose their membership lists.

The voice of the Christian Coalition, perhaps the most effective lobbying group of the era, and which had specifically protested the disclosure clause, spoke through him. Ralph Reed, the executive director of the Christian Coalition, had sent faxes to one thousand chapter chairmen in fifty states asking them to swamp the Congress with calls. He also had turned to Pat Robertson, the Coalition's founder, who denounced the bill on his weekly *700 Club* television program, which reaches ten million viewers. Robertson said the bill is "one of the most shocking attempts to limit your freedom of speech, and the rights of Christian people and other groups concerned about the out-of-control government."

In the wake of Gingrich's intervention, thirty-five Democrats crossed party lines and voted with him on a procedural rule prior to the bill's final passage. The Senate then refused to pass the bill, after Gingrich rallied three hundred radio talk-show hosts, the Christian Coalition, and the *Wall Street Journal* editorial page to oppose the measure.

He later told lobbyists that they should contribute to the G.O.P. out of gratitude for his killing the lobbying-reform bill.

Senator Jesse Helms led a filibuster of the bill in the Senate. When he ended his speech, he was applauded by the lobbyists gathered in the gallery.

"There's something wrong when a senator can filibuster that bill and walk off the floor of the Senate and be cheered by lobbyists," President Clinton stated. The bill passed the House but died in the Senate, where the Republican filibuster could not be broken.

The incident shows the amazing synergy Gingrich had managed to create among his political supporters, financial backers, and congressional allies. It also showed that he would not hesitate to wield this awesome power to achieve his own ends. And he did not hesitate; later in October, Gingrich warned representatives of political action committees that if he became House speaker in January 1995, "For anybody who's not on board now it's going to be the two coldest years in Washington."

Some say that Gingrich's greatest accomplishment

as a politician has not been as a lawmaker or in constituent services, but in the creation of an interlocking set of powerful vehicles allowing him and like-minded Republicans to acquire political power, culminating in the sweeping victory of 1994.

While gradually taking over the Republican Congressional Campaign Committee in the mid-1980s, Gingrich began to develop a theory that in order to win a majority, Republicans needed to coordinate legislative and campaign strategies, and to nationalize House elections instead of just targeting a few seats at a time. They also needed a machine to develop winning candidates.

That machine was, essentially, dropped into Gingrich's lap when in 1986, Delaware Governor Pierre S. "Pete" DuPont, preparing for his 1988 presidential bid, asked Gingrich to take over his political action committee, GOPAC. GOPAC had operated since 1979, bundling together donations to state Republican parties and candidates.

DuPont said Gingrich was "head and shoulders" above other candidates for the job, even though up to then he had played no role in the organization. He had the right ideas, the right drive. DuPont offered to hand GOPAC over to Gingrich over breakfast one day in Washington.

"He said, 'Are you serious? Let me think about it,'" DuPont told the *Washington Post*. "He was on the phone an hour later saying it was a wonderful idea."

Under Gingrich's leadership, GOPAC began to develop a farm team of candidates at every level. It became a kind of idea machine for the Republican Party, with free campaign tips for candidates, like the car cassette tapes of Gingrich's speeches and the tapes teaching candidates how to "talk like Newt." Critics charged that within a few years, GOPAC was merely an extension of Newt Gingrich, which allowed him to groom an entire generation of G.O.P. politicians in his own image.

Democrats say that GOPAC, with its $2 million annual budget, was a way for rich supporters to fill the coffers of Republican consultants and finance Gingrich's travels around the country building up a cadre of like-minded Republican candidates. But Gingrich has described GOPAC, which has spent nearly $8 million since 1991 in recruiting, training, and campaigning for G.O.P. candidates, as the Bell Labs of G.O.P. politics. The two explanations don't necessarily contradict each other. For GOPAC, with its motivational tapes, its reading lists, its training sessions, and its lexicon, could very well be called the Newt Gingrich Information Superhighway.

In the years leading up to the 1994 elections, Gingrich traveled constantly for GOPAC. He spoke to conservative groups and young Republicans, developing a sometimes automatic-seeming spiel that was part motivational training, part history lecture, and part pure Gingrich gospel. It was based on five hundred pages of thoughts and ideas—musings on the "liberal welfare state" and the "conservative opportunity society," updated every now and then to take the appropriate digs at whatever Democrat needed dressing down and aimed at training a generation of young Republicans in the tactics of pit bulls. He called the House a "corrupt institution," called the Democratic leadership "decadent" and "sick."

"I'll do almost anything to win a Republican majority in the Congress," Gingrich would vow on his travels. "I will not rest until I have transformed the landscape of American politics. . . . I want to shift the entire planet, and I'm doing it."

In the 1992 elections, despite losing the White House, the Republicans gained ten seats in Congress, largely thanks to GOPAC's training. "My strategy was always [that] you just kept building momentum and building momentum and you would capture seventy to eighty percent of the incoming freshmen every two years and at some point you would have transformed the whole structure," he told the *Washington Post* late in 1994. His theory was borne out by the 1994 elections. In his December speech accepting the G.O.P. nomination for Speaker, Gingrich asked the 230 Republican conference members to raise their hands if they had been helped by GOPAC. All but a few held their hands high, proving that after nearly ten years it had become the most powerful political machine in America.

"Newt used GOPAC to create the strategy for what is really a revolution in American politics," former Representative William Dannemeyer says.

"If you look at the people that Gingrich helped elect this time, many, if not most of them, did not have any prior political experience," said a Democratic political consultant. "And what GOPAC does is it pierces the veil of mystery around how politics and campaigns work for these people who did not have a great deal of background or experience in it. GOPAC says that some forty-three members of the current Republican class were GOPAC recruits. They have a list of nineteen thousand people they call their farm team. And I think, in the prior Congress they said some thirty were, and in the prior one, some twenty. So you have close to half the Republican conference who have some ties, allegiance, loyalties to Gingrich and GOPAC."

In the wake of its overarching successes, the PAC's finances remain somewhat mysterious. In 1992, for example, GOPAC announced that it would compile $17 million for Republican congressional candidates; it ended up contributing directly about a tenth of that amount. The rest was spent on training sessions, videotapes, and cassettes and travel by Gingrich.

Early on in his political career, Gingrich had sworn to remain independent of financial interests and to keep all his fundraising activities out in the open. In 1974, running in his first congressional race, he had said that he would "file at regular intervals with every public and high school library in the district" the records of his and his staff's campaign activities. He said he would strictly follow the $1,000 contribution limit from individuals "so that special interests cannot dominate my actions."

But over the years GOPAC has operated by peculiar financing arrangements that have allowed Gingrich to collect millions of dollars from a small pool of wealthy businessmen without disclosing their names.

GOPAC has long claimed that because its funds are not directly used to aid candidates for federal office, it does not need to register as a federal PAC and comply with FEC disclosure laws. (Under federal law, any group that raises or spends more than $1,000 to influence federal elections must register as a political committee with the FEC.) The Democratic Congressional Campaign Committee forced the issue in September 1990, filing a complaint with the FEC alleging that GOPAC had been raising and spending funds for the purpose of influencing federal elections without registering as a federal PAC. As evidence, the DCCC offered a solicitation letter from GOPAC signed by Gingrich that asked for money to help "break the Democrat's [sic] iron grip on Congress by building a new Republican majority in the House of Representatives." The letter added that GOPAC's Campaign for Fair Elections "will defeat or seriously weaken a large number of Democrats in 1990," and said that GOPAC was "dedicated to building a Republican majority at all levels of government."

When the complaint was first issued, Gingrich denied the charge, saying it "is as phony and as inaccurate as everything else the DCCC has said about me. . . ." Nonetheless, on May 8, 1991, GOPAC registered as a federal PAC, one day before the FEC announced that it agreed with the claim filed by the DCCC.

The FEC has no enforcement power, and in cases that violators of election laws refuse to abide voluntarily by its rulings, it has to rely on the courts. On April 14, 1994, after a two-and-half year investigation, the commission filed a complaint in U.S. District Court for the District of Columbia, alleging that GOPAC violated election law over a two-year period from 1989 to 1991 by not registering as a federal PAC and not reporting more than $500,000 in financial activity. The FEC asked the court to declare GOPAC in violation of federal election law on three counts, force GOPAC to pay a fine of at least $500,000, and require GOPAC to disclose its finances for the two-year period after it allegedly became a federal committee in 1989.

GOPAC argues that as long as it doesn't support specific candidates, its role is to educate and train candidates, which is protected by free speech and thus not subject to FEC regulations on disclosure.

Contradicting himself somewhat in response to the allegations, Gingrich noted that the Democratic Leadership Council "produced Bill Clinton." Then, in September 1994 when the Georgia Democratic Party filed a state ethics complaint alleging that GOPAC violated state law by failing to report nearly $500,000 donated by about a dozen Georgians, and that same month the FEC fined Gingrich's 1992 campaign $3,800 for failing to disclose in a timely way more than $30,000 in contributions, Gingrich grew nervous. In October he said he planned to step down and recommend that GOPAC find a new head.

In December, shortly after Gingrich was nominated Speaker, GOPAC sought to have the lawsuit dismissed, saying that the fund-raising letter cited by the DCCC complaint was not an attempt to influence a federal election because it did not endorse a specific candidate. "GOPAC said 'Hey, we would love to get a Republican majority in Congress,'" GOPAC's lawyer said. "We didn't expressly ask you to vote for a particular candidate."

In January 1995, GOPAC allowed a list of "non-federal" contributors to be examined. The list showed that it had received $236,000 in the 45 days since the election. A spokesperson for a Democratic organization said GOPAC staffers were clearly uncomfortable with this unique peek into their finances. They refused to allow reporters to Xerox or film the list, forcing reporters to copy it by hand. A staffer from the Democratic National Committee who ran out of paper while copying the list was told GOPAC couldn't lend her a sheet of paper.

At this time GOPAC still has not fully disclosed all its donors through 1995. In addition, GOPAC has never shown how the money it collected was disbursed.

"They could be doing anything with their money," said one Democratic source. "They could be investing in gold futures; there's no disclosure."

GOPAC is the jewel in the crown of Gingrich's vast political empire. It was GOPAC that gave him money to put where his mouth always was. It was GOPAC that gave him power, that built his "farm team" of followers, that propelled him to the Speakership of the House.

And yet these days Gingrich says that it is not strengthening GOPAC—it is not even being Speaker of the House—that matters most to him. It is instead teaching a Saturday morning lecture course at Reinhardt College, a tiny, private business college located about fifty miles north of Atlanta in Waleska, Georgia.

In his course lectures Gingrich elaborates on his idea that because of its unique history and demographics, America has a leading role to play in the modern world if it doesn't succumb to the decay brought on by the liberal welfare state, a "second-wave model" of society ill suited to the challenges of the twenty-first century. The characteristics of the liberal welfare state—big government, regulation, and welfare—are foreign to the American character, Gingrich says, because they sap individual initiative and ultimately lead to degeneracy. If the nation's current downward slide is to be arrested, and if America is to avoid the tragic fate of other great civilizations and lead the world into the "third wave information age," the country must embrace its inherent characteristics.

The central points that Gingrich makes are often reiterated by graphics in block letters on his videotapes and the companion materials that accompany them, breaking down his abstract thoughts into concrete, bite-sized chunks of information.

For example, according to Gingrich, the Five Pillars of American Civilization are:

1. Personal strength
2. Entrepreneurial strength
3. The spirit of invention and discovery
4. Quality as described by Deming
5. The lessons of American history

Those qualities, he says, must be reflected at all levels of American society if we are to maintain our competitiveness in world markets and therefore our freedom. To illustrate these points, Gingrich often refers to actual companies or persons, some of whom are GOPAC or Renewing American Civilization contributors.

Which is why, stumped by the obvious shallowness of the course, ("[Gingrich] throws around lists of American values and American characteristics. . . . They're not highly controversial or provocative; they're essentially meaningless," says Alan Brinkley, a professor of history at Columbia University who is familiar with the lecture series) many critics have called Renewing American Civilization little more than a twenty-hour advertisement for sympathetic corporate entities.

The course, as originally conceived by Gingrich, contained substantive mentions of major contributors to GOPAC or to the Progress and Freedom Foundation, a thinktank created in April 1993 that raised $400,000 to fund Renewing American Civilization's first semester at a Georgia state school, Kennesaw College, and still funds the course. Although Gingrich is not paid for the course, its costs are high because it is also offered at 132 sites in 31 states via satellite.

Gingrich's course is carried on National Empowerment Television, a cable network founded by Free

Congress Foundation Chairman Paul Weyrich, a conservative stalwart who was one of the leading members of the Moral Majority in the 1980s and a founder of the Heritage Foundation. Weyrich is one of the leading lights in the Christian right's battles against gay rights, abortion, the Equal Rights Amendment, and the foes of tax breaks to private schools, all of which he calls part of "the age-old conflict between good and evil, between the forces of God and the forces against God." His goal, he has said, is "Christianizing America."

Weyrich says Gingrich doesn't altogether share this goal, but he is willing to work with him nonetheless. "I think [Gingrich's vision] is sort of New Age conservatism which I don't entirely share," says Weyrich. "I come from a profoundly different point of view than Gingrich does. My views are religiously based, they are rooted in a theological view of the world and his are not, and we have a coincidence of interest and cooperation on our allies, but we are by no means coming at this from the same direction. So his conservatism is . . . anti-liberalism wedded with new technology and hoping in science."

Weyrich's connection with Gingrich dates back to 1974, when Gingrich approached the Free Congress Foundation for help with his first campaign. Despite their differences, Weyrich says he has supported Gingrich because, "I recognized long ago that one must not let the perfect be the enemy of the good, and Newt will end up doing some good for this country, and therefore I think it is proper that we support him and advance his interests even though they are not totally coincidental with our own."

At least two major GOPAC contributors, Robert Krieble and Richard DeVos, are affiliated with the Free Congress Foundation.

National Empowerment Television, a twenty-four-hour conservative cable network, carries both excerpts from the course and *The Progress Report*, a talk show co-hosted by Gingrich, where he answers

telephone calls à la Larry King. That program is
sponsored by the Golden Rule Insurance Company,
whose chairman and president gave $117,076 to GO-
PAC between 1991 and 1993. At the time of the 1994
election, the House Energy and Commerce Committee, led by Democrat John Dingell, was investigating
allegations that Golden Rule failed to pay off claims.
With the replacement of the chairman by a Republican, Democratic Hill staffers told *Newsweek* that they
doubt the investigation will continue.

Gingrich has also reached an agreement to broadcast the course on the Mind Extension University
cable network, which is owned by Glen Jones of
Jones Intercable. In addition, John Malone, owner of
Telecommunications Inc., the country's largest cable
distribution system, has said that he is interested in
picking up NET programming, including Gingrich's
productions, for his cable system. Malone and other
cable system operators have been lobbying Capitol
Hill for years to force the deregulation of the cable industry.

The Progress and Freedom Foundation assumes full
financial responsibility for the distribution of Renewing American Civilization via satellite and tapes. The
foundation also receives royalties from the sale of the
text and videotapes of the course.

At the time that the course was first put together,
Roll Call has reported, solicitation letters were sent
out to companies, guaranteeing that contributors of
$25,000 or more would be able to assist in developing
the course. In "Quality and Deming's Profound
Knowledge," for example, one of the lectures contained in the video series version of the course,
Gingrich spends fifteen minutes praising textile mag-
nate Roger Milliken—listed among the donors to the
course. Milliken and his father, Gerrish, have given at
least $345,000 to GOPAC since 1985. In the course
Gingrich also praises Thomas Kershaw, the owner of
the Cheers bar in Boston, who has contributed at least
$63,000 to GOPAC. HealthSouth, a Birmingham-based

rehabilitation center chain, is featured at length in one of the lectures titled "Health and Wellness." The company has contributed at least $15,000 to the course.

In addition, a course memorandum may show that corporate sponsors may have donated to the course in return for Gingrich's expressing support for specific political ideas. The May 10, 1993, memo from Pamela Prochnow, GOPAC finance director, is addressed to Jeff Eisenach and Joe Gaylord and describes a meeting with Richard Berman, of Berman and Company, a lobbying firm that represents restaurant chains. "I think there is a very real possibility of $20,000–$25,000 if the course can incorporate some of the ideas mentioned in the *Journal of Labor Research*, volume XIV, number 3," Prochnow wrote. "[Berman's] primary concern is a discussion of what he call "genesis employment opportunities—the idea that entry-level positions are not necessarily 'dead end.' ""

While the course does not mentions any of Berman's clients, last year's version does contain the following comments by Gingrich, who has opposed Clinton's plan to raise the minimum wage: "The welfare state, they say, 'Well, you're just going to worry about getting a hamburger flipping job.' Well, it's a first step. It's not a last step. It's not the journey. It's the first step."

After the press got wind of the story, Gingrich removed some of the endorsements from the course. But the entire notion of such political paybacks having a place in a college course caused an uproar. The commercial plugs, though, were just the tip of the iceberg.

Almost from its inception, Renewing American Civilization had drawn fire. Gingrich began teaching the course at Kennesaw State College in September 1993. But by January 1994 the implication that the course had political content was too strong for the publicly funded college to allow it to continue to be broadcast from its campus. Gingrich was forced to move Renewing American Civilization to Reinhardt College after the Georgia Board of Regents ruled that a public office holder could not teach at a public university such as Kennesaw.

There were problems, too, with the Progress and Freedom Foundation. The nonprofit, ostensibly non-partisan "thinktank" is headquartered in downtown Washington and has a half-dozen staff members. It was set up to help usher in the "third wave" described in the works of Heidi and Alvin Toffler, whom Gingrich has known since the 1970s and greatly admires. According to the Tofflers' philosophy, the first wave is the conversion from hunter-gatherer to agricultural society. The second wave is the Industrial Revolution. The third wave, which we are currently entering (or stumbling into under Democratic leadership) is the information revolution. It is this transition, from the second wave to the third wave, that the Progress and Freedom Foundation studies. Gingrich has said that the way to the "third wave" is through the abolition of the welfare state. Gingrich has defined himself as a "conservative futurist" and is thrilled by Toffler's concept of "triliteracy," combining the traditional three R's with media and computer literacy. References to the Tofflers and their work are staples of Gingrich's speeches. The Progress and Freedom Foundation published Toffler's latest book, which includes an introduction by Gingrich.

As Morton Kondracke, executive editor of *Roll Call* puts it, foundations often turn into slush funds allowing "politicians to travel, entertain, hire staff and distribute propaganda beyond House limits." The Progress and Freedom Foundation in 1994 estimated that in the coming year it would collect $2.25 million in donations from corporations, foundations, and individuals. Because the foundation is officially a public charity supported by tax-deductible contributions, it is not subject to FEC regulations. This means it can get away with revealing almost no information about its finances and can accept contributions from almost any source. It also means that the foundation is not supposed to have any specific political agenda, and is certainly not supposed to be a funding arm of Newt Gingrich, Incorporated.

Last year Ben Jones, Newt Gingrich's opponent for the Sixth congressional seat in Congress, filed a complaint with the FEC alleging that the Progress and Freedom Foundation was all of that. Jones' September complaint alleged, "Mr. Gingrich fabricated a 'college course' at Kennesaw State College . . . intended, in fact, to meet certain political, not educational, objectives. Because the college did not have or wish to make available funding, Mr. Gingrich directed the creation of a tax-exempt organization which claimed a charitable educational purpose, but which operated under the control of Mr. Gingrich's political organization, GOPAC, for purely political purposes. As a result, through the tax-exempt, tax-deductible contributions solicited through this charity, the taxpayer paid the cost of Mr. Gingrich's political mission."

The links between GOPAC, the Progress and Freedom Foundation, Renewing American Civilization and Gingrich are many and complex, and range from the obvious and above-board to the downright questionable. The Progress and Freedom Foundation was created in April 1993 as a nonprofit, "nonpartisan" thinktank, by Jeffrey Eisenach, the former executive director of GOPAC. Although Gingrich is not officially associated with the foundation, it is almost entirely run by old Gingrich associates, including Eisenach and Vin Weber. West Georgia College professor Steve Hanser is also listed as being on the board, although he says that he recently resigned that position. The foundation's single biggest project is to fund Gingrich's college course, Renewing American Civilization, and Gingrich is usually the main attraction at the foundation's functions.

Critics have charged that Gingrich, the foundation, and GOPAC are far too intimately linked. Indeed, while Eisenach was setting up the foundation, he continued to work from and use the facilities of GO-PAC until October, when the foundation moved into a new office and it was announced that Eisenach had resigned his post at GOPAC. Eisenach denies any connection between the foundation and GOPAC, saying that his presence at GOPAC headquarters during the foundation's beginnings was purely a matter of convenience while he searched for appropriate office space. He said that during the time he was using GOPAC office space to set up the foundation, he was off GOPAC's payroll.

To substantiate the charge that the foundation, Gingrich, and GOPAC are one, critics point out that several GOPAC staffers and consultants, including Steve Hanser, have been, or are currently, on the foundation payroll. Gingrich says that the course was inspired by Owen Roberts, a Belleair Bluffs, Florida, businessman, who along with his wife, Susan, has given at least $324,513 to GOPAC and other Gingrich-affiliated ventures, making him GOPAC's second-largest contributor.

Democrats have subpoenaed 1,400 pages of records of the course from Kennesaw College, some of which showed that letters, including solicitations, pertaining to the course were often sent on GOPAC letterhead from a GOPAC fax machine.

In addition, there are charges that three members of Gingrich's House staff were involved in launching the course. This allegation is particularly troubling since it would indicate that the course was partially financed with taxpayer money.

The Progress and Freedom Foundation also raises red flags because as a tax-exempt institution, it is supposed to be involved in purely educational work and not in advancing any specific political agenda. But Jones and other critics point out that Renewing American Civilization has been, from its inception, political in intent and not purely educational. They point to a 1993 letter sent to one thousand college Republicans, in which Gingrich described the need for conservatives to define the future and said, "In that context, I am going to devote much of the next four years, starting this fall, to teaching a class entitled Renewing American Civilization."

The goal of the course, according to a 1993 fund-raising letter signed by Eisenach, was to train by April 1996 "200,000-plus citizens into a model for replacing the welfare state and reforming our government."

In addition, records show that more than forty-five percent of those who contributed to the foundation are also contributors to GOPAC. This presents a potential ethics violation because if Gingrich or GOPAC are found to be tied to the foundation, contributions from donors could be construed as having been solicited in exchange for "the prospect of legislative access."

One case in which questions of this sort have been raised involves a company called Direct Access Diagnostics. In January 1995, *Roll Call* reported that Gingrich had intervened with the White House and the Food and Drug Administration to endorse a home AIDS test manufactured by Direct Access Diagnostics, a subsidiary of Johnson and Johnson. Gingrich was approached in 1994 by the company, whose product was then under review by the FDA, and in September he wrote a letter to White House Chief of Staff Leon Panetta urging him to look into the FDA's handling of Direct Access Diagnostics application.

"I hope as you review the issue in the next few days you will agree that the delay must end immediately and that the FDA should approve the home test without any qualifications," Gingrich wrote in the letter, which was then passed on to FDA chief David Kessler.

Afterward, the company and its president made contributions to the Progress and Freedom Foundation. Direct Access Diagnostics' parent company, Johnson & Johnson, has also contributed to the foundation.

A government official familiar with the case said that both Gingrich's method of going through Panetta and the content of his letter are highly unusual in terms of how congressmen typically approach FDA product-approval issues.

"Not many would go through Panetta, especially when you are in the opposition party. Unless you think it's critically important," the source said. "Most congressmen would avoid interfering with the legal process."

Instead of arguing for approval without delay, a representative is more likely to have a staffer write a letter to Kessler to request that he meet with a company official. Kessler's office forwards such letters to the FDA's legislative affairs office for handling.

Most Congressmen would not make the case [for approval], the source said.

There's some speculation that Gingrich approached the FDA through the White House because his relations with the agency had become strained after it was disclosed that the Progress and Freedom Foundation was conducting a study of the FDA and could recommend that the agency be dismantled or, at the very least, privatized.

Direct Access Diagnostics was not the only company he had tried to help out, though. In February 1995, the *Wall Street Journal* disclosed that Gingrich interceded with the FDA on behalf of Solvey, the Georgia subsidiary of a Belgian drug company that had donated money to the foundation. According to the *Journal*, Gingrich wrote to FDA Commissioner Kessler in July 1994 to find out why the agency had delayed approval of Luvox, a drug for treating obsessive-compulsive disorder.

The call for an investigation grew even more urgent when it was revealed that in September 1992, Timothy Mescon, the dean of the Kennesaw State College School of Business Administration, wrote to Gingrich asking him to assist him in being introduced to the director of the Bureau of Private Enterprise at the State Department. Apart from his position of dean at Kennesaw, he also ran a consulting company, The

Mescon Group, which specialized in fledgling companies.

In October 1992, Gingrich confirmed that he had contacted State Department officials on Mescon's behalf, adding "I am very interested in working with you after the election," with the word *very* underlined. On October 1, Gingrich wrote to Ronald Roskens, then head of the Agency for International Development. His letter praised Mescon and his associates, saying they were "pioneers who have worked so diligently in promoting private enterprise in West Africa."

In December, Mescon met with AID officials, and three weeks later he extended an offer to teach the course at Kennesaw to Gingrich. Both Gingrich and Mescon insist the letter to AID and the offer to teach the course are unrelated.

"Mescon is a constituent," Allan Lipsett, a spokesman for Gingrich told the Associated Press, "and [Gingrich] asked the same kind of question he would ask for any constituent. There was no quid pro quo about a course."

Jones alleges there was a quid pro quo for arranging the meeting, because three weeks later, the dean offered to let Kennesaw host Renewing American Civilization.

The biggest bombshell would fall in December 1994, when Gingrich announced that he had accepted a $4.5 million advance for two books from Rupert Murdoch's HarperCollins. At that time, Jones amended his complaint to show that the book advance was tantamount to influence-peddling, since Murdoch had met with Gingrich shortly after the election to discuss a case before the Federal Communications Commission that involved his Fox television network. As a result of the uproar, Gingrich subsequently turned down the advance, but Jones said that the case remained valid, as Gingrich still stood to gain financially from the sale of the books, which were to be largely derived from Renewing American Civilization, which, he alleged, may have been developed with the use of taxpayer money.

The House Ethics Committee has not yet determined how it will investigate the charges, for some of the members of the committee are themselves contributors to GOPAC. The Democrats, along with several newspaper columnists, have called for the appointment of an outside counsel.

Little is known about the sources of funding of Newt, Inc., and it is not certain that in the future, under FEC pressure, the different entities will disclose their funding and their spending pattern. A look at three families that count among the highest-known GOPAC contributors provides insight into the corporate and ideological underpinnings of Newt, Inc.

Although highly secretive, GOPAC's most important backer is the Kohler family of Sheboygan, Wisconsin. Terry J. Kohler has given $578,157.19 in personal contributions to GOPAC since 1985. Terry Kohler is the son of a former governor of Wisconsin and bathroom-fixture magnate who now operates Windway Capital Corp. Kohler was once rejected for a spot on the board of regents of the University of Wisconsin because of disparaging comments he made about South African blacks in 1988. Mary Kohler, Terry's wife, who had been widowed and was involved in G.O.P. politics before she married Terry, has given $137,300.00 in personal contributions since 1988.

They are described as "staunch conservatives" who have frequently been criticized for trying to "buy" involvement in the political process.

Sources say that Gingrich, at the invitation of the Kohlers, was in Sheboygan around Christmas of 1994 to attend a dinner meeting of the Sheboygan Economic Club, a group of conservatives who meet "quietly." Members are mostly "senior business people—bankers, industrialists," an observer of the Wisconsin political scene said, commenting on Gingrich's visit.

"As much as they give, they have a few chits to call in."

Another major contributor to GOPAC is Roger Milliken, who, with his father, Gerrish, has given Gingrich's organization at least $345,000 from 1985 to 1993. Milliken & Co. is a privately held textile conglomerate based in South Carolina with sales of more than $2.5 billion annually. Gingrich and Milliken have known each other since 1964, when they were both involved in the Goldwater campaign. Milliken was a partner in the 1984 book deal.

Milliken, who has a personal fortune estimated at $600 million, is a fervent opponent of the General Agreement on Tariffs and Trade. According to the *Washington Post*, before the November elections, he met with Gingrich and raised his objections to the pact. Gingrich favors GATT in principle but last year supported efforts to delay a vote on it.

Since the late 1980s, the textile industry has come under tremendous pressure from cheaper imports from abroad and has frequently lobbied Congress for bills to impose tough trade restrictions on imports. Gingrich has been a frequent speaker at textile industry meetings.

Although he refrained from commenting on trade issues, at a 1989 conference of the American Textile Manufacturers Institute, Gingrich placed the blame for the American textile industry's woes squarely on the shoulders of its workers and of the "corrupt welfare state."

"We spend far more money than the Japanese for education," Gingrich said, according to the Associated Press. "We just get less for it. . . . Why do we get less for it? Because of the incredibly stupid union work pool."

If there has been a single backer sustaining Gingrich from the beginning of his political career, it is the Richards family, the owners of Southwire, the nation's largest copper wire producer based in Carrollton, Georgia.

According to the *New York Times*, from 1986 to 1993, Jim Richards, Southwire founder Roy Richards' son, who now operates the company, gave $80,200 to GOPAC. In total, members of the Richards family have given more than $100,000 to various Gingrich enterprises.

Southwire, which operates a copper-smelting factory employing two thousand workers at five plants in Carrollton, has a long record of environmental and occupational-safety violations. The company's environmental violations, in fact, are the reason Gingrich first came to their notice: In his first congressional campaign he denounced the emissions from the plant's five-story chimney, which dominates the town.

"You used to be able to see the air at night," West Georgia College professor Don Wagner recalls. "In the summertime I used to walk my dog at night, and I couldn't believe all the junk that was in the air. Somebody told me that that was when they burned all the stuff that's illegal."

As a professor in the environmental studies department of the college, Southwire's pollution was a natural and popular cause for Gingrich to take up in his first races. At that time the company was run by its founder, Roy Richards, a self-made man and autodidact who was so wedded to his creation that he lived on the grounds of the plant.

Roy Richards, who died in 1985, leaving his company to his two sons, was a "country boy" who grew up working at his family's saw mill. He was driven enough to try to go to college, and went to Georgia Tech before he served in World War II. When he came out of the service there was no electricity in Carroll County except in Carrollton. It occurred to him that there was a lot of surplus wire left over in military stocks. So he started buying the surplus wire and making telephone poles at his family's sawmill and running lines for the Rural Electrification Administration.

The company grew on federal contracts. Richards

created and patented an assembly-line process for installing electric utility poles and was awarded a number of contracts by the Rural Electrification Administration. These contracts made him rich, and in the early 1950s he created Southwire, which has since averaged twenty percent annual growth, and now has annual revenues between $1.3 billion and 1.5 billion, employing four thousand people at ten plants in five states. In the beginning the company made aluminum and copper rod, then added an aluminum smelter and a copper refinery. It later added a compound blending plant, a large fleet of trucks, a machinery division, a wood-products division, and a hydroelectric plant.

Residents of Carrollton recall that the elder Richards ran the town very much like a mill town of the last century. He owned the bank, newspaper, car dealership, radio station, was chairman of the board of the hospital and a power unto himself in the town. "Every time another business tried to come in, he'd keep them out," one Carrollton resident recalls. "He even kept out McDonald's."

There have been allegations that Richards' paternalism extended well beyond legal limits. When, for example, some workers at the plant tried to organize a union in the mid-1970s, "some of the union supporters had had very unfortunate things happen to them," recalls Dr. Jack Birge, a Carrollton physician who has treated a large number of Southwire employees and had more than his share of conflicts with Roy Richards. "Some ended up in jail on trumped-up charges, some were fired and were blackballed by other local employers because Richards would call other sources of employment locally and tell them if they dared hire these people, they would have his wrath. He owned the bank, so mortgages were foreclosed."

"Roy Richards always swore that there'd never be a union in his place," says Glen Thomas, who taught environmental studies with Gingrich at West Georgia College in the early 1970s. "And he did it on the basis of, 'I can guarantee you work, the union can't, and I don't fire people.' And he didn't, as a matter of fact. He kept them; when times got hard they had to push the broom for a while.''

When, in the late 1970s, the Georgia Environmental Protection Department began an investigation of Southwire, the few employees who were willing to discuss conditions at the plant had to be interviewed twenty-two miles from Carrollton, so great was their fear of Richards' reach.

The company also has a record as a polluter. While most copper refining plants use primary ore, Southwire uses mostly reclaimed or scrap copper, which usually comes from motor armatures, plumbing, and refrigeration coils, which contain toxic heavy metals. The process creates toxic waste that the company has always had difficulty disposing of.

The *Atlanta Constitution* reported in December 1994, "Industrial waste from Southwire Co. that was used by a Carroll County school for erosion control in the 1970s has been found to be tainted with lead levels up to thirteen times government-recognized safe levels." It said that EPD has urged all 1,183 students at the school, the Oak Mountain Academy in Carrollton, to be tested for lead in their blood. Sources say the tainted soil was brought to the school by Southwire as a favor to help them build a playing field. Southwire has said it will clean up the waste.

Despite Gingrich's initial attacks, Richards saw something in the young man and contributed $1,000 to his first campaign in 1974. "Newt has an ability to impress a lot of these self-made entrepreneurs, guys that didn't have much of an education but admire the hell out of anybody who did," Howell says.

The attacks on the company's environmental practices stopped instantly.

By the time Gingrich got to Congress, he was largely perceived in Carrollton as having close ties to Southwire. "It was local knowledge that when Newt Gingrich went to Congress, he went with an anchor to one leg labeled Southwire," says Birge.

In the late-1980s, Gingrich voted against the Super-
fund, which gave the government power to require
businesses to pay for cleaning up pollution. While
Richards had already personally contributed to
Gingrich projects, twelve days after the vote Southwire gave the first PAC donation in its thirty-year
history—a $250 PAC contribution to Gingrich's cam-
paign. Gingrich had to deflect criticism from his Democratic opponent, Dock Davis, that he was "too
interested in helping Roy Richards to dump his
waste."

Gingrich's association with Southwire and the Richards continued. Roy Richards was one of the partners
in Gingrich's *Window of Opportunity* book deal.
Throughout this period the Carrollton bank controlled
by Richards allowed Gingrich to roll over his campaign
debts several times over several years.

"Southwire automatically has my attention every
morning," Gingrich said in 1989.

At the same time Southwire began to attract the
attention of federal regulatory agencies both for its
illegal disposal of waste and for labor law violations.
In 1981 and 1982, some employees of the company
charged that they suffered from lead poisoning incurred while at work in the plant. At the same time
medical analyses showed that Edward Kelley, a
worker at the plant who the company claimed had
died on the job of a heart attack in 1978, in fact died
of "arrhythmias or a fibrillation that is a consequence
of heavy metal exposure." The company was also
cited by the federal Occupational Safety and Health
Administration for the on-the-job deaths of two
Southwire workers in 1985.

In 1989, Southwire was fined $1,289 and cited for
"serious violations" of two health and safety standards after two workers were severely burned.

A source who has done a close study of Southwire
says no reliable study has ever been done of health
conditions in the local population, adding that the
company offers on-site primary care for employees

and dependents "so they can pretty much control what's diagnosed and reported as far as exposure to both the heavy metals and the polyvinyl fluoride jacketing for wire."

But a study of the area's toxicity and its effect on health has been completed by the federal Agency for Toxic Substances and Disease Registry, and is expected to be released at some time in 1995.

In 1990, two Southwire waste treatment plants were added to the EPA's national list of "toxic hot spots." The two plants discharge into nearby Buffalo Creek and a tributary.

In November 1992, Southwire and a South Carolina subsidiary, Gaston Copper Recycling Corporation, pled guilty to violating federal environmental rules for mixing toxic ash from the smelting operation with fertilizer, which was then exported to Bangladesh. As a result, in November 1993, Southwire was fined $190,000 and received two years' probation, and Gaston Copper received a fine of $600,000 and had to pay $200,000 restitution to the state of South Carolina. Gaston was ordered to take out full-page ads in South Carolina newspapers to apologize for their misdeeds. The fertilizer has still not been entirely disposed of.

In addition to the $1 million criminal fine, the *New York Times* reported that "hundreds of thousand of dollars in other fines and payments, the result of more than two dozen civil actions by regulators, are catalogued in federal and state environmental files in Georgia, Kentucky, South Carolina, Mississippi, and Connecticut in the last three years alone."

In February of this year, Gingrich was confronted at a press conference by Russell Mokiber, editor of the *Corporate Crime Reporter*, who asked him how he could receive money from a company that had been pled guilty to criminal violations of environmental laws, and had a record of violations of OSHA regulations.

"You're talking about the biggest employer in Carroll County," said Gingrich. "And you know, I fully

support the federal government prosecuting companies when they break the law. But I hardly think that,
given the complexity of our environmental and OSHA
regulations, that having been convicted of a violation
turns one into a 'criminal company,' as you describe
it. They are good citizens. They work very hard. They
provide very good jobs for over three thousand
people."

He said it would have been "irresponsible to not
have a concern for that particular corporation and for
the jobs that corporation provides."

Newt, Incorporated, with its interlocking entities, has
inaugurated a new era in U.S. politics in which candidates will increasingly seek ways to raise money without having to disclose where it comes from or how it
is spent. But as GOPAC and the Progress and Freedom
Foundation come under increasing scrutiny, particularly if an outside counsel is named to investigate
Newt, Inc., Gingrich could find himself exposed to the
same kinds of charges that brought down Speaker
Jim Wright.

In the meantime, even if GOPAC is slapped with a
$500,000 fine, Newt, Inc., is unlikely to go bankrupt
anytime soon. In mid-February, Arianna Huffington,
author and wife of failed California House candidate
Michael Huffington, announced plans to host a gala
event to raise money for National Empowerment Television with a $500,000 per couple sticker price. She
is also scheduled to open the Center for Effective
Compassion, a thinktank that will focus on replacing
public programs with charity. The center is described
as an offshoot of the Progress and Freedom Foundation.

CONCLUSION
The Newt World Order

At the time of this writing, only one of the provisions of the "Contract with America"—a bill subjecting Congress to the same labor laws that govern private employment—had been signed into law by the President. Two other bills had cleared the House: the Fiscal Responsibility Act—calling for a balanced-budget amendment and for the presidential line-item veto—and the Taking Back Our Streets Act—calling for greater damages for crime victims, loosening federal laws of evidence to allow evidence obtained without a search warrant into court, restricting the ability of state prisoners to appeal convictions, providing more money for prison construction, and streamlining the deportation of criminal aliens. And a provision to make it harder for Congress to impose requirements on states and cities without providing federal money to pay for them was on its way to the President.

But while the House was moving on at a fine clip, it wasn't at all clear what the prospects for the Contract with America would be in the long term. The balanced-budget amendment was stalled in the Senate. The line-item veto, which would give the president the power to knock spending items out of a bill without killing the whole thing—a bill that would sharply strengthen the power of the presidency—was believed to have an iffy chance of passage in the Senate for just that reason. Many senators were balking at the wisdom of cutting taxes while working to balance the budget. And where Social Security would fit in budget balancing was an issue that stuck in everyone's throat.

It's impossible to tell at this point just how successful as a legislative document Gingrich's Contract with America will be. But then, Gingrich has never made any real promises about his commitment to its long-term success. As he reiterated to the *New York Times* in mid-February, "I've said all along this is not written in stone."

Writing legislation never really was Newt Gingrich's chief concern. He's an ideologue, a king maker, a catalyst, who crystallizes the national mood into political form. And the Contract, after all, *was* ideology, was atmospherics. It was a prop for the Newt & Co. traveling stage show. A blue print for an alternative New World Order.

What is the Newt World Order?

On the one hand, it's "New Age Reaganism"—an anti-intellectual, pro-big business, highly ideological way of Thinking Big Thoughts that simplifies nicely into slogans and videotapes for mass consumption. A kind of mix of "Ten Steps to Thinner Thighs" and the Strategic Defense Initiative. An example:

On January 11, 1995, the cultural elite picked up their *New York Times* and got a smirking peek at Gingrich's thought and the people who inspired it. Under the front-page headline "Capital's Virtual Reality: Gingrich Rides a Third Wave," Maureen Dowd delivered a scathing review of a conference entitled "Democracy in Virtual America" that had been organized by the Progress and Freedom Foundation at the Mayflower Hotel in Washington the previous day. The article described Washington as ringing "with the opinions of futurists and spiritualists, self-improvement experts and cyberspace cartographers—all billing themselves as friends, advisers and even 'gurus' to the new speaker."

Times readers chuckled into their coffee as they read of the closing address titled "From Virtuality to Reality" delivered by Gingrich, which Dowd described as roaming "in verbally complicated ways, from Pitt the Younger to downloading from cybernetic systems."

"In a sense, virtuality at the mental level is something I think you'd find in most historical periods," Gingrich said in his speech. "But in addition, the thing I want to talk about today, and that I find fascinating, is that we are not at a new place. It is just becoming harder and harder and harder to avoid the place we are."

The conference and its participants, with their talk about "virtual economy, virtual government, and virtual America," Dowd wrote, "serve as a window into the culture of the new congressional leadership, reflecting Newtonian notions far more quirky than the tax- and budget-cutting talk that led to Mr. Gingrich's election as Speaker of the House."

The article also included abstruse, if not nonsensical, quotations from comments made by conference participants such as Alvin and Heidi Toffler and Arianna Huffington, author of *The Fourth Instinct*, John Roger cultist and wife of Michael Huffington, a California oil baron who spent $28 million of his own money in a quixotic 1994 campaign to obtain a seat in the Senate. The less than flattering article belied the picture Gingrich had tried to present as a conservative, but presented him instead as an illuminated zealot who has opened the highest reaches of the U.S. government to kooky "gurus" and sycophants.

Another window of opportunity to glimpse into Newt Gingrich's intellectual world was offered when he announced his appointment of Kennesaw State College professor Christina Jeffrey to the post of House historian. Jeffrey's appointment came as something of a surprise, since the old employees of the House historian's office had been fired just after Christmas and were told the office was being abolished

in an effort to economize. Gingrich hired Jeffrey along
with her husband, Robert, who would work without a
salary as Gingrich's personal "chronicler"—a move
that, for Thomas Mann, a congressional scholar at the
Brookings Institution, "raises all the questions about
a Gingrich machine being lodged in the House."

Gingrich dismissed Jeffrey after he learned that she
had once helped to deny federal financing of an educational program about the Holocaust because, she said,
it did not present the views of the Nazis and the
Ku Klux Klan, and suggested that, because of its
limitations, it "may be appropriate for a limited religious audience but not for wider distribution."

In the wake of her evaluation, then Deputy Assistant
Education Secretary Robert Preston had labeled her
comments "appalling" and his department had her
removed from the list of teachers who advise it about
school curriculums.

"It wasn't the kind of thing I would have said if I
had known it was going to be in the *New York Times*,"
she said in her defense in January 1995.

The Jeffrey debacle was eye-opening not because it
suggested that Gingrich espouses the beliefs of Holocaust revisionists (he claims he knew nothing of Jeffrey's views on the curriculum—a point that Jeffrey
and her supporters have hotly contested) but for the
questions it raised about the company he keeps and
how well he applies his much vaunted belief in "quality" to the people he gathers around him profession-
ally. Jeffrey's predecessor, Dr. Raymond W. Smock,
who was named House historian when the job was
created in 1983, had been a lecturer in history at
the University of Maryland, had co-edited fourteen
volumes of the *Booker T. Washington Papers*, served
as president of Instructional Resource and was president of Research Materials Corporation. Jeffrey herself was a graduate of the University of Plano, an
unaccredited school near Dallas that no longer exists.
An example of her own academic writing appeared in
1994 in *The American Experiment: Essays on the*

Theory and Practice of Liberty, edited by Peter Augustine Lawler and Robert Martin Schaefer. In an essay called "Public Policy," which basically argues against it, she appears to endorse phasing out Social Security in favor of Individual Retirement Accounts. Jeffrey also published articles as a staff writer for the very (if sophomorically) right-wing *Kennesaw Spectator,* which is the kind of newspaper where a sympathetic letter to the editor can go: "Why is it that conservatives, especially Christian conservatives (of which I am one), are viewed by liberals as close-minded and unable to tolerate diversity? If you ask me, that is the pot calling the kettle black. (Oh, sorry, African-American.)"

Jeffrey was a political scientist, not a historian. She told *Congressional Quarterly* she did not have a "tremendous amount" of background in congressional history and, defending herself, told the *New York Times* that she "didn't know anything about the Holocaust" at the time that she wrote the course evaluation. More troubling than her lack of credentials, though, was the fact of how obvious a payoff her appointment was. Jeffrey had helped Gingrich set up his course at Kennesaw College and had defended his right to continue lecturing there when the political content of the course had been criticized. She also had written a letter to the *Atlanta Journal and Constitution* saying GOPAC should not be obligated to disclose its donors because it would add to the already unfair advantages enjoyed by incumbents (mostly Democrats, in Congress, at the time of the writing). "Government is so powerful that many of us do not want incumbents to know that we supported their opponents, hence the difficulty that challengers have raising money," she wrote in September 1994.

It's been said many times that Gingrich will have to change the way he operates now that he is speaker. He will also have to be more aware of the company he keeps. Mainstream America does not want a House historian like Christina Jeffrey, nor does it want to see the United States turn into a "Christian Nation," as some of Gingrich's supporters desire. Gingrich, it seems, has tried to establish a kind of intellectual legitimacy by connecting himself to thinkers like the Tofflers and academic institutions like Kennesaw. And he's given himself a solid and wide-reaching political base by connecting himself to the Christian Coalition and conservatives like Paul Weyrich. But when payback time comes, whether in the form of positions granted or a school prayer amendment, he may find these choices shortsighted—particularly if his eyes are set on the national political stage.

Will he, in fact, run for president?

He used to say no—not ever. But now he says no—not now. "I think I should stay and focus on what I am doing and get things done," he said in February 1995. "I hardly need to run for president to get my message out."

He said he thought about it, discussed it with Marianne after Dan Quayle dropped out of the race, then decided that the speakership had been too long awaited to be dropped so quickly. If we won't see a Newt Gingrich candidacy in 1996, could we see one in the year 2000 (a perfect year, it would seem for a futurist) or in 2004? Given the fact that Gingrich has said that, in deference to the House's new term-limit rules, he would step down from his office as Speaker in eight years, the latter prospect seems most likely.

But could he win? If he ran right now, he might have a shot. Polls conducted in the first week of February showed him with a favorable rating of forty-three percent—considerably higher than the President's. Where he'll be eight years from now remains to be seen.

For now, there's something not quite presidential about Newt Gingrich. He still doesn't quite fit in. In February, while the real President of the United States entertained German Chancellor Helmut Kohl over dinner at the White House, the virtual presidents of the Republican party held an inaugural gala. At a fund-raising dinner in a huge Washington convention center, 4,200 contributors, paying upwards of $1,000 per dinner, ate raspberry mousse out of white chocolate Capitol domes, applauded delightedly for songs by Natalie Cole, and feted the Republican takeover of Congress last November with unbridled glee.

"There are so many of us," Senate Majority Whip Trent Lott of Mississippi crowed. "It's such a rare and special occasion."

The dinner event, which drew money from some 10,000 donors, raised so much ($11 million, the most ever collected in a single evening) and was so popular that most of the guests, seated far from their representatives and senators in the enormous convention space, had to watch the proceedings on four giant video monitors hung from the ceiling.

And while protesters outside the convention center railed against "fat-cat money" of the sort donated by the evenings corporate sponsors like Coca-Cola, Philip Morris, and the American Meat Institute, possible president Bob Dole attempted to take the high road. Wearing an elegant dinner jacket, and striking the appropriate tone for a presidential stand-in, he said, "We look forward to great days for America. It's not the power we seek. It's the ability to make changes, to change someone's life in a better way because we have a better philosophy."

Applauding on cue, grinning as is his wont, Newt Gingrich was the only man on the dais wearing a business suit rather than a dinner jacket. He was seated alone, his wife, Marianne, having flown off to Jerusalem in pursuit of cementing business connections between Israeli and American companies.

Marianne's new job with the Israel Export Development company, to locate businesses in a free-trade zone favored by Gingrich, had raised eyebrows and the specter of another onslaught of ethical inquiries like the ones that followed her participation in his *Window of Opportunity* book deal. Outside, beyond the protesters, the press waited.

Will Newt Gingrich ever be able to wear the role of statesman without strain? Will he ever *really* be enough of an insider to rise further within the ranks of the tuxedoed, moneyed, teflon-coated crowd that surrounded him that night?

Or would the familiar world of virtual reality be the stopping-off point for him?

"For my taste, Gingrich is too futuristic, too psychobabble, too technobabble—he's a weird mishmash of all kinds of things," a leading conservative told journalist David Rasnick in December 1994. "There is an ongoing attempt to try to keep Newt from going off the deep end. There's a certain grandiosity to his self-understanding which comes from Toffler, and end-of-an-era, the whole-world-is-changing feeling he projects. The Republican presidential candidates being proposed are really more conventional than Newt."

They probably are *cleaner,* too.

In between the time that he was reelected in November and when he was actually sworn in as speaker, ethical problems continued to build.

First, on December 8, 1994, Democratic Minority Whip David Bonior, following statements by Joan Claybrook, president of Public Citizen, formally called for an outside counsel to investigate Gingrich, citing the fact that the House Ethics committee was considering an investigation on him based on the Ben Jones compliant and the outstanding FEC lawsuit. Bonior was joined in his call by acting DNC chair Debra DeLee and Richard Phelan, the outside counsel who investigated the charges against Jim Wright. Gingrich and Democratic Minority leader Richard Gephardt of Missouri agreed to appoint a special ethics panel of ten current committee members to review the Jones complaint.

Then there was the now famous Murdoch book deal. On December 22, 1994, the *Washington Post* reported that Gingrich had signed a two-book deal with Harper-Collins for in excess of $4 million, nearly all of which was for a book articulating his political vision, tentatively entitled "To Renew America." The advance, for a political book, was second only to Ronald Reagan's. HarperCollins is owned by Rupert Murdoch's News Corp., which has interests in a variety of regulatory matters before the federal government. On CNN, Common Cause President Fred Wertheimer said: "It certainly seems like Representative Gingrich is out to capitalize on the office of speaker before he even enters the job." Gingrich called criticism of the book deal "silly," but after David Bonior cited a December 9 *Daily Variety* article entitled "G.O.P. in Fox's Corner," with the jump headline, "G.O.P. may rally to Murdoch's aid," and even Republicans Bob Dole and Jack Kemp began to question the book deal, Gingrich announced he would take just one dollar as his advance and have his share of the books' royalties adjusted upward.

And finally, in late January, Ben Jones amended his complaint against Gingrich to include his new book deal and his pitches before two business groups to purchase tapes of his college course. He claimed the book deal violated House rules because of the bidding war that Gingrich's agent started after election day and charged it was improper for Gingrich to meet in November with Rupert Murdoch, who has billions at stake in business before the government. He said he also violated House rules when he urged two business groups "with interests in legislation" to buy tapes of his college course.

If Gingrich ever does get all his ethical problems straightened out, he'll have other problems to face, if he should decide to run as a candidate beyond the conservative Sixth District of Georgia. There's a fault line that runs through the center of his alliance— between the *Wall Street Journal*—reading fiscal conservatives indifferent to social issues as long as taxes stay low and the Christian conservatives striving to scale back the secular state. Paul Weyrich admits as much: "Right now there are lots of things that both camps agree on like defunding a lot of institutions and people and so on, so the coalition can be held together. If you get into specific social issues that impact on people's behavior, then you would have a significant difference. It's going to be very tricky, there's no question about it.''

Gingrich, whom Pat Robertson's political adherents in Georgia once derided as "immoral," has never entirely been embraced by some factions of the religious right—despite the fact that the Christian coalition gave him a one hundred percent approval rating in 1994.

"When you look at the voting record of Gingrich. I don't think you could realistically call it conservative,'' says William Dannemeyer, the former representative from California who is currently working with a Christian evangelical group, Wallbuilders, in an effort to develop co-sponsors for a constitutional amendment to reinstate voluntary prayer in America. Dannemeyer's definition for a conservative, however, may well go beyond Gingrich's.

Gingrich "has voted for NAFTA, GATT, foreign aid, welfare programs, IMF, aid to Russia, elevation of EPA, Clean Air Act, Endangered Species Act, Americans with Disabilities Act, and the creation of a national police corps,'' Dannemeyer says, citing some of the recent issues that have rallied the far right of the Republican party. "He's a member of the Council on Foreign Relations, a leftist world futurist society. He's a member of NAACP and some New Age congressional clearinghouse on the future. He collaborated in the 1970s with the radical left: globalists, environment extremists, humanists and New Age organizations.

"Now, somebody who has that in their background is no conservative," he concludes.

Gingrich will also undoubtedly face a challenge from the left, which will do whatever it can to heighten public awareness of the far-right-wing strands of Gingrich's alliance.

"Our first counterattack is going to be over the

choice issue," says Barney Frank, the unabashedly liberal representative from Massachusetts.

This strategy has started already.

The abortion-rights issue arose more quickly than anticipated, in February 1995, when President Clinton announced his nomination of Dr. Henry Foster for Surgeon General. Foster at first claimed to have performed only a small number of abortions over the course of his career as an obstetrician and gynecologist. But documents obtained by anti-abortion groups showed that he once said he had performed hundreds of them—causing an uproar by anti-choice legislators.

There is some speculation that the Democrats may have encouraged the choice issue to come to the fore and were willing to sacrifice Foster in order to show the public that opposition to abortion, despite efforts by the Republican party mainstream to downplay it, has not decreased in the least. Moderate, pro-choice Republicans were put in a difficult spot, one that is likely to become more and more familiar to them in the coming months.

There's some speculation, too, that if Gingrich isn't embraced by his own party as a presidential candidate down the line, he might run as a Perot-type independent or third-party candidate.

And, in the meantime, the man whom *Time* magazine called the "virtual president" isn't being shy about consolidating his power.

Gingrich has set the House rules so that he has more power than any other speaker since Sam Rayburn. The very first measures passed by Congress in January—rules that eliminated three committees and twenty-five subcommittees, cut the size of committee staffs by a third, limited committee chairman to terms of six years on the job and the speaker to a term of eight years—consolidated his power and pulled it away from the committee chairman. Also, by eliminating or diminishing committees, he eliminated some of the opportunity for PAC money to reach lawmakers from the industries they oversee. This means that he has to contend less with beholdenness to outside interests and can command party loyalty more easily. Not that he's had any problems with loyalty, once he'd made his own committee assignments, filling seats with allies, often ignoring seniority. And not that he has any problems with lobbyists per se—or with "friendly" industry committee heads.

Newt Gingrich has all of the "imperial" tendencies that he accused his former nemesis, Speaker Jim Wright, of harboring. He is used to being an outsider, to operating in the relative obscurity of C-SPAN fame. It's a habit of mind that won't work anymore. Gingrich will spend the next two years under the sharpest exposure. If he wants a shot at the presidency, he can't play emperor.

Acknowledgments

We owe our greatest thanks to Arnold Dolin and Matthew Carnicelli at Dutton Signet for their remarkable patience and faith in us. We also want to thank Kim Witherspoon and Maria Massie for all their help, Chris Pratt, who made it physically possible, Liza Featherstone, for her unusual talent and good humor, Beverly Larson, for giving us time she didn't have, Barbara Findlen, who made it possible for us to even consider getting started, and Robert Kovacik, belatedly.

We are indebted to John Barry for his account of the Jim Wright affair in his October, 1989, Esquire article, *Anatomy of a Smear,* and to the reporting of Dan Balz, Charles R. Babcock, Dale Russakoff and Serge F. Kovaleski in the *Washington Post.* We cannot, unfortunately, thank all the people who helped us out with time and resources but would like to express our gratitude to Chip Berlet at Progressive Research Associates, Gary Ruskin at the Center for Congressional Accountability, Skipp Porteous at the Institute for First Amendment Studies, Matt Casey, Bill Shipp, Emma Edmunds, Peter Applebome, David Worley and the West Georgia College archives, the Tulane University archives, and the Emory University archives. We are especially grateful to the Gingrich family for their kind cooperation.

We owe special thanks, too, to Grace Mirabella and Deb Futter for giving us that most precious commodity: time.

American History Titles from MENTOR

☐ **JEFFERSON, A GREAT AMERICAN'S LIFE AND IDEAS. Saul K. Padover.** In this definitive biography of the great American statesman, Padover uses many of Thomas Jefferson's own writings to paint a rich and provocative portrait of the author of the Declaration of Independence. (627970—$4.99)

☐ **A DOCUMENTARY HISTORY OF THE UNITED STATES. Richard D. Heffner.** From the Declaration of Independence to Ronald Reagan's second Inaugural Address, here—available for the first time in a single inexpensive edition—are the documents, speeches, and letters that have forged American history, accompanied by interpretations of their significance by a noted historian and scholar. (624130—$6.99)

☐ **THE OXFORD HISTORY OF THE AMERICAN PEOPLE. Samuel Eliot Wilson.** Three-volume edition. This comprehensive analysis by the Pulitzer Prize-winning historian includes: Volume I which covers the period from the earliest Indian civilizations to the beginning of George Washington's first administration, Volume II which extends through the troubled era of Reconstruction following the War Between the States, Volume III which closes with the assassination of John F. Kennedy.

Volume I (626001—$5.95)
Volume III (628187—$5.99)

Prices slightly higher in Canada.

By the year 2000, 2 out of 3 Americans could be illiterate.

It's true.

Today, 75 million adults...about one American in three, can't read adequately. And by the year 2000, U.S. News & World Report envisions an America with a literacy rate of only 30%.

Before that America comes to be, you can stop it...by joining the fight against illiteracy today.

Call the Coalition for Literacy at toll-free **1-800-228-8813** and volunteer.

Volunteer Against Illiteracy. The only degree you need is a degree of caring.